Professor Stephen Francis Frowen KSG
Photograph by Anthony Buckley and Constantine Ltd

50 Years of the German Mark

Essays in Honour of Stephen F. Frowen

Edited by

Jens Hölscher
University of Brighton

palgrave

in association with
Anglo-German Foundation for the Study of Industrial Society

First published 2001 by
PALGRAVE
Houndmills, Basingstoke, Hampshire RG21 6XS and
175 Fifth Avenue, New York, N. Y. 10010
Companies and representatives throughout the world

PALGRAVE is the new global academic imprint of
St. Martin's Press LLC Scholarly and Reference Division and
Palgrave Publishers Ltd (formerly Macmillan Press Ltd).

ISBN 0–333–75267–8

This book is printed on paper suitable for recycling and made from fully managed and sustained forest sources.

A catalogue record for this book is available from the British Library.

Library of Congress Cataloging-in-Publication Data
50 years of the German mark : essays in honour of Stephen F. Frowen / edited by Jens Hölscher.
p. cm.
Includes bibliographical references and index.
ISBN 0–333–75267–8
1. Mark, German—History. 2. Money—Germany—History. 3. Monetary policy—Germany—History. I. Title: Fifty years of the German mark. II. Frowen, Stephen F. III. Hölscher, Jens.
HG999.5 .A154 2000
332.4'943—dc21
00–052420

10 9 8 7 6 5 4 3
10 09 08 07 06 05 04

Printed and bound in Great Britain by
Antony Rowe Ltd, Chippenham, Wiltshire

Contents

List of Tables

List of Figures

Acknowledgment

This volume is based on a conference held at the Institute for German Studies at the University of Birmingham. The editor of this volume wishes to express his gratitude for generous financial help given by the Fritz Thyssen Stiftung and the Anglo-German Foundation. The participants enjoyed the hospitality of the University of Birmingham, which is also gratefully acknowledged. Many thanks go to Corinne Nativel for organizing the event and to Marcus Clayson for his editorial assistance. Linda Auld did the professional copy-editing in a most thorough way and Karin Ermert's assistance is gratefully acknowledged for the production of a proper name and subject index.

The Editor

Word of greeting

Anybody looking into the corpus of Stephen Frowen's work cannot fail to be impressed by the number of publications as well as by the wide range of issues addressed in his books and articles. As a central banker and a colleague, I would refer first to his contributions to monetary theory and monetary policy, covering almost all aspects of this field. Over time his interest has moved more and more to issues beyond economics. In this capacity Stephen has not only made important contributions by virtue of his own writing, but also by organizing conferences and proposing subjects to be addressed by other participants.

Stephen's suggestions were always stimulating – I think everybody who has participated in these conferences has benefited from the deep insights of an erudite man. His 75th birthday is a proper occasion to thank him and to wish him all the best – *ad multos annos*.

Otmar Issing*

* Professor Issing is currently an executive board member and Chief Economist of the European Central Bank.

Notes on Contributors

Jörg Bibow is a Lecturer in Economics at the University of Hamburg and Visiting Scholar at the Jerome Levy Institute of Bard College, New York. He was educated at the Universities of Hamburg, Witwatersrand and Cambridge. He received his PhD from the University of Cambridge in 1996, where he taught European integration and monetary economics. He has published a number of articles on Keynesian monetary economics. Current research interests concentrate on central banking and financial systems and European Integration.

Samuel Brittan is a columnist at the *Financial Times*. His most recent books are *Capitalism With a Human Face* (Edward Elgar 1995, Fontana 1996) and *Essays, Moral, Political and Economic* (Edinburgh University Press 1998). He is an Honorary Fellow of Jesus College, Cambridge; an Hon. Doctor of Letters (Heriot-Watt University; Edinburgh); and an Hon Doctor of the University of Essex. He has been visiting Professor at the Chicago Law School, a Visiting Fellow of Nuffield College, Oxford, and an Honorary Professor of Politics at Warwick. He has been awarded the George Orwell, Senior Harold Wincott and Ludwig Erhard prizes. He was a member of the Peacock Committee on the Finance of the BBC (1985–86). He was knighted in 1993 for 'services to economic journalism' and also became in that year a Chevalier de la Légion d'Honneur.

David Cobham is a Reader in Economics at the University of St Andrews. His main research areas are UK monetary policy, European monetary integration and financial systems. Recent publications include 'The post-ERM framework for monetary policy in the UK', *Economic Journal*, July 1997; and (with Stefania Cosci and Fabrizio Mattesini) 'The Italian financial system: neither bank-based nor market-based', *Manchester School*, June 1999. He has also edited (with George Zis) *From EMS to EMU: 1979 to 1999 and Beyond*, Macmillan 1999.

Stephen F. Frowen, KSG is a Fellow Commoner of St. Edmund's College, University of Cambridge, Senior Research Associate of its Von Hügel Institute, Honorary Professor at the Institute for German Studies, University of Birmingham, and Honorary Research Fellow in the Department of Economics, University College London. He was formerly

Bundesbank Professor of Monetary Economics in the Free University of Berlin. Prior to this appointment he was Visiting Professor at the Universities of Frankfurt and Würzburg, and for many years held senior teaching posts at the Universities of Greenwich and Surrey, following appointments as Research Officer at the National Institute of Economic and Social Research, London, as Economic Adviser to the Industrial and Commercial Finance Corporation (now 3i) and as Chief Editor of *The Bankers' Magazine* (now *Financial World*). In 1980-81 he served as a Special Adviser to UNIDO, Vienna. He has published widely in monetary and macroeconomics and in banking. He is the editor of numerous collective works and a Contributory Editor of *Central Banking*. In 1993 he received the Grand Cross of the Order of Merit of the Federal Republic of Germany, and in 1996 was honoured with a Papal Knighthood of the Pontifical Order of St. Gregory the Great.

Charles Goodhart, CBE, FBA is the Norman Sosnow Professor of Banking and Finance at the London School of Economics. Before joining the LSE in 1985, he worked at the Bank of England for 17 years as a monetary adviser, becoming a Chief Adviser in 1980. In 1997 he was appointed one of the outside independent members of the Bank of England's new Monetary Policy Committee. Earlier he had taught at Cambridge and LSE. Besides numerous articles, he has written a couple of books on monetary history, and a graduate monetary textbook, *Money, Information and Uncertainty* (2nd Edition 1989); and has published two collections of papers on monetary policy, *Monetary Theory and Practice* (1984) and *The Central Bank and the Financial System* (1995); and an institutional study of *The Evolution of Central Banks*, revised and republished (MIT Press) in 1998.

Jens Hölscher is Senior Lecturer in economics and Head of the research group 'Economics of Transition' at the University of Brighton. Previously he taught at the Universities of Berlin, Swansea, Birmingham and Chemnitz. He held Visiting Professorships at the Universities of Halle (IWH), Bonn (ZEI) and Almaty (KIMEP). He is interested in monetary and transition economics, both areas in which he published widely.

Anke Jacobsen is Research Fellow at the Free University of Berlin and has published in the area of international economics.

Elias Karakitsos is Professor in Economics at the Management School of Imperial College, University of London and is also Chairman and Managing Director of European Reliance Finance. He was Head of the Economics

Section 1987–97. He has pioneered work on the design of economic policy and is the author of two books and 65 papers in learned journals. In the 1980s he gave evidence to the House of Commons on monetary policy and international monetary arrangements and was an adviser to HM Treasury between 1980–87. Between 1992–95 he was a consultant to DG II of the European Commission on monetary union, economic convergence and the issues of a multi-speed Europe. In the last ten years he has worked in the areas of asset price determination and volatility, and investment strategies for globally diversified portfolios. He has acted as an economic and investment adviser to many institutional investors, including Citibank/Citicorp (New York), Oppenheimer (New York), Allianz (Munich), Nestle (Switzerland), Banque Indosuez (Luxembourg, Australia, New Zealand, London).

Norbert Kloten was President of the Land Central Bank in Baden-Württemberg and an *ex officio* member of the German policy-making Central Bank Council from 1976 to 1992. He has been a member of the Econornic Advisory Council at the Federal Ministry of Economics since 1967 (Chairman from 1992 to 1996). Other present activities include membership of the Board of Acadernic and Non-Academic Associations and the Trilateral Commission. His Professorship at the University of Tübingen (1960–76) was combined with membership of the Gerrnan Council of Economic Experts (Sachverständigenrat) from 1969 to 1976, being its Chairman from 1970–76. He has published extensively on the principles of economic policy and in the area of monetary and international monetary economics, on the theory and policy of transition and development, and on the methodo1ogy of economics. He holds two honorary doctorates from the University of Karlruhe (1980) and the University of Stuttgart (1993) respectively, and is the bearer of the Grand Cross with Badge and Star of the Order of Merit of the Federal Republic of Germany.

Reiner König has been Head of the Department of Economics at the Deutsche Bundesbank since 1991. He joined the Bundesbank's headquarters in 1972, holding various positions in the Monetary Policy and Balance of Payments Division. He gained his initial practical experience at a savings bank and at regional branches of the Deutsche Bundesbank. Dr König holds a PhD in Economics from the University of Cologne.

Andy (A. W.) Mullineux is Professor of Money and Banking in the Department of Economics at the University of Birmingham and was Head of the School of Social Sciences (1997 to 2000). He has published numerous books and papers on topics including: business cycles; international banking; small business financing; and financial sector reform in Central and Eastern Europe and East and South East Asia.

Eric Owen Smith is a Visiting Professor, Universität of Trier and Visiting Fellow at the Institute for German Studies, the University of Birmingham and at the Centre for International Financial and Economics Research, Loughborough University. His current research interests are focused on comparative studies of the German and British economies. As well as numerous publications in these fields, he has written the definitive English study of the German Economy (1994). A series of essays edited by one of his former ERASMUS students (Lothar Funk) was written in his honour in 1999. He enjoys applying his academic expertise as an ACAS arbitrator and member of Employment Tribunals.

Geoff Pugh is a Principal lecturer in Economics at Staffordshire University Business School. Geoff has recent publications on the real economy effects of long-run exchange rate movements as well as on the German economy. He is co-author, with Thomas Lange, of *The Economics of German Unification* (published by Edward Elgar).

Hajo Riese is the founder of the Berlin school of thought of 'Monetary Keynesanism'. He has directed the Institute for Economic Theory of the Free University of Berlin for many years and his many disciples are active in academia, politics and the financial world alike. His iconoclastic ideas have turned out to be thought-provoking, although they were not always well understood.

Hans Tietmeyer, former President of the Deutsche Bundesbank, economist and civil servant; born 1931, Metelen; educated at the Universities of Münster, Bonn and Cologne; Manager of the Bischöfliche Studienforderung Cusanuswerk 1959–62; Federal Ministry of Economics 1962–82, Head of Division of German Economic Policy 1973–82; member of Economic Policy Committee of European Community and OECD 1972–82; Secretary of State, Ministry of Finance 1982–89; member of the board of directors of the Bundesbank 1990, Vice-President 1991–93, President 1993–99. Multiple honorary doctorates. Publications: several books and more than 100 articles on economics.

Keith Tribe, born 1949, studied at the Universities of Essex and Cambridge, and has taught at Keele University since 1976; 1979–80,

1982–83 Alexander von Humboldt Stipendiat in Heidelberg and at the Max Planck Institut für Geschichte, Göttingen. Present position Reader in Economics, Keele University. Author of a monograph on Cameralism (*Governing Economy*, Cambridge UP 1988) and a collection of essays on German economics from the eighteenth to the twentieth centuries (*Strategies of Economic Order*, Cambridge UP 1995). At present completing a research project on the development of the economics discipline in Britain 1805–1970.

Horst Tomann is Professor of Economics in the Economics Department, Free University of Berlin. His main field of research is applied economics with particular focus on economics of integration and development. He holds a Jean Monnet Chair 'European Economic Policy'.

Geoffrey Wood is currently Professor of Economics at City University London. He has also taught at the University of Warwick, and has been with the research staff of both the Bank of England and the Federal Reserve Bank of St. Louis. He is the co-author or co-editor of ten books, which deal with, among other subjects, finance of international trade, monetary policy, and bank regulation. Among his professional papers are studies of exchange rate behaviour, interest rate determination, monetary unions, tariff policy, and bank regulation. He has also acted as an adviser to the New Zealand Treasury. He is a Managing Trustee of the Institute of Economic Affairs and of the Wincott Foundation.

Introduction

Jens Hölscher

This volume reviews birth, life and death of one of the three key currencies of the second half of the twentieth century, the German Mark. The contributions are based on a symposium held in honour of Stephen F. Frowen at the University of Birmingham, where the editor served as DAAD Senior Fellow at the Institute for German Studies. The work is dedicated to Stephen Frowen and reasons for that are presented within the first two chapters of the book. *Hans Tietmeyer*, who gave his laudatio when he was still president of the Deutsche Bundesbank at a reception arranged by the Bundesbank in honour of Stephen Frowen and to mark his 75th birthday, outlines the achievements of Stephen F. Frowen in the academic and public sphere. *Norbert Kloten* gives a more personal account on Stephen F. Frowen, whom he calls an 'inspired mediator in turbulent times'.

In his keynote speech, *Charles A. E. Goodhart* reflects on the future of the Euro against the background of the success story of the Deutsche Mark. His main concern is, whether fiscal policy in Euroland will be ready for action in case of an economic downturn. He also wonders, whether the European Central Bank will be the same safeguard against inflation as the Bundesbank was. On the same issue of stability orientation *Hans Tietmeyer* reviews the 50 years' lifetime of the German Mark pointing out that the Bundesbank will continue to have a say within the European Central Bank. In particular, he emphasizes the vital part of the Deutsche Mark as cornerstone of the so-called *social market economy* in postwar Germany. *Keith Tribe* looks at the roots of this success story by an analysis of the 1948 currency reform. The inauguration of the Deutsche Mark introduced a clear system of price formation under market conditions, which was not in place in Germany since the mid 1930s. In his comment, *Horst Tomann* reflects on the theoretical foundation of the 'primacy of monetary policy', which he sees in sharp contrast to the neoclassical assumption of the 'neutrality of money'. *Reiner König* in his chapter comes to the conclusion that over the 50 years there was no paradigm change in monetary policy of the Bundesbank, because stability was priority throughout the years. This policy was pursued under varying circumstances, most considerable were the transitions through exchange rate regimes of the Bretton Woods era, European Monetary Systems and finally the introduction of the Euro. In his comment, *Andy Mullineux*, extends König's point on exchange rate policy and questions whether the European Central Bank will be in charge of exchange rate policy of the Euro or whether this will be decided by politicians.

In the following Chapter 5 *Geoffrey Wood* asks the question, whether the European Central Bank would be too independent. He is particularly interested in the question to whom the ECB is accountable and points out the importance of institutional embededness of central banks. In her comment *Anke Jacobsen* proposes to rephrase this question to ask whether there are political decisions outside the ECB, which could undermine its monetary policy. In Chapter 6 *Norbert Kloten* investigates the implications of the Euro for Germany and Europe. He develops an optimistic scenario in general, in which Germany and Europe would be put on test for rational economic policy making, but warns that the historically unique chance for Europa might become jeopardized be political shortsightedness and internal quarrels, in particular if they are caused by ideological stubbornnes. *David Cobham* takes the analysis further by reviewing historical experience of European monetary policy with reference to the 1992 ERM crisis and calls for an approach of economic analysis in the tradition of political economy. In Chapter 7 *Hölscher, Owen Smith* and *Pugh* show that the undervaluation of the German Mark substantially contributed to the high growth rates throughout the 1950s and 1960s. In his comment, *Jörg Bibow* agrees with the analysis, but finds the demystification of the Bundesbank has not gone far enough. He points at the deflationary policy in the aftermath of German unification. In Chapter 8 *Stephen Frowen* and *Elias Karakitsos* explain the background and relative role of the Deutsche Mark and the euro and analyze the fate of key currencies employing a policy-choice model. Their game theoretical model, using a strategic approach to expectations, leads them to the conclusion that the European Central Bank should adopt a more balanced view between inflation and growth, like the Fed. *Hajo Riese* looks at the British Pound under the global monetary system of a bipolar monetary regime. He finds that British economic policy is still rooted in its imperial past and foresees that Britain would become more and more like a developing country as become integrated into the leading Western world. In the epilogue *Sir Samuel Brittan* reflects upon the meaning of sound money. After a *tour de horizon* through the history of monetary economic thought he expresses his hopes that the new European Central Bank will employ a new bag of tricks. He is particularly concerned about the dangers of deflation.

This book concludes with a collection of bibliographical data of *Stephen F. Frowen*. The reader should however be aware of the fact that this is an interim report only. As Stephen is relentlessly continuing his scholarly activities, further milestones are to be expected. I greatly enjoyed editing these essays written in honour of my former teacher, colleague and friend Stephen F. Frowen.

Jens Hölscher, Brighton

Laudatio on the Occasion of the 75th Birthday of Professor Stephen F. Frowen*

Hans Tietmeyer

It is a particular pleasure for me to welcome you here today to a dinner at the Deutsche Bundesbank in honour of the 75th birthday of Professor Stephen Frowen.

The relationship between the Deutsche Bundesbank and Stephen Frowen has in fact a long and multifaceted history. It has also been shaped by intense personal contacts and so has been far more than the exchange of ideas which often exists between a critical scholar and the decision makers at a central bank.

Stephen Frowen certainly deserves prominent mention as one of the scholars who have accompanied us for a long time.

But, in addition, Stephen Frowen may also take credit for something else. More than almost anyone else, he has always been keen to give an international public, too, some idea of German monetary policy.

A recent example is his initiative for a special issue of *Central Banking* journal devoted to the subject of 'Understanding the Bundesbank'[1] It is particularly for this aspect of his work that Stephen Frowen deserves our special gratitude.

If one searches for the potential reasons for this outstanding interest, Professor Frowen's biography offers an initial indication. His eventful life – he was born in Germany in 1923 but has lived in Great Britain since 1949 – has made it possible for him to gain deep insights into both German and British monetary policy.

Certainly, his many visiting professorships in Germany have also contributed to this. We were naturally particularly lucky to win Stephen Frowen in 1987 as the first holder of the professorial chair for international currency issues and monetary policy endowed by the Deutsche Bundesbank at the Free University of Berlin.

However, if one takes a closer look, an astonishing correlation becomes apparent behind the biographical facts which are well known to all of us, a correlation which links Stephen Frowen to German monetary policy.

---

* Held at the Deutsche Bundesbank on 22 June 1998 (after dinner speech).

The day before yesterday, 20 June 1998, was the 50th anniversary of the currency reform in which the atrophied monetary system in the three Western occupation zones of Germany was radically reformed and the Deutsche Mark came into being. This year is also the 50th anniversary of Stephen Frowen's graduation from Bonn University, which marked his entry into the active professional life of an economist.

Perhaps it is precisely this coincidence of events that made Stephen Frowen a critical and esteemed companion of German domestic and external monetary policy.

This applies all the more since Stephen Frowen the economist and the German postwar currency have more in common than just the date of his graduation. In fact, an astonishing parallelism marks their further development, too.

The 1950s was a period of maturing for both of them. The Deutsche Mark had to find its role in the international system of currencies. The reputation it enjoys today thanks to its stability was by no means a matter of course.

For Stephen Frowen, too, it was imperative to find his role as an economist. He also operated at an international level, with his editorial activities for *The Bankers' Magazine* (now *Financial World*), which is published in Great Britain.

For both of them the course for the future was set in the early 1960s. With the first revaluation of the Deutsche Mark in 1961 under the Bretton Woods exchange rate system, the commitment to stability of German monetary policy became very clearly visible. The relative strength of the Deutsche Mark *vis-à-vis* the other currencies involved in the system of fixed exchange rates became fully apparent.

At that time Stephen Frowen made a decision which was both far-reaching and also had major consequences: following several advisory activities, he decided to return to the field of scholarship for good.

In 1960 there were already signs of this reorientation, when he moved to the National Institute of Economic and Social Research. With the assumption of full-time lecturing obligations in 1962 and the resulting re-entry into the academic world this reorientation became definite.

The further course of life of both the Deutsche Mark and Stephen Frowen is ultimately distinguished by the fact that the path taken at that time was thereafter pursued steadfastly. I think it is no exaggeration to say that for both of them this was performed with great success!

Thus, Professor Frowen can today look back on a comprehensive scholarly opus, which is distinguished above all by the quality of his empirical work in the field of monetary theory.

Moreover, he also always succeeded in keeping his eye on the currently most urgent monetary policy problems and in making his theoretical work understandable as a help and guide to practical monetary policy. Titles such as 'The Unsolved Deutschmark Problem' (1970), 'The Demand for and Supply of Money in the Federal Republic of Germany 1965–1974', 'The German Currency Union of 1990' and 'An evaluation of inflation targeting in Germany and the UK' speak for themselves.[2]

But in addition, promoting mutual understanding of British and German monetary policy – as I mentioned earlier – has always been at the heart of the work of Stephen Frowen.

His endeavours to bring about a better mutual understanding particularly of German and British monetary policy is attested by his academic work. Other evidence is his activity as an editor of several collected editions which serve this purpose, and particularly his efforts in bringing about a personal exchange of Britons and Germans, which was officially recognized by the award of the German *Grosses Bundesverdienstkreuz*, the Grand Cross of the Order of Merit of the Federal Republic of Germany, in 1993.

Stephen Frowen also organized a multitude of conferences, which brought together theoreticians and monetary policy practitioners for an intensive exchange of views.

We at the Bundesbank recall above all the Berlin Monetary Conference in 1988, which was initiated by Professor Frowen in connection with his activities at the Free University of Berlin. The volume containing the proceedings of that conference, which was published later,[3] testifies to the extremely fruitful discussions. Many of the subjects discussed there have lost none of their topicality. This applies particularly to the contribution by Stephen Frowen and Herbert Buscher on money demand in some industrialized countries.[4] After all, as the start of European monetary union is drawing nearer, we are experiencing an intensification of the debate to decide what is the proper monetary policy strategy.

The basis of any monetary targeting strategy, as a possible option for the European Central Bank, however, centres on the empirical properties of the demand for money, which Stephen Frowen has helped us to understand.

Finally, speaking of European monetary union, this gives me the opportunity to speculate briefly about the future work of Stephen Frowen. The close correlation between the Deutsche Mark and the economist Stephen Frowen I have demonstrated may give rise to concern that with the replacement of the Deutsche Mark by the Euro we could be deprived of an important academic commentator. Luckily, however, strong arguments speak against this hypothesis.

First, Stephen Frowen's unceasing commitment to economic research suggests that the idea of what would be a certainly well-deserved retirement is far from his mind. After his return to Great Britain in 1989 he accepted the post of an honorary research fellow in the Department of Economics at University College London. In addition, he is a senior research associate of the Von Hügel Institute and Fellow Commoner of St Edmund's College, University of Cambridge, as well as an honorary professor at the Institute for German Studies, University of Birmingham.

Second, the title of an article by Professor Frowen also shows what will possibly be the focus of his further academic work after the foreseeable end of the Deutsche Mark in 1999: 'Inflation and the World Demand-for-Money Function'![5]

All that remains for me to do, therefore, is to wish you, dear Stephen Frowen, all the very best for your future both in your private and professional life. Regarding the Euro as the successor of the Deutsche Mark, I hope that it will become as stable as it was envisaged by the politicians who brought it into being.

Notes

1. 'Understanding the Bundesbank', *Central Banking*, VI 1, 19–76. Revised and updated versions of these papers are included in *Inside the Bundesbank* (Stephen F. Frowen and Robert Pringle eds), (London: Macmillan; New York: St Martin's Press, 1998).
2. S. F. Frowen 'The Unsolved Deutschmark Problem', *The Bankers' Magazine*, 209 1515 (March) 137–43; S. F. Frowen and P. Arestis, 'The Demand for and Supply of Money in the Federal Republic of Germany 1965–1974', in S. F. Frowen, A. S. Courakis and M. H. Miller (eds) *Monetary Policy and Economic Activity in West Germany* (London: Surrey University Press in association with Intenational Textbook Co; New York: Wiley/Halstead Press; Stuttgart: Gustav Fischer Verlag, 1977) pp. 129–46; S. F. Frowen and J. Hölscher (eds) *The German Currency Union of 1990: A Critical Assessment* (London: Macmillan; New York: St Martin's Press, 1997); S. F. Frowen and E. Karakitsos 'An Evaluation of Inflation Targeting in Germany and the UK', *Kredit und Kapital*, 30 4 (1997) 501–32.
3. S. F. Frowen (ed.) *Monetary Theory and Monetary Policy: New Tracks for the 1990s* (London: Macmillan; New York: St Martin's Press, 1993).
4. H. Buscher and S. F. Frowen (1993), 'The Demand for Money in Japan, the United Kingdom, West Germany and the USA: An Empirical Study of the Evidence since 1973', in S. F. Frowen (ed.), *Monetary Theory and Monetary Policy: New Tracks for the 1990s* pp. 123–170.
5. S. F. Frowen and G. Kouris (1980), 'Inflation and the World Demand-for-Money Function', *Kredit und Kapital*, 13 1, 21–37.

Stephen Frowen – an Inspired Mediator in Turbulent Times

*Norbert Kloten**

I

This volume of essays is published in honour of Stephen Frowen. His 75th birthday was a welcome occasion for the authors to show their affection and admiration for Professor Frowen by participating in the symposium '50 years of the German Mark', the papers of which form the present volume. With their contributions they honour a man who as scholar, teacher and editor has significantly advanced his subject and has always put himself wholeheartedly at the service of public concerns. He has grown to feel as much at home in the intellectual climate and way of life of his adopted country, Great Britain, as in the intellectual ambiance of his native Germany. He has always been a good and reliable friend to all those who have approached him.

Even the appearance of Professor Frowen attracts attention: his figure tall for his generation and slim in appearance, the small scholarly head, the extremely lively and alert eyes, also the corners of his mouth which signal an immediate readiness to articulate his views. Conversation with him shows a sharp mind, a rapid grasp of complex issues, a comprehensive cultural background and a remarkable flexibility during wide-ranging discussions. A feeling for language and an admirable gift of formulation combine with rare distinction; and there is an inquisitive streak regarding every current trend. Pride of place belongs to politics, economics and culture, but all are brought together within a comprehensive and unifying vision. The fascination with intellectual exploration, of both professional and personal matters, occasionally tends to induce Stephen Frowen to forget time and place as well as deadlines and other commitments on his agenda; in principle he is constantly searching for something – hence suffering from lack of time. The reason is not least the multitude of engagements he has accepted at one time or other. His commitments and

* Former President of the Land Central Bank in Baden-Württemberg and member of the Policy-Making Central Bank Council of the Deutsche Bundesbank.

obligations, however, are in the end dealt with in time – to be honest, almost in time. It borders on the miraculous that despite deadlines and commitments, Stephen and Irina, his wife, manage to find so much time for travelling, for contemplative hours and for participation in social life. Yet what makes one marvel is not such a great mystery. In Stephen's case, numerous activities simply convert into a unity somewhat related to his personality. The *multa* is in harmony with the *multum*. He satisfies his true nature in everything he does, so that all combines well with his talents accorded to him at birth and developed by him throughout his life. I only realized and began to understand this with the passing of time, but to clarify those points requires from me a more personal approach than is normal and perhaps allowed for on an occasion such as this.

II

I first met Stephen in the winter term 1946–47 at the University of Bonn. Its main building, the former Palace of the Kurfürsten, had been bombed. The Faculty of Economics, a subject we both read, had been evacuated to the upper floors of a public school in Bad Godesberg, south of Bonn. Stephen, one term ahead of me, offered me and other students lessons in double entry book-keeping and the construction of balance sheets – subjects he had studied during a previous apprenticeship. This was the immediate postwar period with limited supplies of food, empty shops, a flourishing black market and a cigarette currency; not surprisingly, the remuneration was expected in the form of something useful or eatable. Stephen, fairly thin and pale, but handsome and good looking, quite obviously an intellectual, proved himself to be a born teacher and was regarded by us as a forthcoming academic scholar. Quickly we established good personal relations. Then, suddenly, soon after Stephen's graduation in the summer of 1948, he just disappeared. According to rumours Stephen was suffering from an open tuberculosis (the aftermath of damage to his lungs resulting from his services as a medical orderly during the Second World War). Additional rumours also claimed that Stephen had established contact with a charming young lady, at that time lecturing at an international summer course at the University of Bonn as a colonel in the British Army of the Rhine. At the time she was teaching German literature at the University of Leeds and academics then had to have a military rank in order to visit occupied West Germany. People talked about Stephen having escaped with the lady to Switzerland for medical treatment. As a matter of fact, they went for a honeymoon to the Ticino after they got married in Switzerland in March 1949. After

Stephen's departure from Germany, I often enquired among English friends and German economists visiting British universities as to his whereabouts, but without success. He remained a missing person. As it turned out, when we – that is my wife Annemie who had been a fellow student of ours at the University of Bonn and I – finally met Stephen Frowen again by chance during the 1980s at the home of my then colleague at the Bundesbank's Central Bank Council, Claus Köhler (previously Professor of Economics at Hanover University), he had by then become an established scholar and writer well known even in Germany. He was in contact with a whole range of German academic economists and was well informed about the Bundesbank, the German banking scene generally and about the political conditions and ramifications in Germany. The solution to the problem of Stephen's disappearance was simple and at the same time perplexing: Stephen's German name had been Horst Otto Frowein (the Froweins being a highly respected German family of industrialists). In England he had anglicized his name by dropping the 'i', thereby reverting to an early-medieval version of his family name. In addition, when (coming from a traditional Protestant family) he converted to Roman Catholicism in England in 1952, he was baptised at St Anne's Cathedral, Leeds, under the name of 'Stephen Francis' and thus became Stephen Francis Frowen (and a British subject by naturalization in February 1956). It is not surprising, therefore, that my searches for him had remained unsuccessful. In any case for me and for my wife Annemie, it was a joyful reunion. The years lost did not seem to count. The previously student-like familiarity deepened rapidly into a friendship now well established, which also includes our wives. What is it that fascinates me and others about Professor Frowen – now 75 years old?

III

The late Professor G. L. S. Shackle, Stephen Frowen's greatly admired academic mentor and personal friend, characterised him 'as the gentle and quiet scholar', who 'has shown himself a man of steel in face of the difficulties which this turbulent and restless century has thrown in his path' (Shackle, 1988. p. x). This sentence brings to light the toughness of part of Stephen's personality expressed in affectionate terms. Both characteristics are essential parts of Stephen's personality. He does, indeed, pursue his aims and everything that in his view is due to him with never-ending single-mindedness, combined with a readiness to be open to new discoveries, in order, so to speak, to remain part of the game. But all this is by no means subject to chance but, rather, in harmony with the possibilities which have previously presented themselves to him and are still doing so today. These opportunities are scarcely realizable without ambition and without a striving for self-realization. But in all this he is conscious of the motto *'Geist sucht Glaube'* (intellect seeks faith) which he himself has chosen as a motto accompanying his old family coat of arms recently granted anew by the College of Arms on behalf of Her Majesty the Queen. The normal attitudes and behaviour of people in retirement certainly do not fit this model. To withdraw to the solitude and ease of a pensioner's life, whatever form this may take, is not for Stephen. This is part of that approach to life which Professor Shackle recognized with his sharp mind. Already the young Horst Frowein, a practising Christian, leaves his school in opposition to the compulsions under the Nazi regime and starts an apprenticeship in the offices of a shipping company. Being discharged later from his duties as a medical orderly in the army after having been infected first with diphtheria and subsequently with severe and long-lasting tuberculosis, he catches up with his *Abitur* (the German equivalent of A-levels in the UK) and starts his university studies in economics, first at the University of Cologne, then Würzburg and finally, after the war, at the University of Bonn. It was here – in 1946 – where, in collaboration with the geologist Professor Hans Cloos, he founded the 'Club of Bonn Students' (later incorporated in the International Student Club) aiming to restore German relations to foreign countries. Later, I learned that in 1950 Professor Cloos had recommended him for a career in the German diplomatic service: 'I know of few young Germans', he wrote, 'on whose character and personality I would so confidently rely in all frontier-crossing questions as on Horst Frowein'. His first years in England were – as he sometimes jokingly says – comparable to a 'male war-bride'. He experienced and absorbed the English way of life with such intensity that to him everything English from the idiomatic language to the details and intricacies of English social life became in the course of time an element of his personality. Five years after settling in England, after further postgraduate studies and a training in bank management, he was appointed first assistant editor of *The Bankers' Magazine* (now the *Financial World*) in 1954, and in 1956, following the death of the then editor, took over the editorial chair himself. One of his predecessors, the distinguished financial journalist G. L. Schwartz, 'saved and re-established it [*The Bankers' Magazine*] after the war and set it again on the road to success' (Shackle, 1957, p. v). Stephen Frowen bestowed upon the periodical, already with a fine reputation since its foundation in 1844, 'a modern shape and content ... [a new] lustrum' (Shackle,. 1960, p. 290). The same tenacious perseverance, the same intellectual muscle and the same intuitive grasp of the specific English ambience marked his career as a senior academic at the universities of Greenwich and Surrey, and when on reaching the official retirement age, as a honorary research fellow in the Department of Economics at University College London (since 1989), as a senior research associate of the Von Hügel Institute, St Edmund's College Cambridge (since 1991) and as an Honorary Professor, Institute for German Studies, University of Birmingham (since 1995). In 1999 he was elected a Fellow Commoner of St Edmund's College, University of Cambridge. But this is not by any means all.

IV

What I have to emphasize more than anything is Stephen Frowen's successful endeavour over decades of the postwar period to get German and British scholars, German and British experts of central banking and banking generally, around the same conference table. He was anxious to achieve an exchange of experiences and academic discussion, even in the presence of divergent concepts regarding the conduct of economic and in particular monetary policy between Great Britain and Germany. Building bridges between the two countries has always been in the forefront of his mind. He sought a personal engagement at German universities (in Würzburg 1983–84, in Frankfurt 1987, and in Berlin 1987–89) and at many professional conferences, such as the meetings of the European Forum Alpbach organized by the Austrian College, Vienna (1960–88). I well remember the exploratory discussions at the Bundesbank's Central Bank Council which led to Stephen Frowen's appointment as the first holder of the Chair of Monetary Economics which the Deutsche Bundesbank founded at the Free University of Berlin in 1987 on the occasion of the 750th anniversary of Berlin.

In order to bring experts from Great Britain and Germany together, he repeatedly initiated conferences in monetary and generally in political economics. His ingenuity in deciding on topical subjects of pressing importance enabled him to persuade initially reluctant participants and also to give the conferences a unique personal flair. It was this which has been the source of far-reaching personal bonds. As Bundesbank Professor in Berlin he pursued, in his own words, 'the idea of establishing Monetary Conferences organized by successive incumbents of the Bundesbank Chair'. This endeavour which would have accorded to the Bundesbank Chair a very special image, could not be realized. The successors of Professor Frowen on the Bundesbank Chair and the Economics Faculty of the Free University of Berlin had unfortunately no wish to carry a burden which Stephen had carried with such ease and willingness by organizing the first of such envisaged monetary conferences.[1] Papers presented at Stephen Frowen's conferences laid the basis for publications routinely, receiving attention in relevant quarters of political, economic and academic life. They were published mainly by his favourite publisher, Macmillan Press Ltd (London) and its subsidiary in the United States, the St Martin's Press (New York) – now combined under the name Palgrave. But a positive widespread echo has been awarded to Stephen Frowen's own writings. They are part of an extensive literary and scholarly *oeuvre*, mostly contributions to books, journal articles, short notes, reviews, letters to newspapers and obituary notes, but also notable translations, for example an English translation of Knut Wicksell's *Über Wert, Kapital und Rente* (*Value, Capital and Rent*). Among his publications in macroeconomics which still have the greatest significance for Stephen are his extensive studies on the demand for and supply of money, on inflation and on related subjects in the field of central banking. His intense interest in the works of G. L. S. Shackle will no doubt lead to further publications on expectational economics. I have read many of Stephen Frowen's publications and have actively participated in quite a few of his conferences. We have repeatedly discussed British and German views on current issues of monetary policy. Stephen Frowen was and is an excellent exponent of German monetary policy. Helmut Schlesinger, then President of the Deutsche Bundesbank, stressed the 'special ties' with Professor Frowen and appreciated 'his excellent contributions to monetary policy issues' (Schlesinger, 1993, p. vii). But although Stephen Frowen consistently emphasized the efficiency of German monetary policy and is well informed about its background, there has always to me been a Keynesian residue. In the last analysis he seemed to lean more on traditional British thinking on monetary policy issues than the puritanical German money supply logic.

V

Stephen Frowen's course of life cannot be understood without reference to his wife who was born Irina Minskers, in Moscow, and who left Russia with her parents in 1919 after the Revolution. She went first to Baden-Baden and then Berlin where she grew up, took her *Abitur* and began her studies of German literature until her move to London in 1938 where she continued her studies and graduated with first-class honours at University College London in 1941. This was followed by an outstanding career as a lecturer first at the University of Durham, then at the University of Leeds and finally at University College London where she is still an honorary research fellow in the Department of German. One of her former students, Richard Hosburn, married Stephen's and Irina's daughter Tania, now a well-known psychotherapist, and through them Stephen has been blessed with three granddaughters Carly (now Mrs Raby), Josie and Cassie and great granddaughter Kaiya Raby who bring much sunshine into the lives of the proud grand and great grandparents, especially after the tragic death of their only son Michael, an economist and computer analyst whose subsequent dream was a career in psychiatry. Irina Frowen is well known in Germany and elsewhere as a brilliant exponent of two of the most important German poets: Johann Wolfgang von Goethe and Rainer Maria Rilke. She also evoked in Stephen a deep interest in their work. Irina in particular, but Stephen, too, are both prominent participants at symposia and conferences on German literature. Irina is an honorary member of the Rilke-Gesellschaft and is much acclaimed for her inspiring temperament. She was honoured herself on her 75th birthday by her own *Festschrift* entitled *Heimat im Wort* (edited by her former student Rüdiger Görner (now Director of the Institute of Germanic Studies at the University of London). Stephen has been honoured in a variety of ways. He is a member of the Reform Club and also (together with Irina) an elected member of the International Pen-Club. For his work as a senior member of the Von Hügel Institute, Cambridge – undertaken in close collaboration with his esteemed colleague and friend, the Rev. Frank McHugh, Director Emeritus of the Institute – he was awarded a Knighthood of the Pontifical Order of St Gregory the Great by Pope John Paul II (1996). Acknowledging his contributions to German economics and building the foundations of the Bundesbank Chair in Berlin, the President of the Federal Republic of Germany honoured him by conferring on him the award of the Grand Cross of the Order of Merit of the Federal Republic of Germany (1993).

VI

Honours of this kind have always delighted Stephen Frowen. He quite rightly took them as recognition of the path he has followed and of his published work, which still does not seem to be completed. He remains active, initiating and supporting events of a scholarly and charitable nature. At the same time, it seems to me, he has been eager in various ways to reap the harvest of his life. These things are of great importance to him. What he treasures are his accomplishments, the respect extended to him and the honours bestowed, but perhaps even more the personal aspects of life and his friends – all those he loves and feels indebted to. In this way, significant circles in his life have merged over the years. This also applies to his intellectual vita, which made him drop well-founded anchors in the academic world, and to his wanderings between the country of his birth, Germany, and the country where he has found his identity, Great Britain. Let us hope that this *Festschrift* will be the source of both delight and satisfaction to Stephen Frowen.

Note

1. Of the numerous incumbents of the Bundesbank Chair after Stephen Frowen, only Emil-Maria Claassen and more recently Victoria Chick managed to organize further Monetary Conferences under the auspices of the Bundesbank Chair at Free University of Berlin. [Ed.]

Bibliography

Schlesinger, H. 'Foreword', in P. Arestis (ed.) *Money and Banking: Issues for the Twentieth Century – Essays in Honour of Stephen F. Frowen* (London: Macmillan; New York: St. Martin's Press,) pp. vii–x (second and extended edition of *Contemporary Issues in Money and Banking*, 1993).

Shackle, G. L. S. 'Foreword,' in S. Frowen and Hillman H. C. (eds) *Economic Issues: A financial and economic debate in the critical years 1954–57* (London: Waterlow & Sons, 1957) p. v.

Shackle, G. L. S. *Stephen Frowen – Editor of The Bankers' Magazine 1955–1960. The Bankers' Magazine*, CLXXXIX 1393 (March 1960) p. 290.

Shackle, G. L. S. 'Foreword,' in P. Arestis (ed.) *Contemporary Issues in Money and Banking – Essays in Honour of Stephen Frowen* (London: Macmillan, 1988) pp. ix–x.

1
Keynote Speech: The DM and the Future of the Euro

Charles A. E. Goodhart

Introduction

One of the trivial statements, purported facts, from perusing the Press, that sticks in my mind is that, if you assume the continuation of present trends in mortality, then the expectation of life of every white American baby girl born after the year 2000 AD will be over 100 years. We used to worry what people would do to fill up their added life span. In the case of American women, Alexander Graham Bell's useful invention resolved that problem, just as Rupert Murdoch's Sky Sports relieves all such worries for British men.

Be that as it may, the choice between work and leisure is little understood, perhaps little studied, by economists. Large segments of society, including our own academic community, are working harder and more hours now than we would have done 20 or 40 years ago, and that is so despite an income level that is much higher in real terms, even if we academics are racing down the comparative income ladder with a speed reminiscent of the clergy's relative decline in the previous century.

Professor Stephen Frowen

Is all this extra work voluntary, or compelled? In the case of Stephen Frowen, it is patently voluntary. In the last three years, and since reaching the age of 72, he has jointly edited no less than five books, with one of these published in June 1998, entitled *Inside the Bundesbank*; he has contributed seven chapters to some of these and to other books, and completed four journal and discussion papers, the last of which, a discussion paper from the Birmingham University's Institute for German Studies, Stephen sent to me a month ago. Stephen's energy is phenomenal. I think that I first met him in 1975, when as a senior lecturer at the University of Surrey he organized the excellent conference 'Monetary Policy and Economic Activity in West Germany', but Stephen's memory is much better than my own, and he may recall even earlier meetings.

That conference illustrates several of Stephen's manifold great qualities. One of these is his organizational and administrative skills. The conference also covered the academic topics which Stephen has made his great speciality, both in his early years on *The Bankers' Magazine* and subsequently as an academic, to wit the study of monetary economics, policies and institutions in Germany and in the UK. As his many honours eloquently testify, Stephen has, and continues, to do great work in this field, explaining German issues to us in the UK, and, what is much harder, explaining the twists and turns of British monetary policies in Germany. His long and illustrious career, holding chairs in some of the top universities in Germany, and here, and his life-long studies and publications, these make him into a one-person Anglo-German institution. I was privileged to be invited to the dinner at the Bundesbank, in honour of Stephen's 75th birthday, earlier this week, where Hans Tietmeyer made an eloquent and memorable speech, or rather a laudation, about Stephen. In the course of this, he said that,

> [Stephen's] endeavours to bring about a better mutual understanding particularly of German and British monetary policy is attested by his academic work. Other evidence is his activity as an editor of several collected editions which serve this purpose, and particularly his efforts to bring about a personal exchange of Britons and Germans, which was officially recognised by the award of the German *Grosses Bundesverdienstkreuz,* the Grand Cross of the Order of Merit of the Federal Republic of Germany, in 1993.

Be that as it may, the conference organizers asked me to concentrate my remarks not on Stephen's anniversary, but on another anniversary, that is the 50th year of the Deutsche Mark. Although, as Tietmeyer also mentioned, the course of the mark has been intertwined with Stephen's own career. As Tietmeyer stated,

> ... on June 20 [1998], was the 50th anniversary of the currency reform in which the atrophied monetary system in the three western occupation zones of Germany was radically reformed and the Deutsche Mark was called into being. This year is also the 50th anniversary of Stephen Frowen's graduation from Bonn University, which marked his entry into the active professional life of an economist.

However, if one takes a closer look, an astonishing correlation becomes apparent behind the biographical facts which are well known to all of us, a correlation which links Stephen Frowen to German monetary policy. There would be a splendid symmetry if, with his birth having preceded that of the Deutsche Mark by 25 years, he was to outlive the DM by as much again. Again, as Tietmeyer said,

> Finally, speaking of European monetary union, this gives me the opportunity of speculating briefly about the future work of Stephen Frowen. The close correlation between the D-Mark and the economist Stephen Frowen I have demonstrated may give rise to concern that with the replacement of the D-Mark by the euro we could be deprived of an important academic commentator. Luckily, however, strong arguments speak against this hypothesis.

The Deutsche Mark

Anyhow, over these last 50 years, the Deutsche Mark has been the most successful currency in the world. First, if we compare the Consumer Price Index in Germany, USA and UK you can see a slower pace of inflation in Germany. The period of greatest comparative advantage, not surprisingly, is between the end of the Bretton Woods era at the end of the 1960s and start of the 1970s, to the current decade, with convergence to low inflation worldwide at the same time as German reunification. That earlier period of much better contra-inflationary performance in Germany, in the 1970s and the 1980s, was, naturally, mirrored in a strengthening nominal exchange rate. This stronger performance has been achieved by better long-term monetary control. Various structural and definitional changes make it difficult to illustrate this (e.g. for narrow money, M1, in the UK), but it is clear that growth of broad money has been slower in Germany than in the UK since 1956.

This success has been due in some large part to the statesmanship and leadership of the Bundesbank's presidents. My own memory goes back to Karl Blessing, president during 1958–69, and both he, and his successors as presidents, Klasen, Emminger, Pöhl, Schlesinger and now Tietmeyer, provide a roll-call of great monetary leaders of Europe and the world. It is also due to the calibre and advice of their chief economists, and, since 1964, they have had three outstanding men in this role, Heinrich Irmler, Helmut Schlesinger, and, until 1 June this year, Otmar Issing. I would also like to use this opportunity to recall the memory of my close friend and colleague in the Economics Department of the Bundesbank, Hermann-Josef Dudler, who, sadly, died a few years ago.

Despite the success of the DM, synonymous with the stability, reliability and strength of the German economy and its people over these years, its days are numbered.

Sometimes currencies disappear because of economic failings, the peso becomes the nuevo peso, and then the grande peso, the peso real, and so on; and more and more people use the US dollar. But that was far from the case here. As is well understood in Germany, the main determinants of the birth, life and ending of currencies owes much more in most cases to political considerations than to economic factors.

Let us take the case of a single currency for Europe. What would have been the overwhelmingly most efficient *economic* way to achieve this? The answer is obvious and straightforward. When they had met agreed criteria, and were willing to do so, each candidate country should have adopted the DM as its own currency and also sent an appropriate number of directors onto the Direktorium of the Bundesbank. This would have eliminated any transitional costs for the largest nation in Europe, have been evolutionary, minimized reputational and credibility problems, and had a variety of other economic advantages. But politically it was unthinkable.

The future of the Euro

The future of the Euro does not really depend on the extent of asymmetry in economic shocks. Instead it depends on the *political* cohesion of its constituent members, although this latter will be somewhat influenced by asymmetric shocks. Let me give you an example. The issue of whether the UK can, and should, join monetary union is far less affected by the question of whether cyclical convergence has been achieved, than by whether the main opposition party, or indeed Mr Rupert Murdoch personally, has become reconciled to that eventuality. Why should the participating nations welcome entry by the UK, if a major party, liable to regain office shortly thereafter, was then threatening to take us out again? But if you see monetary union essentially as a political act, as I do, for example in my forthcoming article 'The Two Concepts of Money' in the *European Journal of Political Economy*, then how would one assess its chances of future success?

I have to say that, while I greatly admire the vision and principles which have inspired EMU and the single Euro currency, I remain somewhat dubious and sceptical of its long-term success. Let me try to explain why. The easiest way to do so is to note what appears to me to be a contradiction between the adoption of a supra national European *monetary* system, and the recently re-enforced determination to place national considerations first and foremost in *fiscal* policies.

I was privileged to serve as an outside expert on a European Commission (EC) working party which had been set up at the outset of this decade to review and reconsider the fiscal changes that could and should support the move to a single currency, a kind of 'MacDougall Mark 2'. Alongside my co-author, Stephen Smith of the Institute of Fiscal Studies (IFS), we proposed, and expert economists then on the EC, notably Alexander Italianer, Marc Vanheukelen, Jean Pisani-Ferry and Roland Leseure, worked out the details for a modest and focused EC stabilization scheme, whereby countries facing asymmetric output and employment losses, would receive some financial assistance, via the EC, from their more fortunate colleagues. All this was set out in papers published in *European Economy* among the 'Reports and Studies' on *The Economics of Community Public Finance* at the end of 1993.

There were the standard adverse responses to any such proposals. For example, moral hazard was once again raised in opposition – in my view one of the more overstated concepts in modern economics, whose most vocal adherents often embody a large streak of unpleasant Victorian rigidity – and then again the claim that asymmetric downturns often result from idiosyncratic bad policies or stupid behaviour (for example trades union intransigence), so why should virtuous us hand over good taxpayers money to help out misguided you.

But the main criticism, at least among economists, was that asymmetric shocks could usually be expected to affect especially particular industries, and/or particular regions. Most countries within the EC are sufficiently large and heterogeneous to be able to provide such stabilization internally, and, in view both of the virtues of subsidiarity, and the various administrative and bureaucratic disadvantages of operating at the federal level through the EC budget, it would be better to leave it that way.

From an economic standpoint that argument has quite a lot of force, but to me it misses the key *political* economy factor. Try and imagine for the moment a participating nation state within Euroland that has, for one reason or another, got itself into a deteriorating economic condition. What can it do to help itself? Interest rates and exchange rates are determined centrally, and its fiscal policy is supposed to be constrained by the Stability and Growth Pact. Of course, if that country has been fiscally virtuous in the past, that constraint would not be severe, but are you confident that such fiscal virtue will be the future commonplace in Euroland?

If not, then demand management in all its main forms will be hog-tied in a deflated country within Euroland. There are surely, I would suggest, going to be politicians who will ask, under such conditions, exactly what benefits do we, in our own country, get from membership in Euroland? In my paper, with Stephen Smith, I was trying to provide an opportunity for politicians who want to stay with Euroland to point to something concrete, even if modest, to point to in response. They could then say, 'When we get into real and special difficulties, our Euroland partners are prepared to help us out. Why even yesterday EC President Gonsalez handed over a cheque for X billion Euros to Prime Minister Peter Mandelson'.

To return to reality, to my mind the crunch for the euro and the EMU process will come at the moment when and if a downturn causes the budgets of some member countries to overstep the limits set by the Stability and Growth Pact. What will happen? If the pact becomes, in political practice, unenforceable, at least against the larger countries, will it then be possible to avoid fiscal indiscipline in some countries, with possible consequential crises in bond markets. But if the pact is rigidly enforced, fines and all, what will be the political consequences in the country at the receiving end. Can you seriously imagine a major, proud country, for example France, in a situation where its fiscal position has been adversely affected by serious economic problems, then voting to impose an extra Eurotax on itself for having failed to undertake sufficient *pro-cyclical* expenditure, or tax changes. Quite honestly, the mind boggles.

Conclusion

Perhaps such a crunch will never arise, but it will be good fortune if it does not, and in economics we should never rely on luck. The successful management of the DM did not occur because of luck. As I said earlier, the Bundesbank enjoyed great leadership, but also its themes and handling of monetary policies in Germany went with the grain, and reflected the priorities, of German society and its people. Making a central bank independent does not take it out of politics; rather the reverse, it plunges it much more immediately into the political process, which is one reason why the issues of accountability and transparency are of such vital importance for the ECB to get right. The Bundesbank was seen by the people of Germany as their defender and bulwark against the scourge of inflation; they relied, and rightly so, on the Bundesbank for protection in a dangerous world. Will those who are following, and trying to emulate the Bundesbank, whether the Bank of England or the ECB, be able to do as much, or even enough? Time will tell.

2
Fifty Years of the Deutsche Mark – a Currency and its Consequences*

Hans Tietmeyer

I

Fifty years – it almost seems that this span of time is something of a magic number for German currencies. Fifty years was the age reached by the first German common currency: the Mark, which was created in 1873 after the German Reich was founded and perished amid the chaos of hyperinflation in 1923. Twenty-five years – that is, exactly half the magic number 50 – lay between the currency change of 1923 and the currency reform of 1948 which overcame the inflationary legacy bequeathed by Hitler's war financing. Finally, 1998 is the 50th anniversary of the Deutsche Mark, and this will be its last birthday as an independent currency. But could the end of these three eras of German currency history have been more different? Surely not! In 1923 the currency that was abandoned was already ruined. Not only the currency but also the Reichsbank itself was compromised. Its conception and understanding of monetary policy were negated by reality. At the same time, the inflation of 1923 left a terrible legacy for the future fate of our country. In 1948 the inflationary ruins of the Hitler regime had to be cleared away and the foundations laid for a new beginning. A new currency had to be created from scratch, that is it had no successful tradition on which it could build. Its birth was marked not by jubilant celebrations or firework displays but by the dry, repetitive words of the control officer and announcer on Radio Frankfurt, Robert Lochner: 'The new money is called the Deutsche Mark. Each Deutsche Mark is divided into 100 Deutsche Pfennigs. The old money – the Reichsmark, the Rentenmark and the Allied Military Mark – will no longer

* Address to the meeting presented at a ceremony commemorating 'Fifty Years of the Deutsche Mark' in the Paulskirche, Frankfurt, June 20 1998.

be legal tender as from June 21'. What a world of difference to the situation today! At the end of 1998 the Deutsche Mark will be integrated as a highly esteemed currency into a new, larger currency: the Euro. It will take with it its internal and external strength. And although the Bundesbank will then surrender its responsibility for monetary policy decision-making, it will do so as an institution which is held in high repute both at home and abroad. The most important thing is that no one will lose anything through the conversion to the new currency. On the contrary, the Germans, too, will be among the winners if the Euro is stable. So for the first time in Germany's turbulent monetary history this century, a new currency will be launched not with the mandate to bring order into chaos or to correct old mistakes. No, the new currency, the Euro, will begin its life with the mandate to uphold, continue and augment the existing legacy of stability.

II

Naturally, many people will be sorry to see the end of the DM because it has become a part, and indeed a powerful symbol, of German postwar development and of the new republic in Germany. While it is true that every national currency represents its respective state, the ties between the DM and the Federal Republic of Germany are closer than is usually the case. In the consciousness of the German people, the currency reform of 20 June 1948 symbolizes the fresh start after the war. It is a land 'mark' in the true sense of the word. Many people in the western part of Germany who witnessed that 20 June date events in their own lives at that time on the basis of 'before and after the currency change'. Similarly, for many East Germans 1 July 1990 was at least equally as important as the following 3 October. The currency reform of 1948 was a turning point for the later Federal Republic of Germany, perhaps even more so than the formal establishment of the republic itself. But just as the currency reform marked the beginning of the new West German state, it also marked the deepening of the split that divided postwar Germany. That was rather tragic. As in Greek tragedy, the currency reform became tainted with guilt through no fault of its own. And this fate was predetermined from a certain point in the postwar years. For what were the alternatives given the increasingly clear-cut East–West divide in Germany and the looming Cold War? Should the currency reform have been postponed? That would have meant deliberately prolonging the agony. Should we have continued to pin all our hopes on a four-zone currency union? At the risk of an even more protracted, painful tug-of-war? Or at the price of letting the East influence the currency and economic system in the West? No, the divide was already too deep. It is not the trizonal currency reform which split Germany. It was the other way round: the already existing political East–West divide limited the currency reform to 'Trizonesia'. The DM and the East Mark which was soon established in its wake thus became the visiting cards of their respective systems. In the West the freely usable and increasingly internationally accepted currency; in the East a currency with limited functionality which never managed to free itself from the straitjacket of the centrally planned command economy. For East Germans the DM – almost more than for West Germans – soon became a symbol of prosperity and freedom. For more than 40 years, however, it was mostly a distant, unattainable symbol. Then, in 1989, the previously unattainable suddenly came closer. The people in the East demanded freedom and equal chances in life. Their strident demands were encapsulated in the formula 'If the D-Mark does not come to us, we will go to the D-Mark'. With the introduction of the DM in the eastern part of Germany on 1 July 1990, the currency anticipated the political reunification that was to follow soon after. And so the D-Mark sealed not only the division of Germany but also its reunification. And you will go down in the history books, Chancellor, for having boldly seized the chance offered by events.

III

Today the Deutsche Mark is an integral part of this republic. It is thus simultaneously a part of this state's dedication to democracy, liberty and social justice. Joseph Schumpeter once famously said that a nation's monetary system mirrors everything that that nation wants, does and suffers; and at the same time the monetary system exerts a fundamental influence on that nation's actions and destiny. And so the DM is a mirror of the largely happy postwar history of the Federal Republic of Germany. That means it enjoys an enormous privilege because, unlike its predecessors, it has been spared the trauma of negative historical fractures. The DM has invested this starting capital with which history endowed it very capably, for it is not only a mirror and reflection of the Federal Republic but has also itself undoubtedly made an important contribution to our political and social stability. This is because the stable DM helped our free society to achieve broad economic prosperity. In this way the stable DM became a cornerstone of the stability of our society and of our free democracy. For the stable DM promoted the development of key civic virtues. Without a stable currency it is hard for self-reliance and self-responsibility to take root. And let us not forget either that the stable DM has also made an ongoing contribution to social welfare, for the erosion of the value of money always hurts the weakest members of society most. That is the cruel law of inflation, a fate which postwar Germany was spared. In this same building 150 years ago the representatives of the separate German states demanded national unity and liberty and some of them called for social justice, too. This is therefore a very fitting place to recall that unity, the rule of law and liberty cannot flourish in the long run without a currency that is lastingly stable and without a currency that is acknowledged and accepted by the country's citizens. That is why the German words for unity, law and liberty which are stamped around the edge of some DM coins are so meaningful. In this sense, too, the DM is a positive legacy for the euro; and also a challenge for Europe.

IV

Above all, of course, the Deutsche Mark is associated with the rise and success of the German economy. In this respect it is also the result of a series of fortunate basic economic policy decisions. That began with the currency reform itself. The decisions concerning the new currency were undoubtedly enormously important: the clean and definitive break with the previous currency, the careful technical and organizational preparations – including, notably, the work in Bad Homburg and in the heavily guarded barracks in Rothwesten – and, not least, also the decision to entrust monetary policy responsibility to a central bank independent of political bodies in Germany. These were favourable factors which owed much to the influence of the American military agencies in Germany at the time. Specifically, Edward A. Tennenbaum, a young officer and scholar who unfortunately met an untimely death, made an unforgettable contribution.

Nevertheless, the launching of the Deutsche Mark would not have been the memorable event that it was without the simultaneous far-reaching release of prices. Of the fundamental economic policy decisions taken by Germans after 1945, the release of prices was shaped more than any other decision by a single man – Ludwig Erhard.

Currency reform and economic reform were two sides of the same coin. New money without free prices would have had little impact, for what new effects can new money achieve if the channels of the market economy are blocked? Conversely, free prices without a preceding currency reform would have opened the floodgates of pent-up inflation overnight. It would have resulted in rampant inflation. How could the market-based economy and the monetary system have gained public confidence in such circumstances? The signal of free prices ushered in what later became known as Germany's economic miracle. Ludwig Erhard set that signal, and he did so against fierce opposition – initially even from the American side. This signal also put the new money to a 'make or break' test. It was both a challenge and a chance, for a currency can gain popular confidence only if it proves it can cope with free prices. The DM embraced that signal of the indispensable role played by prices in the allocation of resources; and, with its high level of domestic stability, it has carried that signal like a flame for five decades. The social market economy, the great efficiency and effectiveness of German businesses and the stability of the DM – these were the three components of the powerful economic triangle in Germany for most of the postwar years. The DM has made a crucial contribution to that successful triangle. Its stability has helped to keep the market economy viable even in critical periods. And its growing international reputation also brought benefits: a broader capital market, relatively low interest rates and the privilege for German enterprises of being able to invoice most of their foreign trade dealings in their own currency. But of course it was not always sunshine in the past 50 years. There were also phases in which the DM's stability record was not satisfactory; for example, in the early 1970s. On occasion domestic misalignments jeopardized monetary stability. At other times there were external constraints through the exchange rate. Safeguarding and regaining internal stability also often required unpleasant measures. From time to time the Bundesbank came into conflict with the politicians, for the first time back in the early 1950s. But there have been periods, too, in which the exchange rate parity of the DM was inappropriate. During some phases the external value of the DM was too low. That sometimes led to an excessive monetary expansion, especially during the crisis period of the old Bretton Woods system. That in turn sent wrong signals and gave rise to illusions about our international performance – for instance, at the beginning of the 1990s. Conversely, there were also periods in which the DM tended to be over-valued. This had a correspondingly negative impact on the price competitiveness of the German economy. It must be said, though, that these blemishes regarding internal stability and the external value of the currency were in the main short-lived episodes. Over the past 50 years, taken as a whole, the DM – and with it German monetary policy – has been a good and reliable partner both for industry and trade and for political decision makers in our country and also at the international level. And that is all a currency can hope to achieve in the long run. It cannot replace the political process – nor should it seek to do so. In fact, a currency's strength is always determined in part by the strategy pursued by policy makers in other fields. A stable currency can only provide a solid foundation. It is the business and political leaders who determine how solid that foundation remains and what kind of edifice they construct upon it.

V

Besides its links with the political and economic fields, the Deutsche Mark is also tied to Germany through an important element of social culture. The stability of the DM was never purely the concern of technocrats. The objective of stable money was and is deeply rooted in our society. It is based on a wide consensus in broad sections of the population. It is based on a culture of stability. That is why German public opinion – particularly in critical periods – again and again proved a loyal ally of a stability-oriented monetary policy. Similarly, the Bundesbank has helped to shape that culture of stability in Germany and to underpin it in institutional terms. The experience of 1948 certainly contributed much to the creation of that culture of stability. People saw that a sound currency quickly led to a restoration of economic order. This was no doubt reinforced by the long tradition in Germany of preferring decentralized and separate structures to an absolute concentration of authority. That is perhaps one reason why there is no difficulty in our country about accepting the independence of monetary policy.

In future the subject of anchoring an independent stability-oriented monetary policy in public opinion and in the culture of society will become an important issue throughout Europe, including for the European Central Bank and the European System of Central Banks. It must be said, too, that, taking a long-term view, the Bundesbank was not immune to making the occasional misjudgement. But when its track record as a whole is assessed, it has made a decisive contribution, with its frequently long-term perspective, to maintaining the orientation towards stability in Germany – and that is a verdict which even its international critics share; in fact, the Bundesbank has become a model which others copy. And there can be no doubt that this orientation to stability has benefited Germans over the past 50 years.

VI

Fifty years of the Deutsche Mark – that is a rather special anniversary, and not only because it is a round number. Today's review is also something of a final report. The great French palaeontologist and philosopher Pierre Teilhard de Chardin once said: 'The magnitude of a river cannot be gauged at its source but only at its estuary, where it flows into the sea'. Well, we have almost reached that estuary where the DM will flow into the great ocean known as the Euro. But looking back, one can see all the more clearly what a respectable heritage it is that the DM will bequeath. Besides comprising the largest share of the capital and reserves of the European Central Bank, the DM will contribute something more: its international reputation in the markets, the independent central bank as a reference model, important monetary policy traditions, above all, the culture of stability among the population.

In the event of a conflict, internal monetary stability is more important than an external exchange-rate relationship. The best monetary policy contribution to growth and employment is lasting stability. And, not least, the lesson that if the process of making monetary policy decisions is kept at arm's length from day-to-day political influences, that is also in the longer-term interests of industry and trade but also of the political leaders themselves. Therefore, perhaps the most important lesson of all is: let the monetary policy makers do what they are there to do: that is, to do everything in their power to ensure monetary stability and thus to lay the basis for economic and social stability. Within this overall monetary framework, the politicians can and must then decide and act in accordance with their responsibilities. But they must not undermine the basis of monetary stability. Otherwise they would jeopardize the very democracy, freedom and social justice on which our society is based. At the same time, it must be remembered that the balance between freedom and social justice must be continuously redefined. That is particularly true of the future given the burden of a still excessive level of unemployment and the challenges posed by the growing global integration of the economy. But in the economic conditions of tomorrow, as in the past, finding the right equilibrium between freedom and social justice can only succeed with a stable currency. This legacy of the DM will now be passed on to the Euro. Naturally, each of the 11 participants will contribute its own heritage. However, the DM's legacy is undoubtedly not the least important. President Duisenberg has recently again emphasized just how important that legacy is as a foundation for a stable Euro. The Euro will be helped on its way by other important sources of support. Monetary convergence in Euroland is today more extensive than it has been for a very long time. And inflation rates are gratifyingly low. Under the Treaty the European Central Bank is just as independent as the Bundesbank. And the Stability and Growth Pact is to provide extra support against the danger of misguided national fiscal policies that could jeopardize stability. The Euro also represents a great historic chance for Europe, a chance for greater economic flexibility and dynamism, and for greater and more durable political harmony – in short, for an economically competitive and politically united Europe.

Chancellor Kohl, I clearly recall something you said in spring with reference to the euro. If I remember right, you said at that time: 'I hope and wish that our descendants in fifty years' time will view the decision to launch monetary union just as positively as we look back today on the decision of 1948'. I certainly second that. And I would add that the Bundesbank will remain a vigilant advocate of stability. Within the new framework in which it will now operate, it will continue to make its contribution towards ensuring that the value of money, both in this country and in Europe, remains lastingly stable in the future.

3
The 1948 Currency Reform: Structure and Purpose

Keith Tribe

Introduction

The Currency Reform (the 'Reform') of 20 June 1948 represents a turning point in the development of the post war German economy. The abolition of a money supply denominated in the Reichsmark and its replacement with the new Deutsche Mark was a symbolic act whose political, cultural and economic impact has resonated throughout the latter half of the twentieth century. The inauguration of the DM as a stable currency reinstated the conditions for regular price formation and economic calculation absent in Germany since the mid-1930s. Contemporaries witnessed the overnight disappearance of disorderly market phenomena – goods shortages combined with currency excess, fixed prices, exchanges in kind, and the black market – and the dawn of a new day with fresh currency, goods in the shops, and an incentive to earn money wages. In popular mythology this event stands therefore at the inception of the Economic Miracle; it is thought of as the founding moment of West Germany's political and economic recovery, and it is generally linked to the elaboration of a social market economy as the foundation of prosperity. The Reform also had profound political effects: it pre-dates the Federal Republic, but precipitated its formation. Introduced by the three Western military governments subsequent to the breakdown of efforts to reconstruct the German economy on a four-power basis, a parallel currency reform in the Soviet Zone sealed the monetary division of Germany and foreshadowed the partition of post-war Germany, whose territory then became for the next forty years the focus of a Cold War confrontation between western and eastern blocs. In 1990 this relationship between monetary and political sovereignty was played out once more; in early July the creation of a unitary German state was foreshadowed by the replacement of the currency of the (still extant) German Democratic Republic with the DM. The experience of postwar European reconstruction was often recalled during the progressive dismantling of eastern European state socialist economies that followed. Politicians and economists who favoured a 'big-bang' approach to the creation of market-led growth turned instinctively to the 1948 Currency Reform as a model for economic reform. And finally, of course, the Reform serves as a model for the European Currency reform, in which the Euro is cast in the role of the DM.

In all these stories it is customary to treat the Reform as a starting point.[1] Dissent from the ruling assumption that the Reform was instrumental in the initiation of economic recovery – most cogently (and aggressively) argued shortly afterwards by Balogh[2] – has pointed to the impact of Marshall Aid, abundant supplies of labour, the overall recovery of the European economy and therefore of export markets, and the impact of the Korean War as associated factors affecting the rate and timing of economic recovery.[3] Analysis of the design and impact of the Reform itself therefore becomes ensnared within a more general discussion of the leading features of German postwar economic growth. This is especially true of those accounts which treat the Reform as the inaugural moment of a Social Market Economy, overlooking the fact that Reform was designed and introduced by the Western allies, and that there was nothing unique about the Reform in a European context, apart from its timing.[4] This paper adopts a different strategy: it considers the genesis of the Reform against a background of prewar and wartime financial policy, and also as one of the last in a series of contemporary European currency reforms. The purpose of this is to sharpen our appreciation of the agenda to which the Reform was addressed, as well as provide insights into the exact timing and properties of the Reform.

The paper will be in four main sections. For the sake of orientation, the exact terms and conditions of the 1948 Currency Reform will be outlined first – many accounts of the Reform[5] are both cursory and inexact, and a return to the text of the relevant paragraphs is called for. This will be followed by a review of the domestic economic and monetary consequences of the manner in which the National Socialist regime pursued rearmament, territorial expansion and, finally, wars of conquest. Contemporary German discussion of this will be examined, followed by a survey of other post war European reform measures aimed at the reconstruction of functioning market economies. The conclusion considers some of the more general implications of the arguments which were advanced for and against a currency reform during the 1940s.

The currency reform: terms and conditions

The German Currency Reform involved both the substitution of one currency for another, and the sterilization of monetary assets. The process began on Friday 18 June 1948 with the promulgation by the three western Military Governments of the first two laws, to come into force on Sunday 20 June 1948. Article I of Law No. 61, the 'First Law for Monetary Reform (Currency Law)', established the Deutsche Mark as the legal currency from Monday 21 June, with Allied Military Marks of 1 and ½ mark denominations, and Rentenbank notes of 1 mark, being recognized until 31 August at one-tenth of their face value – resolving the problem that no small coin for the new currency yet existed.[6] Where existing laws and ordinances employed the Reichsmark (RM), Rentenmark or Goldmark as a unit of account this should in general be henceforth read in DM (Art. II). Monetary obligations arising from application of these laws and ordinances were therefore to be written on 1:1 from the old to the new currency. A deadline of midnight on 26 June (i.e. the Saturday of the week following the Reform) was set for all RM obligations (Art. IV). Article V provided for wages and salaries due later than the end of June, and this concluded Part One of the Law, subtitled 'Conversion of Currency'. It should be noted that it includes two conversion rates, 1:1 under Article II and 10:1 under Article I.

Part Two of the Law dealt with the allocation of new DM to individuals above and beyond the conversion of their pending wages and salaries. Here commentary is often rather blurry, and so it is worth quoting Article VI in its entirety:

> Every inhabitant of the specified area shall receive in cash Deutsche Marks, in exchange for old currency notes as defined in Article IX paragraph 1(i)[7] of the same nominal amount to a maximum of 60 Deutsche Marks (quota per capita), of which not more than 40 Deutsche Marks shall be paid immediately and the remainder within two months. Where the person entitled can claim amounts in Deutsche Marks as a result of the subsequent conversion of old currency as defined hereinafter (Altgeld), the quota per capita shall be charged against the amount thus due.

The quota was to be issued to ration card holders, who in turn were required to surrender 60 RM in order to receive 40 DM immediately, and a further 20 DM at a later date. The 60 DM was an exchange for a nominal equivalent amount of cash denominated in the old currency; it was a maximum, so that if you did not have 60 RM in cash[8] you did not get the full 60 DM allocation. Furthermore, where individuals held accounts which were to be converted from old to new money, the quota was to be charged against these accounts. As we shall see, this meant that account holders could end up paying 600 RM for their 60 DM quota, instead of 60 RM, although they would not have become aware of this until the following October.

The old currency became invalid for new transactions from 21 June (Art. VIII), and all RM credit balances held in specified financial institutions became defined as 'old currency' along with RM notes and Allied Military Marks (Art. IX). All old currency was, as we have already seen, to be declared and surrendered by 26 June 1948, the obligation to do so being laid upon juridical and natural persons, the latter taxable subject[9] then acting on behalf of any dependants (wife and children). Currency was to be surrendered at specific institutions, primarily banks and buildings societies of various kinds, but not the Postal Cheque Office and the Postal Savings Institute (Art. XII). Large private and government places of employment were also authorized for this purpose on behalf of the *Land* central banks. On receipt of the form declaring monetary assets the identity cards of those included on the form were punched in a defined manner to obviate future claims (Art. XII.5), and the balances placed in a Reichsmark Liquidation Account (Art. XIV). Procedures were also outlined to cover misreporting of various kinds. Part Five, the final substantive section of the First Law, dealt with the issue of new currency to public authorities and businesses. The Land central bank was made responsible for supplying agencies and offices with a sum of DM one-sixth of *Land* receipts during the last quarter of 1947 and the first of 1948, to which was added one-sixth of Zone receipts during the same period (Art. XV). For the ensuing half a year, therefore, public authorities received an allocation about one third of former annual receipts, introducing a further variation on the rate of exchange between DM and RM. Businesses were entitled to claim 60 DM per employee payable against their balances of old money, a requirement being that payment so made '...shall not exceed one Deutsche Mark for every Reichsmark of old currency credit balances'.[10]

It could therefore reasonably be inferred that these balances were to be converted at 1:1. Supplementary regulations covered acceptance of RM postage stamps on letters in transit, the continuing validity of season tickets, and extraordinary procedures for the payment of quotas.

Law No. 62, the 'Second Law for Monetary Reform (Issue Law)', likewise to come into effect on 20 June, was much shorter, and outlined the terms of reference of the Bank deutscher Länder, the newly formed central bank for the three Western zones of occupation. This dealt with the issue and withdrawal of notes, the replacement of the existing small change with proper coinage, it limited notes and coin in circulation to 10bn DM (Art. V) and established reserve requirements for the Land central banks (Art. VI). The first and second laws came into effect on Sunday 20 June, and when public trading resumed on the Monday all transactions were made in DM, former RM wages, prices and rents simply being redenominated at the rate of 1:1.

As we have seen, the First Law contained more than one exchange rate between the DM and the RM, but made no mention of the future treatment of the Reichsmark Liquidation Account balances, which brought together all existing monetary assets. This was clarified by Law No. 63, the 'Third Law for Monetary Reform (Conversion Law)', which was announced later during the week of the conversion and came into force one week after the beginning of the Reform, on 27 June:

> In principle, old currency credit balances pertaining to Class I[11] shall be converted so that the owner is credited with one Deutsche Mark for every ten Reichsmarks. Of this, one half shall be credited to a free Deutsche Mark account (*Freikonto*) and the other half to a blocked Deutsche Mark account (*Festkonto*), with regard to which regulations will be issued within 90 days.[12]

This Law came into force the day after all RM currency became invalid, acting therefore directly on the established RM liquidation accounts. The Third Law also decreed that where such accounts had sufficient balances a further 540 RM per capita was payable in respect of the 60 DM quota allocation,[13] and by ten RM for each DM received as an advance by employers in respect of their employees under Law No. 61 Art. XVII. Balances, where they existed, were freed for conversion subject to clearance from the tax office, up to a limit of 5000 RM for individuals and 10,000 for members of trades or professions (Art. V).[14] Article XVI stated the principle that all RM financial claims were to be converted into DM at 10:1, with an exception being made for social insurance payments pending reform by the German authorities (Art. XXIII). The residual 20 DM cash allocation was made in September, and then in October 70 per cent of deposits in blocked accounts was liquidated, 20 per cent released and 10 per cent made available for investment. A new rate of exchange with the dollar was also established, at 1 DM = 30 cents.[15]

The general monetary objective of the Reform had been to cut the money supply by 90 per cent through the surrender of RM for DM at the rate of 10:1, a rate originally established in the Colm-Dodge-Goldsmith

Plan of May 1946 on the basis of a comparison of the existing national product and the money supply with that prevailing in 1938.[16] As we shall see, the appropriateness of the 10:1 ratio was disputed by British officials at the time, and today a more balanced appreciation of the relationship of economic activity to money supply raises doubts about the necessity of a 10:1 cut in money supply in 1948. Furthermore, as noted in note 7, since 1945 monetary assets would have been redistributed through the black market towards those able to obtain goods or who could sell produce, and so the impact of the Reform was perhaps more inequitable than might at first appear. In fact the Colm-Dodge-Goldsmith Plan had recognized the impact of war and post war dislocation upon household incomes and provided for a general redistribution of assets. In the 1948 version, however, the Allies merely called upon the 'appropriate German legislative bodies' to deal with the equalization of non-monetary losses and assets by 31 December 1948, proposing a levy on property which would readjust the balance between real and monetary assets.[17]

The text of the three laws was published in English and German, column by column, with the German version being the official text.[18] Working through the text as above draws attention to the fact that this was a military law, a scheme devised by the Western Allies, although drafted in detail by German experts. This requires emphasis, for the Reform is often run together with several parallel measures which liberalized the economy of the three western zones, but where we need to be careful in attributing the source of the initiative. On 18 June the Bizonal Economic Council[19] adopted an ordinance cancelling existing economic controls, and in the course of the summer this was given effect in a series of directives. Price ceilings were maintained for a limited number of essential foods, rents and some basic materials, such as coal and steel. Clothing and footwear were freed of controls but subject to rationing.[20] For the time being existing wage controls continued in force. This initiative was therefore German in origin, albeit surrounded with mythology concerning the relation of Erhard and Clay, the military governor. In addition to these measures a number of changes to direct and indirect taxation were made immediately following the start of the Currency Reform, with the objectives of restoring work incentives and encouraging saving.[21] These liberalizing measures were however the prerogative of the military authorities, not the German Economic Council; the schedules relating to the changes are printed directly after the three Currency Reform Laws.[22] Most of these last changes simply reversed significant increases in taxation introduced by the military authorities during 1946 in an early effort to erode the monetary overhang through fiscal measures. Income taxes were reduced by some 33 per cent overall, and there was a general shift from direct to indirect taxation, with the former accounting for 47 per cent of the 1949 total.[23] Of the three principal components of the June measures – Currency Reform, abolition of controls, and taxation reform – the first and the third were introduced by the Allies without consulting the Bizonal Economic Council, while the actual deregulation of prices and wages was undertaken in stages over a period of many months.

At the Potsdam Conference, the four Allied powers had agreed to treat Germany as a unitary economy, and negotiations on a pan-German currency reform, based on the Colm-Dodge-Goldsmith Plan, had continued from the autumn of 1946 to the early spring of 1948. The unilateral declaration of a Currency Reform for the three Western zones therefore broke openly with the Potsdam Agreement, and the Soviet Authorities responded forcefully in kind. On Wednesday 23 June the land blockade of Berlin was begun, and a separate Currency Reform for the Eastern Zone was announced. The preamble to 'Soviet Military Administration Order No. 111 on Currency Reform in the Soviet Zone' stated that 'A crushing blow has been dealt to German unity', and that the Soviet administration, '. . . conceding to the demands of the German democratic republic' was compelled to take measures to protect the interests of the German population and of the economy of the Soviet occupation zone.[24] Like the Western reform, the Soviet Currency Reform involved both the substitution of one currency for another (in the absence of new notes effected through the gumming of coupons on to RM notes) and the sterilization of monetary assets. The actual course of the reform mirrored the procedures already outlined. The basic rate of conversion was 10:1, as in the West, but with a differential rate of exchange applied so as to implement a measure of redistribution. A rate of 1:1 was used on the first 70 RM surrendered, with savings deposits being converted at a rate of 1:1 on balances up to a value of 100 RM, and 5:1 up to 1000 RM. Deposits of between 1000 RM and 5000 RM were converted at 10:1, while balances above this level were to be subject to investigation in respect of the legality of their source, earnings from black market dealing or war profiteering being subject to confiscation.[25] As in the West, wages and prices were written on 1:1 from their former values. A Germany divided into two economic zones was therefore created in late June 1948, to be followed in 1949 by the establishment of two governments, each of which laid claim to sovereignty over a united Germany.

The 1948 German Currency Reforms were by European standards considerably delayed by inter-Allied argument over the future of

Germany, but as reforms go this is their only idiosyncratic feature – apart of course from the fact that all other European reforms were carried out by sovereign governments, while the German reforms were devised and imposed by military governments. Moderate and suppressed inflation was a characteristic of the economies of all participants in the war, exacerbated in continental Europe by extensive damage to industrial plant, housing and infrastructure caused by aerial bombardment and land fighting, combined with a variety of short-term problems in labour supply. Output levels for 1945 were everywhere much reduced on pre war figures, but within two years production indices had recovered everywhere – except in Germany. This, despite the post war capital stock being higher than that of 1938, and that demobilization and expulsions, combined with the termination of arms production, provided Germany with a large and highly skilled workforce. German recovery was hampered in part directly by the occupation, and also partly by disagreements among the four Allied powers concerning Germany's economic future. The principal line of cleavage that developed was of course that between East and West, but the Western allies also had their differences, and this emerges clearly in the pre history of the currency reform. None of this alters the fact that, as a currency reform, there is nothing especially unusual about the scheme finally agreed upon by the British, the Americans and the French in early 1948.

In May 1945, following the German capitulation, all banks had been closed, although commercial banks quickly reopened in the Western Zones, local branches of the Reichsbank being placed under central control without the right to issue notes. In the Soviet zone, by contrast, all existing banks remained closed and a new state banking system was created designed to service an administered economy. The Reichsmark continued to circulate in all occupation zones, together with the Occupation Marks which the Allies at their Yalta meeting had agreed to use as a common currency.[26] The Potsdam Agreement of August 1945 had provided for the joint administration of Germany by the four powers, with the Americans favouring rapid decentralization of banking operations under a single currency in the four occupation zones. Despite initial British objections that the system already worked and that decentralization would make supervision more difficult, by October 1946 the French, British and American authorities had agreed to the establishment of *Land* central banks. There was however no agreement with the Soviets over the central authority.

American proposals for a currency reform had already been formulated by November 1945, involving a 5:1 conversion rate together with a capital levy and capital gains tax aimed at war profiteers. The British authorities at this time considered a 5:1 rate draconian, and generally adhered to the position that any reform should be deferred until some kind of equilibrium had emerged in the German economy. The Treasury was concerned at the prospect of a wage–price spiral in the German economy, but generally supported a moderate inflationary approach to the excess money supply, rather than the deflationary approach implicit in a sharp reduction in the money supply. Accordingly, British officials favoured differential price rises of up to 100 per cent, together with controlled wages, any currency reform that was subsequently imposed then being at the much reduced rate of 2:1 or 3:1.[27] British officials therefore favoured a broadly fiscal approach to economic stabilization, but found that the Americans adhered strongly to a monetary approach based upon a radical reduction of the money supply.[28] When the revised American Colm-Dodge-Goldsmith Plan for Currency Reform was published in April 1946 it took no account of British reservations, increasing the conversion rate from 5:1 as in the draft proposal to 10:1. Introduced as a basis for four-power discussion in September 1946, the British proposed instead a 1:1 conversion rate subsequent to price increases, but this was brushed aside by the American delegation. The British responded by suggesting a rate no higher than 2.5:1, combined with the blocking of bank deposits. This was likewise scornfully rejected by the American representatives, and the French proposed a compromise of a 70 per cent cancellation of monetary assets, 20 per cent blocking, and 10 per cent issue of new currency – proportions later imposed on blocked deposits in October 1948.[29]

The Colm-Dodge-Goldsmith Plan became the *de facto* basis for discussion between the Allies, all four powers agreeing on its proposed monetary purge plus compensation for war losses, together with the replacement of the Reichsmark by a new currency unit. Discussions quickly bogged down however over Soviet insistence on printing the new currency in two centres, Berlin and Leipzig. Ostensibly the American representatives considered the proposal to print in Leipzig a security problem, and insisted that all printing should be carried out in Berlin under strict four-power control.[30] There was no agreement on the matter by the end of 1946, and in any case no progress had been made on the future structure of the German banking system.

The Americans went ahead and established a central bank in each of the *Länder* (LzBs) of its occupation zone on 1 January 1947, and these LzBs assumed the major functions of the old Reichsbank, without of course the ability to issue money. In March and October 1947 there was a parallel reorganization of the French zone, but the British zone remained substantially unchanged until 1948, since the British considered that decentralization in the absence of a central authority conflicted with the terms of the Potsdam Agreement relating to the joint administration of a unitary German economy.[31] By this time of course there had been a substantial alteration in the political climate, relations between the four powers increasingly deteriorating into a confrontation between two blocs. This confrontation was reflected in proposals for a German banking system, for the Western allies eventually realized that the Russian demand for a common German central bank would provide them with an instrument through which the entire German economy could be administered along Soviet lines. In this way arguments over a future central monetary authority, the necessity for which all four powers continued nominally to agree upon, turned into a struggle for the future economic organization of a united Germany. Despite the fruitlessness of discussions on the banking system and a common currency since early 1947, in the autumn Bevin and Marshall, respectively British and American Foreign Secretaries, instructed their military governors to convey to the Soviets their preparedness for a common currency. At about the same time rumours began to circulate that the Soviets were preparing to print new banknotes in Leipzig, and that a separate Eastern currency reform was a possibility. This prompted Clay, the US Military Governor, to order the secret printing of new DM currency in Washington, shipment to Germany taking place in late 1947 without the knowledge of the then recently formed German Bizonal Economic Council.

In January 1948 the three Western powers sought once more to come to an agreement with the Soviet authorities on the issue of the future financial structure of Germany, but by this time the Soviet demand for a common central bank had become a point of explicit division. On 20 March the Soviet delegation left the Control Council, the *Bank deutscher Länder* having finally been established as the central bank for the three Western zones in Frankfurt on 1 March 1948. The way was now clear for the organization of a currency reform, for the notes had been printed and were ready for issue in Germany – although this was still a closely guarded secret. At the beginning of April the Allies requested that the Bizonal Economic Council nominate German experts to take part in the planning of the reform, and the group began its work on 21 April under conditions of strict isolation in an American barracks near Kassel.

During the period from 1945 to June 1948 more than 250 proposals for a reform of German currency and finance had been drafted,[32] although there are of course only a limited number of ways in which an excess money supply can be removed. There was therefore a general expectation that, sooner or later, the Allies would introduce a currency reform, and production figures clearly indicate that manufacturers built up stocks of semi-finished goods and raw materials in anticipation.[33] Nevertheless, the long delay and the secrecy with which the Reform had been prepared contributed to the shock effect of its announcement on Friday 18 June.[34] The initial impact upon popular perceptions is typically captured by the following passage:

> The black market suddenly disappeared. Shop windows were full of goods; factory chimneys were smoking; and the streets swarmed with lorries. Everywhere the noise of new buildings going up replaced the deathly silence of the ruins. If the state of recovery was a surprise, its swiftness was even more so. In all sectors of economic life it began as the clocks struck on the day of the currency reform. Only an eye-witness can give an account of the sudden effect which currency reform had on the size of stocks and the wealth of goods on display. Shops filled up with goods from one day to the next; the factories began to work. On the eve of currency reform the Germans were aimlessly wandering about their towns in search of a few additional items of food. A day later they thought of nothing but producing them. One day apathy was mirrored on their faces while on the next a whole nation looked hopefully into the future.[35]

But nothing is ever that simple, and to understand the original purpose of the Reform we need to examine the financial history of Germany under the National Socialists.

Rearmament and wars of conquest: Geräuschlose Finanzierung and its consequences

During the 1930s the German economy became increasingly autarchic, the relationship between the domestic and the international economy being subject to rigorous control of foreign exchange and capital movements. This increasing closure of the German economy was a response to world wide depression, and many of its characteristic features had been introduced before 1933. Exchange controls had for example been introduced in 1931, and on his accession to power Hitler inherited an existing programme of public works and employment creation. In the course of the 1930s, international trading relations became increasingly protectionist – this is for example the period during which Britain adopted

Table 3.1 Arms expenditure 1933–38[38]

	1933	1934	1935	1936	1937	1938	1933–38
Expenditure bn RM	0.7	4.2	5.5	10.3	11	17.2	48.9
Mefo Bills (%)	–	50	49	44	25	–	25
Arms spending as (%)	8.3	39.3	39.6	59.2	56.7	61	49.9
Govt. expenditure as % of GDP	1.2	5	7.1	11.2	12	15.7	9.5

the policy of Imperial Preference – and the Nazi regime took advantage of this development to cultivate a more permanently isolated economy. By the later 1930s the Nazis were able to pursue domestic economic objectives unimpeded by concerns about the balance of payments, the relation of domestic to international interest rates, capital movements or indeed currency depreciation. Domestic prices had been administered since 1931, when a Commissar for the Supervision of Prices was appointed; but it was only after 1933 that a consistent price policy was pursued. In November 1936 a price freeze was imposed, and this remained in effect until mid-1948, although in practice some upward adjustment in prices was possible.[36] A general wage freeze followed in June 1938, and this remained in force until late 1948. To all intents and purposes Germany was a closed economy from the mid-1930s, and this meant that conventional economic principles no longer apply when analysing the regulation of domestic production and consumption.

Recovery from the depression of the early 1930s was in Germany largely effected through public works and arms expenditure, the latter accounting for at least 50 per cent of government spending during 1933–38.[37] The financial arrangements facilitating this were creative, if nothing else. During the mid-1930s, almost one half of arms expenditure was financed by three-month 'Mefo Bills', paper drawn upon the Metallurgische Forschungsgesellschaft mbH and whose bills the Reichsbank was obliged to discount. The Metallurgische Forschungsgesellschaft was no more than a dummy company set up to provide a simulation of commercial activity, enabling the government to finance its contracts with what appeared to be commercial bills of exchange, but which were not.

As can be seen from Table 3.1, by the later 1930s a substantial part of the German economy was dedicated to military purposes. When war was precipitated in the early autumn of 1939 the economy was already at full capacity,[39] so that any further expansion of military-related production had to be at the cost of civilian consumption.

German workers had for many years lived in an economy where resources were directed to rearmament and where the quantity and quality of consumer goods was low in comparison with nominal GDP per head. Any increases in personal incomes in the later 1930s had resulted from longer hours worked, and not from a share in the growth of the economy.[40] By 1939 there were latent inflationary pressures, which were then exacerbated by the manner in which the government financed its military purchases.

Official understanding of the problems of excess purchasing power was coloured by popular memories of the inflationary collapse of 1923, and this inclined policy makers in the early 1940s to soften, rather than harden, the fiscal stance, while at the same time officially discouraging public discussion of war finance, fearing a general flight from money.[41] Fiscal policy remained relatively slack throughout the war, and payments to the dependants of service personnel were generous, involving therefore both a high level of public expenditure not backed by tax receipts, while at the same time providing little incentive for such dependants to seek employment. The outcome was a war financed through the plundering of occupied economies while printing money at home, resulting in a significant RM purchasing power overhang at the end of the war in circumstances where output had dropped to less than half of pre war levels. The allied occupiers extended the 1936 price freeze on the one hand and sought to control the emergent black market, although the extent to which the latter undermined the restoration of normal market relations can be exaggerated.[42]

As is apparent from Table 3.2, relative price stability throughout the period 1932–44 was accompanied by the rampant growth of the money supply, reflected in the strong growth of cash balances. National income doubled from 1932 to 1939, peaked in 1943 but then declined – in 1944 it was little more than that of 1939, and in the following year estimates put it at about half the level of 1938. Money stock began a rapid rise at the outbreak of war, quadrupling over the era of the Third Reich, but was matched by a fall in velocity of circulation since opportunities for using money declined. This continued into the post war years, where exchange in kind became increasingly important for both households and firms.[44] It was therefore a sudden upward move in the velocity of circulation that was the danger in the early post war years, not the existence of a given stock of money. However, as we shall see in conclusion, very few German economists or officials at the time made this simple distinction.

The insulation of the domestic economy from international goods and money markets, coupled with the fact that the public debt which financed rearmament and then wars of conquest was largely domestic in origin,

Table 3.2 Price and monetary indices, Germany 1932–44[43]

	Wholesale price index	Adjusted money stock	Real cash balances (col. [2]/col.[3])	National income (bn RM)	Income velocity (NI/money stock)
1932	100	100	100	45.2	1.35
1933	96.7	96.2	99.5	46.5	1.44
1934	102	99.6	97.6	52.7	1.58
1935	105.5	106.2	100.7	58.6	1.65
1936	107.9	114	105.7	65.8	1.73
1937	109.7	124	113	73.8	1.78
1938	109.5	139.4	127.3	82.1	1.76
1939	110.8	160.6	144.9	89.8	1.67
1940	114	196.9	172.7	92.5	1.41
1941	116.4	257.4	221.1	97.8	1.14
1942	118.5	333.4	281.4	98	0.88
1943	120.4	424.9	352.9	99	0.7
1944	121.9	536.6	440.2	90	0.5

meant that the Nazi regime was consistently able to run considerable budget deficits. Such deficits are financed by the sale of government bonds, which in normal circumstances are bought through financial markets by domestic and foreign financial institutions, and in a modified form by domestic private households. The autarchic and centrally administered nature of the German economy meant however that these markets had lost much of their significance, and domestic financial institutions had no significant alternative for the cash balances building up in their customers' accounts other than the purchase of government bonds. In Britain and in the United States governments sold war bonds to the population, and encouraged towns and cities to contribute directly to the purchase of aircraft and other equipment – excess purchasing power was in this way converted into privately held war bonds whose terms of redemption would be determined after the war, or simply sterilised. Apart from party initiatives such as *Winterhilfe*, the Nazi regime generally sought to conceal the economic cost of war from its domestic population, and relied chiefly on what became known as *geräuschlose Finanzierung*, the sale of bonds directly to financial institutions, a system of 'silent finance' in which the population 'paid' the costs of the war without it being necessary to sell war bonds to them directly, or radically increase taxation. In essence, the accumulation of a very large public debt relied upon the existence of fixed prices and wages, an economy which had few links with international markets, and a banking system entirely subordinated to the government.

From the standpoint of the late twentieth century the evolution of the German government budget summarized in Table 3.3 makes grim

Table 3.3 Reich budget (bn RM)[45]

	1938–39	1939–40	1940–41	1941–42	1942–43	1943–44	1944–45
Total expenditure	31.8	52.11	78.0	101.9	126.6	153.0	171.3 (planned)
Wehrmacht and armaments	18.4	32.3	58.1	75.6	96.9	117.9	128.4
Family support	–	na	na	4.8	5.5	6.5	8.1
Debt interest	1.3	1.9	2.8	4.2	5.9	6.6	10.5
Debt amortization	1.0	1.3	1.7	1.9	2.1	1.8	2.8
Total income	23.8	39.5	57.6	75.0	91.6	96.2	89.7
Taxes, duties	18.2	24.2	27.5	32.3	42.7	38.0	37.5
Locar war contribution	–	0.8	1.4	1.4	1.6	2.0	2.5
Goverment borrowing	7.5	6.6	18.5	22.9	22.0	28.4	21.0
Occupation costs etc.	–	–	6.1	12.2	18.9	20.3	23.6
Annual balance	–3.0	–12.6	–20.4	–26.9	–37.0	–56.8	–81.6
Cumulative shortfall	–5.1	–17.6	–38.0	–64.9	–101.9	–158.9	–240.3

reading, but there are here echoes of the balance sheets of both British and German governments during the First World War. Then, both governments had for a long time believed in the imminent end of the war; neither had a taxation system with a broad enough base and sufficient flexibility to absorb a sudden large and prolonged increase in government spending; while the level of daily expenditure required by modern warfare was completely unanticipated on all sides. The war began about half way through one financial year, and already by the next, 1915–16, the UK current account deficit had risen to nearly one third of national income, continuing on to around 40 per cent in 1917–18.[46] The budget for this fiscal year forecast expenditure of £2290m. with anticipated revenue at £613m; which was however an improvement on the September 1915 Budget, which had raised just 21.6 per cent of expenditure from taxation.[47] These figures lend some sort of comparative perspective to German wartime budgetary practice. It is also worth bearing in mind in this context that the massive expansion of the British public debt which the First World War brought about was paid off in the usual manner without provoking serious economic instability – although the servicing of national debt accounted for 46 per cent of all British government expenditure by 1925–26.[48]

Macroeconomic data has little meaning without the identification of trend relationships within and between economies. When considering German financial and economic statistics over the period 1930–50 we need to set them in some kind of perspective which makes sense of the numbers in relation to the trend performance of the German economy and/or in relation to that of similar contemporary economies. Curiously enough, this very elementary consideration is rarely introduced into discussion of German post war monetary history, which sometimes reads as though Germany were the only country ever to suffer monetary stress. The 1923 inflation certainly played an important role in linking economic instability to a loss of confidence in political institutions; but it is seldom noted that another consequence of this episode was the dissolution of the German national debt. Reparation payments would continue to be a problem for Germany during the 1920s, but after 1923 the direct cost of the First World War for Germany was wiped out. The national debt was therefore at the beginning of the 1930s at a very low level, unlike that of Britain.

Whether the comparison of national debt is made in terms of a proportion of national income or in RM per capita, the German figures are clearly not unique. Even after the Nazis' military spending spree of the 1930s the German public debt was still in 1939, on these measures, below

Table 3.4 Comparison of US, German and UK public debt[49]

Central state debt	Germany			USA			UK		
	1933	1939[50]	1945	1933	1939	1946	1933	1939	1946
In bn. of given currency	12.8	30.8	440	22.5	40.4	265	7.6	8.2	25
In bn. RM[51]	12.8	30.8	440	56.3	100.6	a795 b1325	110	95.7	a300 b500
In RM per capita	194	388	6674	448	768	a5663 b9438	2365	2015	a6276 b10,460
As % national income	28	31	917	53	57	162	224	178	245
National income in bn. of national currency	45.2	98.3	48	42.3	70.8	164	3.4	4.6	10.2

the levels prevailing in the United States and Britain. The principal difference emerges when these statistics are compared for 1945; but here again, what is striking is the rate of increase of debt, not its overall size. German public sector debt is shown here to be approximately four times that of Britain when compared to national income; but this is because in the interim the national income of Germany has been (temporarily) halved while that of Britain has (permanently) doubled. Given the proportion of expenditure and output devoted to the war in Germany – one estimate puts the proportion of GDP dedicated to war expenditure in 1943–44 at around 70 per cent of GDP[52] – it is hardly surprising that the figure for national income in 1945 should have collapsed, for after the cessation of hostilities all German military expenditures ceased, not to be resumed until the 1950s. All combatant economies confronted the problems of economic demobilization, but it is reasonable to suggest that the wartime imbalance between military and civilian consumption was in Germany so extreme that the disappearance of the former brought about a unique recession. This was a fundamental problem of the post war economy, often overlooked when considering the sheer level of destruction to infrastructure, homes and factories.

When evaluating the extent of the problem that the monetary overhang presented this point must be kept in mind, for as we have seen the first post war currency reform proposal, the Colm-Dodge-Goldsmith Plan, used a comparison of money supply with national income over the period 1938–45 to arrive at the conclusion that 90 per cent of the money supply had to be eliminated. This assumption was simply built into the planning of the 1948 Currency Reform. In fact both figures, money supply and national income, prewar and postwar, are somewhat indeterminate. Wolf's calculations (summarized in Table 3.5) indicate that the generally accepted level of postwar money stock can be severely qualified, while on the national income side even before the war the level of government spending on armaments and related projects was close to 20 per cent of GDP. With levels of public expenditure like this it should be no surprise that gross output slumped immediately following the war, since the most significant item of expenditure suddenly disappeared from the accounts. The low levels of output in the immediate post war years reflect this, and can perhaps be compared to the redirection of production and consumption that has recently occurred in the former Soviet Union.

The monetary stock is the obverse of the mode in which the public debt was created, but Wolf's calculation significantly modify the extent of the problem as perceived during the immediate post war period. Of the estimated 300bn nominal money stock at the end of the war, 20 per cent

Table 3.5 Estimated changes in German monetary stock since May 1945[53]

A. Stock in May 1945	300bn RM
Reductions brought about by war, territorial changes, blocked assets	
1. Physical destruction of banknotes	4bn
2. Territorial detachment	56bn
3. Blocked assets in Soviet zone and Berlin	70bn
4. Blocking of assets in Western zones	8bn
Total	138bn
Expansion of stock	
1. Occupation currency	12bn
2. Use of Reichsbank reserves	2bn
3. Credit guarantees to public agencies	2bn
4. Freeing of blocked savings accounts etc.	2bn
Total	18bn
Reduction through contractionary measures	
1. Local administration surpluses	4bn
2. Foreign trade accounts	1bn
3. Reduction in outstanding Occupation Marks	2bn
Total	7bn
Balance of changes	27bn RM
B. Stock early 1947	173bn RM

had either been destroyed or was left behind in Poland, Czechoslovakia or Austria as a consequence of the realignment of frontiers. When combined with those assets frozen in banks closed in Berlin or in the Soviet zone, the net result is to reduce the money supply by more than half. Some additions are necessary, however: the occupation currency freely printed by the Allies had increased the stock, as well as various credits to public bodies. Nevertheless, Wolf estimates that the RM monetary stock in early 1947 was 58 per cent of the assumed 1945 figure, which was the figure implicitly assumed in the 1948 calculation, since this was in turn based on the Colm-Dodge-Goldsmith Plan of early 1946.

Wolf also provides estimates of the location of the money supply, as between cash and deposits, cash in circulation and in banks, and between the occupation zones. Table 3.6 highlights the fact that around one third of the money supply was in savings deposits, and a surprisingly large amount of cash in circulation was in the Soviet zone, whose population

Table 3.6 Stock of notes and coin plus bank deposits in individual zones, September 1946 (bn RM)[54]

	Notes and coin	Notes and coin	Deposits	Deposits
	Circulating	In banks	Savings	Others
British Zone	10	7.0	34.0	27.0
US Zone	8.0	5.7	20.8	18.6
French Zone	4.0	2.3	10.6	5.0
Soviet Zone	14	8.5	2.4	8.5
Berlin	4.0	1.6	0.2	2.1
Total	40	25.1	68.0	61.2

was much smaller than those of British and American zones. While not denying that the excess RM money stock hindered economic reconstruction, the above figures dictate a revision in the customary habit of focusing on the simple existence of a monetary overhang and redirect out attention to more general problems in the functioning of market institutions. This observation is reinforced when we consider the level of national output, which should by 1947 have recovered from the artificially low level prevailing in summer 1945. The specifically German problem was that output had not recovered as quickly as it had elsewhere in Europe. This can in part be attributed to the administration of the economy by military governments, a positive German policy on the part of the Western allies developing in stages as a reflex to the worsening relations with the Soviet Union. The seemingly obvious and direct developmental path – from Nazi war finance to monetary overhang and thence to the need for a currency reform which would abolish this overhang and enable the market mechanism to function properly – turns out on closer examination to be less compelling than was widely assumed at the time, and most modern treatments simply recycle these assumptions. Having established that the case for a radical reduction in the money supply was less compelling than generally thought, we can now turn to consider the institutional and intellectual context which led politicians and economists to argue that conditions did in fact dictate a radical Currency Reform.

The restoration of market relations and economic policy

So far in this account no mention has been made of the role of the Reichsbank in German monetary policy. Following the hyperinflation of

1922–23, the independence of the Reichsbank had been established by the Bank Law of 1924, but this autonomy was short-lived. In October 1933 Hitler, as Chancellor, assumed the right of appointment and dismissal over the Director and members of the Directorate. Succeeding measures progressively limited the scope for independent banking activity on the part of the Reichsbank, and in January 1937 it was explicitly subordinated to the Führer.

As outlined above, already by the mid-1930s the absence of international economic constraints permitted the government to indulge in its own monetary creation. Throughout 1937 and 1938 the Reichsbank struggled to bring government spending into some kind of orderly plan, finally in January 1939 refusing the Finance Ministry a special credit and demanding that the state be declared bankrupt. On 7 January 1939 the President of the Reichsbank, Schacht, sent a memorandum to Hitler, signed by all the directors, stating that unchecked public expenditure was becoming a threat to the currency, that the creation of an orderly budget was being progressively undermined, that state finances had been brought to the verge of collapse despite the unprecedented use of taxation, all of which was tending to undermine the central bank and the currency. He noted that, 'No central bank is able to maintain the currency in the face of an inflationary expenditure policy on the part of the state'.[55]

The memorandum closed with four demands:

(1) The Reich and all other public instances to cease making expenditures, assuming responsibility or issuing guarantees unless backed by tax revenue, or by such loans as can be raised through loans without harming long-term capital markets;
(2) To ensure adherence to this the Reichsfinanzminister must assume full control of public expenditure;
(3) Price and wage controls must be organized effectively;
(4) Resort to gold and capital markets to be the sole prerogative of the Reichsbank.

Schacht and all of the directors were summarily dismissed on 20 January 1939. Later, in June 1939, the *Gesetz über die Deutsche Reichsbank* abolished all regulations on monetary expansion. Subsequently only one third of public expenditures in the period 1939–45 were based on receipts; 12 per cent was raised on foreign and 55 per cent on domestic capital markets. In December 1944 for example 36 per cent of all state expenditure was effected by printing money, leading to an unprecedented expansion of the money supply combined with a steady reduction in the already limited supply of goods to the non-military market.

It is sometimes suggested that the treatment dealt out to Schacht and his directors drove serious discussion of the problems of war finance underground, and it is true that wartime discussion of postwar economic conditions did become a delicate matter. Nonetheless, specialist journals frequently published contributions addressed to this issue right up to late 1943, after which many of them simply ceased publication owing to increasing economic dislocation. In late 1939 several noted German economists put their names to an official memorandum on wartime finance whose line of argument largely coincides with that of the Reichsbank. This 'Professoren-Kriegsfinanzierungsgutachten' was dated 9 December 1939, its authors listed as Berkenkopf, Eucken, Hasenack, Jessen, Lampe, von Stackelberg, Stucken, and Teschemacher. Eucken and Lampe were colleagues in Freiburg and Stackelberg was involved in their discussions during the war; Jessen, originally a dedicated Party member, organized discussions among German economists under the auspices of the Akademie für Deutsches Recht and was executed in the wake of the failed attempt to overthrow Hitler in July 1944. The structure of the memorandum is typical of Eucken: the argument turns upon a contrast of two ideal economic forms, one with free price formation and the other with fixed prices. Just as Schacht in his memorandum sought to establish the principle of a balanced budget and moderate use of the capital market, this December memorandum begins by noting that war finance is constrained by the level and material composition of total income. The state, it is argued, can only make limited use of existing reserves and investments in the economy, since exercise of this prerogative reduces the scope for restocking and accumulation. There is a limit to this, for no amount of monetary creation will call forth additional output unless there are related efforts to secure the level of production to which the government aspired. The only way out of the existing domestic constraints was by imports, but these have to be paid for out of existing balances or foreign credit. Any attempt to bypass these intransigent economic facts through financial manipulation simply renders rational production and a price policy impossible.

There was, the *Gutachten* continues, consequently a right and a wrong way of financing the war. Credit creation resulting in the increase of means of payment without associated increases in the supply of goods has the following consequences:

- qualitative or quantitative alteration in money values
- reduction in production volume
- consumption of reserves and stocks
- exit of smaller and medium-sized firms from the economic process
- destruction of any rational economic management (*Wirtschaftslenkung*).[56]

Expansion of the money supply while prices are fixed leads to a progressive dislocation of economic activity, and to emphasise this point the Memorandum schematically presents the phases of progressive dislocation under increasing degrees of inflationary pressure, assuming that the economy is at the outset already at full capacity. There are several interesting features of this presentation, quite apart from the manner in which it contrasts the consequences of free and of administered prices, the latter directed to the consequences of German government policy in the later 1930s. The criticisms extend beyond the impact upon the retail market to production organization, incentives, levels of output and tendencies to industrial concentration, highlighting the damaging effects associated with suppressed inflation in an economy with fixed prices. And they were quite explicit about the economy they had in mind: 'In the contemporary German economy the problem is principally one of covert monetary depreciation'.[57]

This memorandum is notable not only for the thoroughness with which it spells out the consequences of suppressed inflation, but also for the fact that it does so before a serious purchasing power overhang began to build up. It was not however unique in expressing these problems, although another early discussion approached the matter tangentially through a comparison of current practice with German financial policy during the First World War.[58] In February 1940, a special meeting of the Association of German Economists was devoted to discussion of these matters, and an entire issue of the specialist journal *Weltwirtschaftliches Archiv* was devoted to papers from the conference.[59] Economists generally agreed that war expenditure should only be financed out of the incomes arising from current production, but that the present requirements were so large that taxation was an inadequate instrument. In this way discussion focused upon the nature of inflation as a symptom of shortages in current production for which the printing of money represents no solution. In a later article Terhalle described the developing system of war finance as '... scheinbar fast automatische, im ganzen wenig geräuschvolle'.[60] Another author argued that the capacity for an economy to wage war was a function of its politico-economic system, the market system typical of liberal-capitalist economies being unsuited to the tasks.

A 'guided economy', however, in which money, prices and markets are stripped of the autonomy they enjoy in a capitalist economy, was a much more suitable economic form for the prosecution of a modern war.[61] It was not until 1942 that articles began to appear which directly addressed the problem of the 'purchasing-power overhang', or *Kaufkraftüberhang*.[62] This theme was also taken up in discussions among the Arbeitskreis Erwin von Beckerath, where Adolf Lampe and Walter Eucken consistently argued from the existence of a monetary surplus to the need for its removal if market relations were to be restored in a postwar economy.[63] Implicit in most of these analyses was the assumption that inflationary pressures are directly caused by an excessive money supply, that the dangers of inflation were kept at bay only by a price freeze, and that before market relations could be restored it would be necessary to remove excess purchasing power in some way, preferably through a currency conversion which drastically reduced the money supply.

Some contributors to the debate took a different line, however. In a lengthy article published in 1942 Otto Donner invoked instead the 'new theory of credit', by which he meant the new Keynesian economics. The point of departure for Donner was the fact that by April 1942 public indebtedness had already reached the level prevailing at the end of the First World War; was there then, he asked rhetorically, a level beyond which state indebtedness could or should not go, to be exceeded only at the risk of bankruptcy or inflation? Not according to the new credit theory, argued Donner, citing Keynes' *Treatise on Money* and the *General Theory*. He went on to recapitulate arguments concerning deficit financing, full employment, the balancing of civilian against government consumption and the associated inflationary pressures in the kind of wartime setting laid out by Keynes in *How to Pay for the War*, a text to which he does not however refer.[64] Having discussed the various measures open to a wartime government, he then turns to a postwar economy in which a monetary overhang exists. Switches between military and civil production, and the return of soldiers into productive employment, would result in an expansion of consumer goods output, although some economists had argued that the consequent increase in incomes would prevent a reduction in the wartime purchasing-power overhang. Donner countered this by pointing to the savings ratio, with the observation that if this model of production and consumption were true, then there would never be any cyclical slump in sales. The shift to consumer durables, argued Donner, would be associated with an alteration in expectations: the idea that tomorrow things will be cheaper and of better quality would create a sense of stability and longer-term consumer planning, shifting much of the overhang into savings, assisting the state in its efforts to transform short-term debt into long-term debt.[65]

The ruling monetary orthodoxy among German economists was a simple form of quantity theory, in which surplus money created inflationary pressures which, if left unchecked, would hinder a postwar return to the market mechanism. Adherents of the new Keynesian line of analysis did not deny the problems created by inflation, but were more sanguine in facing the postwar economy, pointing as Donner did to alterations in patterns of consumption and saving, and the expansion of economic activity that could be expected in a peacetime economy. There were however considerations other than the simple existence of a monetary overhang which pointed to the need for a reform of the currency, and these are usefully highlighted by the series of European currency reforms which preceded the German reform of 1948.

Currency reform in postwar Europe

The manner in which the German war economy was financed domestically was made possible by its insulation from international capital and goods markets; but the German war economy was intimately connected to the international economy in a different fashion, namely through conquest. A substantial part of the German war economy was supported by the systematic plunder of those economies which it had occupied, requisitioning labour, transplanting factories, charging occupation costs and managing the 'European Economic Space' to its own best advantage.[66] Naturally enough, the costs imposed upon the European economy as a whole were significant, and during the war the price level in all western European economies advanced at a faster pace than that in Germany.[67] Countries were liberated from late 1944, although there was no uniformity in the economic problems that they displayed. Belgium was the first, liberated in five days, with a largely intact industry but a population close to starvation. Denmark was largely intact, the economy depleted of raw materials but with only a 5 per cent reduction in national wealth since the outbreak of war. The Netherlands was 10 per cent under water, with 75 per cent of its rolling stock lost, a 33 per cent reduction in national wealth, and a population whose near liberation in September 1944 made the following winter under an additionally harsh occupation regime hard to bear. All of these countries made reform of the currency a priority, seeking to establish a firm basis for reconstruction.

The Belgian government launched a currency reform in October 1944. This had as one of its aims the removal of excess liquidity, but it was also thought prudent to issue new currency through an exchange of notes, for it was suspected that the German occupation forces, after their withdrawal, might possess a duplicate set of printing plates with the aid of which the economy could be flooded with currency. It was planned to remove surplus monetary assets above a designated equilibrium level by issuing bonds which would be later amortized through special tax measures.[68] The reform was announced by the Finance Minister by radio on Friday 7 October 1944. All notes above Frs 100 had to be deposited at post offices or banks, and each individual was permitted to exchange Frs 2000 of old notes for new ones. At the end of the following week old notes ceased to be legal tender. All bank deposits were blocked except for those that predated the invasion of 10 May 1940, or an amount not in excess of balances as at 8 October 1944. From 3 November 1944 each person could withdraw Frs 3000 from these blocked accounts, after which all assets in blocked accounts were divided into temporarily (40 per cent) and permanently (60 per cent) blocked accounts. The former were to be freed gradually as production expanded, the latter were to be converted into long-term government bonds, to be amortized through taxation. The total money supply was reduced from Frs 160.7bn to Frs 96.4bn. This undershot the target by 13 per cent; but the major problem turned out not to lie in the execution of the reform, but rather that war had not ended as expected in December. Instead, the Ardennes offensive brought large numbers of Allied troops into Belgium and these were paid in local currency (Frs 12.5bn), and who consumed Frs 16.6bn in goods and services. This pushed the cash deficit to Frs 39.6bn, and since this could not be financed by the issue of bonds inflation began once more. It had been planned to stabilize the price level at 160 of 1938, but by June 1945 it was 343. All was not lost, however, for the Allies reimbursed the Belgian government in foreign exchange for Frs 22.1bn of goods and services supplied to the Allies during the winter of 1944–45, providing Belgium with a windfall of hard currency with which substantial amounts of food were imported, successfully breaking the black market and stabilizing prices, and leading to a rapid restoration of the prewar standard of living.

During the early postwar years this process was repeated throughout Europe. The Dutch reform followed on quickly from that of Belgium because the Benelux agreement of September 1944 linked macroeconomic policy in the two economies. The contraction of the Dutch money supply took longer, beginning on 9 July and terminating on 27 September, when the old notes ceased to be legal tender and a period of progressive deblocking of accounts began.[69] In Denmark a reform was carried out beginning on 23 July 1945, when the banks were closed, new notes were issued in exchange for old up to Kr 500,[70] residual monetary assets being placed in blocked deposits. A principal objective of the reform was a postwar 'cleansing', a census of assets being used to penalize any who had profited from the occupation; the impact upon the money supply was a reduction of less than 15 per cent.

The French story was more mixed. At the time of liberation in September 1944 the key relevant statistics – output and money supply – were no better, if not worse, than those of Germany. Balogh in 1945 estimated that industrial output was 30 per cent of the prewar level, Sherwin in his later study has a lower estimate for all output at 20 per cent of the 1938 level.[71] Money supply is given by Sherwin in the same table as 550 with 1938 = 100, with retail prices at 290. As mentioned in passing above, within three years the economy had recovered to levels of production and consumption prevailing in the later 1930s, but this owed little to consistent and rigorous economic policy. The Free French government had intended to carry out a reduction in the money supply, but were opposed by some French economists who argued that the price level is determined by income levels, not the money supply, rendering a reduction in the money supply unnecessary. Other economists argued that an excess money supply was the result, not the cause, of inflation; while some suggested that a mechanical relationship between money supply and prices did not take account of alterations in the velocity of circulation.[72] Moreover, the incumbent Finance Minister opposed a reform on the grounds that it was technically impossible, given the degree of dislocation to communications. Instead, the government launched a series of voluntary bond drives, lowered the rediscount rate, and announced a note exchange and registration of liquid assets in June 1945. Together, these measures tended to increase velocity, outweighing small reductions in money stock, and over the year following Liberation the price level rose from 267 to 373.

Gurley[73] in his survey of the 24 postwar European currency reforms that took place between October 1944 and May 1952, divides them into three basic types:

(1) Reduction of the supply of liquid assets at the outset without blocking any portion of this supply. This was done by a currency exchange of old for new notes at rates of exchange which substantially reduced the outstanding volume of assets – for example 3:1 in the Austrian programme (8 cases).

(2) No immediate reduction in the supply of liquid assets; instead efforts were made to immobilize a proportion of this supply by blocking

bank deposits. Banknotes were called in and deposits declared by their owners (12 cases).

(3) Combines the primary features of (1) and (2). Currency and bank deposits are converted into new money at deflated rates of exchange, but a portion of amount the residual is in turn frozen in blocked accounts (4 cases).

In all three types, the registration of securities and assets was also required, whether monetary, real or both. Half of the reforms were introduced before the end of 1945, and only three reforms were carried out after mid 1948. Only in a few cases, such as Greece and Hungary, was the introduction of a new unit of currency a response to rampant inflation; in most cases the reforms were part of the process by which governments regained control over their economies after years of occupation.

Klopstock[74] emphasized the historical novelty of the early postwar Currency Reforms for, unlike the sequence of reforms that followed the First World War, they were chiefly designed to pre-empt, rather than contain, hyperinflation. The Polish currency unification of 1920 for example was accompanied by a sharp expansion of Polish marks, and the re-establishment of a stable currency involved an exchange of marks for newly issued gold zlotys at rate of 1.8m: 1.[75] The Czech currency reform of 25 February 1919 sterilized half the circulating medium on its territory by stamping notes of the Austro- Hungarian Bank and then forcibly converting half of them into non-negotiable government bonds. It has been noted in passing above that the First World War had serious financial consequences for Britain, without the consequent economic constraints provoking serious economic or political instability. Jessen alluded to precisely this point in an article discussing Wagner's law of increasing public expenditure, published the year before his execution as a participant in the July Plot.[76] He went rather further back, to the British public finances in the post-Napoleonic era, when the three largest items of British government spending were debt interest, the navy and the army, in that order. During the period 1822–31 an average of 59 per cent of government expenditure was devoted to debt repayment.[77] Until the mid-nineteenth century, interest paid on the national debt took up almost half of all government expenditure; in 1880 it was a quarter and in 1890 11 per cent.[78] This burden was increased once more in the 1920s, and one of the more remarkable features of the evolution of the British national debt during the interwar period is not simply its size, but the speed with which moderate economic growth reduced its impact.

Conclusion

As noted in the introduction, the 1948 Currency Reform is usually judged in terms of its consequences, not its purposes. There are substantial difficulties in attributing the real development of the German economy in subsequent years to individual contributory factors – Marshall Aid, the revival of intra-European trade, the completion of the period of recovery and the onset of the European 'Golden Age', the establishment of a central government in Bonn, or the absence of significant military spending and related atomic energy research. Debate on the consequences of the Reform takes as its variables these and other factors, while assuming that the Reform itself requires little direct discussion, or that the benificent results of the Reform prove that it was economically justified.[79] This paper has approached the matter differently, seeking to understand the nature of the Reform in its context – the real economic developments of the early 1940s, the assumptions governing the framing of policy on the part of German economists and Allied administrators, and the wave of currency reforms which preceded it. From this a rather different picture of the Reform emerges, which in turn has implications for our understanding of its significance.

First, the terms of the Reform were dictated by the military governments – chiefly the American administration. German involvement was restricted to the actual drafting of the laws and regulations, an onerous task certainly, but a strictly subordinate one. Second, the Reform was just one of many currency reforms conducted in the immediate aftermath of war as governments sought to re-establish functioning market economies; as such its terms were a variant on a limited number of variables with a restricted range of permutations. The German reforms were distinguished only by the fact that they were imposed by military governments and took place after some delay. Third, the overall aim of reducing the money supply by 90 per cent was principally based on an assessment of national income and money supply in the period 1945–46. How far this was justified in 1948 is questionable, and in any case the statistics underlying these estimates are open to substantial revision or qualification. Given the general expectation that a currency reform would eventually take place, and the consequent hoarding of cash and goods, by 1948 some kind of reform was needed simply to jolt the money economy back into life. The June Reform certainly gave the jolt, but how far its actual terms and conditions were important in stimulating activity is open to question. Finally, underlying all arguments for a radical reduction of the money supply is a simple quantity theory of money, in which rapid growth of the stock of money in an economy without administered prices leads directly to inflation. Some remarks can be made about this presumption in closing.

Table 3.2 shows that there was a decline in the velocity of money from 1937 onwards, the rate of decrease accelerating in 1940. This reflects diminishing opportunities to use money under a fixed price regime combined with draconian suppression of a black market. All that changed in mid-1945 was an alleviation of the pressure upon black market transactions, while the presence of Allied troops introduced goods which hitherto had been either unavailable or in very limited supply – cigarettes, coffee, and nylon stockings. The principal problem for households and enterprises in the immediate postwar period was the lack of effective market mechanisms capable of regulating the distribution and consumption of goods. The limited uses for money transactions was expressed in the low velocity of money. We measure velocity by comparing the stock of money with national income, and as such it is a statistical construct with tautological implications; but it is more than this, for it expresses the volatility of transactions and hence economic activity. Contemporary economists and administrators tended to link the absolute size of the money stock directly to the flow of transactions, without considering the presence of intermediate institutional factors which dictated variations in flow independently of the size of the stock. The implicit assumption that money stock was the same as money supply – that money supply was also simply a stock – was related to the idea that in equilibrium conditions velocity (a flow concept) would be invariant, and therefore of negligible importance. The conception that velocity would be invariant in equilibrium conditions amounts to asserting that when everything balances nothing changes, and the tautologous nature of the simple quantity theory of money has frequently been noted. However rudimentary such notions might appear today, they represented the principal theoretical underpinnings of the view that excess money supply caused inflation, and that when an excess existed its absence or moderation was due to market imperfections.

Cagan's classic study of seven hyperinflations[80] established that among all the noise of ballooning prices and wages during periods when monthly price changes exceed 50 per cent there was a stable relationship between the average rate of change of prices per month and the average change of cash per month. He observed that it was usual to treat cash balances as a function (not necessarily a linear function) of real income and other variables, but that the erratic behaviour of cash balances in the course of hyperinflationary periods indicated the limitations of this approach. Instead, he proposed that the variations in real cash balances depended mainly on the expected rate of change in prices, and that generally hyperinflations should be explained in terms of the expectations formed by rational actors.[81] Applying the general logic of this argument to the later 1940s, we could say that the prospect of excess money supply bringing about significant inflation depends upon 'rational expectations' formed by an appraisal of institutional developments and the opportunity cost of holding cash. Inflation, we might say, is not a monetary phenomenon, in that it is not mechanically triggered and sustained by excess money stock, but instead by social and economic institutional factors which influence the formation of expectations.

In his introduction to *Studies in the Quantity Theory of Money*, Friedman represented the quantity theory as a theory of the demand for money, and suggested that his representation was based on a Chicago oral tradition of the 1930s and the 1940s separable from the published writings of faculty members, '... a theoretical approach that insisted that money does matter ...'.[82] In this model, Friedman suggests, the demand for money is stable over time, although this does not involve the belief that velocity of circulation is constant over time, although, since he goes on to state that stability is instead located in the relation between the quantity demanded and the variables determining it, this amounts to an adherence to constant velocity in a stable state. In some respects this 'oral tradition' appears congruent with the governing assumptions of German economists during the 1940s, but Patinkin has since shown that this 'oral tradition' presented by Friedman serves mainly to disguise his assimilation of Keynesian theory, and has little to do with monetary orthodoxy in the Chicago of the 1940s. Leading Chicago economists, he argues, never used the expression 'demand for money':

> ... Simons did not spell out the details of the mechanism by which an increase in the quantity of money was supposed to increase the volume of spending on goods and services. Instead, he sufficed with the simple, sometimes implicit, and frequently mechanical statement that an increase in M increased aggregate demand MV.[83]

This sounds rather familiar, especially in the light of Patinkin's argument that Simons treated the quantity theory as a theory relating the quantity of money to the aggregate demand for goods and services and thence to the price level and/or level of output. On the other hand, Simons was aware of the dangers in sudden changes in velocity, due to anticipated changes in the price level and changing states of business confidence.[84] Mostly these observations were developed in the context of the recessions of the 1920s and 1930s, and they did not envisage the consequences of an accumulated purchasing-power overhang as in Germany. But there are three points that can be made in closing.

First, too little is known about German monetary economics of the 1930s and the 1940s. The arguments put forward by German economists and administrators were shaped by this tradition, and this paper has sought to demonstrate that the relation between war finance and the Currency Reform is not as entirely straightforward as usually supposed, since the relationship is mediated by principles drawn from prevailing theories of money and banking which are remote to us today.[85] Second, even cursory examination of contemporary American monetary thought reveals parallel assumptions, from which we could infer that a more detailed study of international monetary thought during the 1930s and the 1940s might throw up further similarities.[86] Third, and finally, a study of this kind might show how far monetary orthodoxy in Germany during the 1940s was simply a reflection of a more international orthodoxy; and, therefore, that the economic content of Ordoliberalism, the foundation of the social market economy, is nothing more than a version of a neoclassical orthodoxy elsewhere eclipsed in the course of the 1950s.

Notes

1. See, e.g., H. Giersch, K.-H. Paqué, H. Schmieding, 'Openness, Wage Restraint, and Macroeconomic Stability: West Germany's Road to Prosperity 1948–1959', in R. Dornbusch, W. Nölling and R. Layard (eds), *Post-war Economic Reconstruction and Lessons for the East Today* (Cambridge, MA: MIT Press, 1993) pp. 1–28. For a more journalistic version of the same story see W. Bickerich, *Die D-Mark. Eine Biographie* (Berlin: Rowohlt, 1998).
2. T. Balogh, *Germany: An Experiment in 'Planning' by the 'Free' Price Mechanism* (Oxford: Basil Blackwell, 1950).
3. See, e.g. W. Abelshauser, 'American Aid and West German Economic Recovery: A Macroeconomic Perspective', in C. S. Maier and G. Bischof (eds) *The Marshall Plan and Germany. West German Development within the Framework of the European Recovery Program* (Oxford: Berg, 1991) pp. 367–409; A. S. Milward, *The Reconstruction of Western Europe 1945–51* (London: Methuen, 1984) ch. V. Abelshauser's argument that the Reform played a subordinate role in German economic recovery was first put forward in the mid-1970s, and has since then engendered much debate. For an overview and assessment see H. Berger and A. Ritschl, 'Germany and the Political Economy of the Marshall Plan, 1947–52; A Re-revisionist View', in B. Eichengreen (ed.) *Europe's Post-war Recovery* (Cambridge: Cambridge University Press, 1995) pp. 199–245.
4. Although of course those German economists most closely identified with the genesis of the social market economy, notably the Arbeitsgemeinschaft Erwin

von Beckerath, had long advocated monetary reform as a route to the re-establishment of market relations – see K. Tribe, *Strategies of Economic Order. German Economic Discourse 1750–1950* (Cambridge: Cambridge University Press, 1995) ch. 8.

5. A recent exception is the account given by C. Buchheim, 'Die Währungsreform in Westdeutschland', *Vierteljahrshefte für Zeitgeschichte*, 36 (1988) 217–20.
6. *Military Government Gazette*, 25, Law no. 61, pp. 848–9.
7. Reichsmark notes, Rentenbank notes greater than 1 RM, and Allied Military Marks with a value greater than 1 mark – *Gazette*, 25, Law No. 61, Art. IX, p. 850.
8. 60 DM was roughly one week's pay for a working man; a skilled worker in Hamburg at this time would have earned 10 RM per eight-hour day, and a six-day week was the official norm (official statistic cited in Buchheim, 'Die Währungsreform in Westdeutschland', p. 193). Mendershausen and Matchett in their estimate of cash and deposit holdings in early 1946 estimated that 66.5 per cent of the population in the US zone and Berlin Sector held less than RM 250 in cash, that 28 per cent of the adult population had no bank accounts, and that another quarter of the population had less than 2000 RM in bank and savings accounts: 'Annex H: Analysis of Size Distribution of Cash and Bank Deposits', Colm-Dodge-Goldsmith Plan, reprinted in H. Möller (ed.) *Zur Vorgeschichte der deutschen Mark* (Tübingen: J. C. B. Mohr (Paul Siebeck), 1961) pp. 459, 457. It is reasonable to suppose that during 1947 redistribution from poorer to richer households, and from urban dwellers to farmers, exacerbated this position. Burchardt and Martin drew attention to this when they noted that '… it must not be forgotten that in contrast to a country such as Britain all goods, bar the most essential ones, have become liquid assets and that the process of inflation continues to be fed by turning household stocks into money or directly into other goods', – F. A. Burchardt, K. Martin, 'Western Germany and Reconstruction', *Bulletin of the Oxford University Institute of Statistics*, 9 (Dec. 1947) 409. It is therefore more than probable that many poorer urban households did not receive their full 60 DM allocation per person.
9. The German text is more precise here; it refers to those natural and juridical persons which are 'steuerpflichtig' rather than 'subject to taxation', *Gazette*, 25, Law No. 61, § 11, p. 850.
10. *Gazette*, 25, Law No. 61, Art. XVII(1), p. 853.
11. That is the balances paid in by natural and juridical persons, excluding the assets of financial institutions and public authorities.
12. *Gazette*, 25, Law No. 63, Art. II(i), p. 863.
13. A supplementary regulation stated that where the balance of an account was below 540 RM, then the holder would receive 60 DM in return for the liquidation of that balance – Regulation No. 1 under Military Government Law No. 63, Art. II(2), *Gazette*, 25, p. 875.
14. Previous European currency reforms had used differential rates of exchange for blocked and free accounts, differing proportions between them and varying rates of release for blocked funds.
15. S. F. Sherwin, *Monetary Policy in Continental Western Europe 1944–1952*, Wisconsin Commerce Studies Vol. II, No. 2 (Madison: University of Wisconsin, 1956) pp. 53–6
16. Reprinted in Möller, *Zur Vorgeschichte* (note 8) pp. 216–54, at pp. 219, 233.
17. Military Government Law No. 63, Art. XXIX, *Gazette*, 25, p. 872.

18. Just as well really, since there is a printing error in the English text of Law 63 Art. IV which does not appear in the German version.
19. A body elected from the eight regional Landtage of the Bizone – see W. Benz, *Von der Besatzungsherrschaft zur Bundesrepublik. Stationen einer Staatsgründung 1946–1949* (Frankfurt a.M: Fischer Verlag, 1984) pp. 60ff.
20. F. H. Klopstock, 'Monetary Reform in Western Germany', *Journal of Political Economy*, 57 (1949) p. 283.
21. 80bn RM had been registered as family accounts in June 1948, which ended up as 4.5bn DM total savings. The post-Reform spending spree, in which it seems households did not realize (prior to the 70 per cent cancellation of blocked deposit accounts in October) that they were in fact spending most of their savings, reduced this figure to 300m DM in three months; in September savings accounted for 2.4 per cent of money stock, as against 48 per cent in 1938 – H. Sauermann, 'The Consequences of the Currency Reform in Western Germany', *Review of Politics*, 12 (1950) 191–2.
22. Schedule to Law No. 64, 22. June 1948 *Gazette*, 25, pp. 890–915.
23. W. W. Heller, 'Tax and Monetary Reform in Occupied Germany', *National Tax Journal*, 2 (1949) 219, 225.
24. 'Soviet Military Administration Order No. 111 on Currency Reform in the Soviet Zone', 23 June 1948, reprinted in B. R. von Oppen (ed.) *Documents on Germany under Occupation*, (London: Oxford University Press, 1955) p. 295.
25. von Oppen *Documents* (note 24), pp. 297–8.
26. The set of plates given to the Soviet Union under this agreement were used to print unknown quantities of notes which were distributed to troops in lieu of backpay, and also to obtain goods in the West, where they in turn found their way into the hands of US servicemen, who then sold it to the US Government as part of a buyback deal, together with their own surplus Occupation Marks. Some $160m was disbursed in this way before occupation pay was reorganized – Sherwin *Monetary Policy* (note 15), p. 49.
27. I. Turner, 'Great Britain and the Post-war German Currency Reform', *Historical Journal*, 30 (1987) 690–94.
28. British officials also found the competence of American financial experts deficient compared with that of Russian and French experts – Turner, 'Great Britain and the Post-war German Currency Reform' (note 27), p. 700, fn. 81. Buchheim ('Die Währungsreform in Westdeutschland' (note 5), p. 205, suggests that the British focus upon fiscal solutions reflected the Keynesian cast of British thinking, but he overstates the influence of economic theory in policy formation. The British officials involved were overwhelmingly senior career civil servants without any formal training in economics, who later went on to be leading business figures; and neither the Treasury nor the Bank of England could at this time be described as 'Keynesian' in their general approach to policy.
29. Turner 'Great Britain and the Post-war German Currency Reform' (note 27), p. 695.
30. H. Möller, 'Die westdeutsche Währungsreform von 1948', in Deutsche Bundesbank, *Währung und Wirtschaft 1876–1975* (Frankfurt a.M., 1976) p. 443.
31. H. Adler, 'The Post-war Reorganisation of the German Banking System', *Quarterly Journal of Economics*, 63 (1949) pp. 322–30.

32. Möller *Zur Vorgeschichte* (note 8), p. 6.
33. Buchheim, 'Die Währungsreform in Westdeutschland' (note 5) p. 196.
34. Although of course the exact timing of all such reforms, if they are to have any chance of success, must necessarily be unanticipated.
35. Jacques Rueff and André Piettre cited in L. Erhard, *Prosperity through Competition* (London: Thames and Hudson, 1958) p. 13 (translation of *Wohlstand für Alle* (Düsseldorf: Econ Verlag, 1957).
36. K. H. Hansmeyer and R. Caesar, 'Kriegswirtschaft und Inflation', in Deutsche Bundesbank, *Währung und Wirtschaft 1876–1975*, (Frankfurt a.M., 1976) pp. 408–9.
37. Historians of the period note that some military expenditures were included in the civilian budget, understating the published figures for arms spending.
38. Hansmeyer and Caesar, 'Kriegswirtschaft und Inflation', (note 36) p. 392.
39. Although female labour was not rapidly mobilized in the way it was in Britain and the United States. According to the 1939 job survey, around 6m women were without employment, of whom 3.5m could be regarded as employable. The Labour Ministry planned for an increase of 2.6m female workers, but in fact over the next few years female participation fell: from 14.626m in 1939 to 14.385m in 1940; and down to 14.186m in 1941. There was a recovery in 1942, the prewar level being returned to only in 1943. There was however a redistribution of female labour, into transport, energy, civil administration and military administration. See L. Herbst, *Das nationalsozialistische Deutschland 1933–1945* (Frankurt a.M: Suhrkamp Verlag, 1996) p. 263.
40. This point needs to be kept in mind when comparisons are made between pre- and postwar levels of production and consumption.
41. Salin draws attention to the paradox that the only detailed study of the inflation of 1923 available as late as the 1960s was by an Italian and translated into English, despite the importance of the episode for the German economy: C. Bresciani-Turroni, *Le Vicendo del Marco Tedesco* (1931) trans. M. E. Sayers as *The Economics of Inflation. A Study of Currency Depreciation in Post-war Germany* (London, 1937). The definitive modern study is by Carl-Ludwig Holtfrerich, *Die deutsche Inflation 1914–1923* (Berlin: de Gruyter, 1980). E. Salin, 'Zur Einführung', in H. Möller *Zur Vorgeschichte der deutschen Mark* (note 8) p. V.
42. Hansmeyer and Caesar estimate that no more than 10 per cent of transactions were conducted on the black market, but 80 per cent of the money in circulation was concentrated here, leading to spiralling prices – 'Kriegswirtschaft und Inflation' (note 36), p.423.
43. J. J. Klein, 'German Money and Prices', in M. Friedman (ed.) *Studies in the Quantity Theory of Money* (Chicago: University of Chicago Press, 1956) Table 1, p. 122.
44. For example, those who worked for the occupation administrations received an off-ration midday meal at the official price, which was the principal attraction of such employment – Buchheim, 'Die Währungsreform in Westdeutschland' (note 5) p. 193.
45. Hansmeyer and Caesar, 'Kriegswirtschaft und Inflation' (note 36) p. 400.
46. Morgan, *Studies in British Financial Policy, 1914–25* (London: Macmillan, 1952) p. 102.
47. Morgan, *Studies* (note 46) p. 92.
48. Morgan, *Studies* (note 46) p. 98. It is today a commonplace to note that so long as the creditors of a national debt are domestic – as was the case in Germany in

1945 – servicing the debt is primarily a redistribution problem between taxpayers and creditors. When a significant part of the debt is held by foreign creditors – as was the case in Britain after 1918 – repayment involves foreign exchange transactions which, if large enough, can have serious macroeconomic repercussions.

49. E. Wolf, 'Geld- und Finanzprobleme der deutschen Nachkriegswirtschaft', in Deutsches Institut für Wirtschaftsforschung, *Die deutsche Wirtschaft zwei Jahre nach dem Zusammenbruch* (Berlin: 1947) p. 202.
50. Excludes Mefo and tax credits; inclusion would raise this figure by *c*.35 per cent.
51. 1933 and 1939 converted at prevailing rate of exchange; for 1946 (a) at 3 RM to $ and 12 RM to £; (b) at 5 RM to $ and 20 RM to £.
52. Hansmeyer and Caesar, 'Kriegswirtschaft und Inflation' (note 36) p.399.
53. Wolf, 'Geld- und Finanzprobleme der deutschen Nachkriegswirtschaft' (note 49) pp. 219–20
54. Wolf, 'Geld- und Finanzprobleme der deutschen Nachkriegswirtschaft' (note 49) p. 221. The total stock adds up to 194.3 RM here, the figure of 173bn being arrived at by the subtraction of assets in blocked accounts in the Soviet Zone and in Berlin.
55. Facsimile copy of letter printed in Hansmeyer and Caesar, 'Kriegswirtschaft und Inflation' (note 36) pp. 382–3.
56. Möller, *Zur Vorgeschichte* (note 8) pp. 29–32.
57. 'In der gegenwärtigen deutschen Wirtschaftsordung handelt es sich überwiegend um das Problem der verdeckten Geldentwertung.' Möller, *Zur Vorgeschichte* (note 8) p. 32.
58. F. Terhalle, 'Die deutsche Kriegsfinanzierung 1914–1918. Ein naheliegender Rückblick', *Bank-Archiv*, 1939 23 (1 Dec. 1939) 549–52.
59. Bd. 51 Heft 3 (1940).
60. F. Terhalle, 'Die Aufbringung der Kriegskosten als volkswirtschaftliche Aufgabe', *Bank-Archiv*, 11 (1 June 1940) 193.
61. K. Burkheiser, 'Kriegsfinanzierung und Wirtschaftsystem', *Bank-Archiv*, (1940) 260–63.
62. As in the title: G. Keiser, 'Die Abtragung des Kaufkraftüberhangs', *Bank-Archiv*, 14 (1942) 273–5. Keiser was chief editor of *Bank-Archiv*. See also O. Veit, 'Geldüberschuß und Wirtschaftslenkung', *Weltwirtschaftliches Archiv*, 57 I (1943) 278–309, and R. Meimberg, 'Kaufkraftüberhang und Kriegsfinanzpolitik', *Weltwirtschaftliches Archiv*, 58 II (1943) 98–130.
63. See my discussion of this in *Strategies of Economic Order* (note 4), pp. 227–32.
64. O. Donner, 'Die Grenzen der Staatsverschuldung', *Weltwirtschaftliches Archiv*, 56 II (1942) 183–224.
65. Ibid., p. 212.
66. See my *Strategies of Economic Order* (note 4), pp. 251–5.
67. With 1938 = 100, the cost of living at the time of Liberation was in Belgium 181, in Denmark 160, in France 290, and in the Netherlands 167, compared with 125 for Germany – Sherwin, *Monetary Policy* (note 15) Table I, p. 7.
68. The problem of what the equilibrium level might be was resolved through a comparison of the Congolese franc, devalued in 1940 by 17 per cent, with the £ sterling, since Britain was Belgium's major trading partner. Equilibrium was therefore thought to lie in a price and wage level 17 per cent above that prevailing in Britain in 1944. In calculating the new money supply constant

velocity and prewar production levels were assumed – Sherwin, *Monetary Policy* (note 15) pp. 11–12.
69. Sherwin, *Monetary Policy* (note 15) p. 24.
70. $1 = Kr 4.81, the note issue was therefore up to a ceiling of $103.95, as compared with the initial German issue to the value of $12. The Danish government was in a position to carry out this reform because new currency was available, the Central Bank having been clandestinely printing new notes since 1943 – Sherwin, *Monetary Policy* (note 15) p. 34.
71. T. Balogh, 'The Economic Problems of France', *Bulletin of the Oxford Institute of Statistics*, 7 (1945) 62; Sherwin, *Monetary Policy* (note 15), p. 35.
72. Sherwin, *Monetary Policy* (note 15), p. 36.
73. J. G. Gurley, 'Excess Liquidity and European Monetary Reforms, 1944–1952', *American Economic Review*, 43 (1953) 76–100.
74. Klopstock, 'Monetary Reforms in Liberated Europe', *American Economic Review*, 36 (1946) 578–95.
75. Ibid. p. 580.
76. J. Jessen, 'Das "Gesetz der wachsenden Ausdehnung des Finanzbedarfs"', *Schmollers Jahrbuch*, 67 I (1943) 164–5. His discussion centred upon England because Wagner's Law could only be tested against a state whose territory had remained unchanged for centuries and where there was also adequate and reliable statistical data.
77. P. Harling and P. Mandler, 'From "Fiscal-Military" to Laissez-faire State, 1760–1850', *Journal of British Studies*, 32 (1993) 49.
78. A. T. Peacock and J. Wiseman, *The Growth of Public Expenditure in the United Kingdom*, National Bureau of Economic Research Number 72, General Series (Princeton: Princeton University Press, 1961) p. 38.
79. Erhard himself took the position that there were no serious problems subsequent to the Reform which were not caused by misguided opposition to his policies. His account of the impact of the Reform misses out the year 1949 altogether, jumping from increasing prices and credit creation in late 1948 to retail price reduction in 1950, then comparing the performance of European economies in the early 1950s with base 1950 = 100 – *Prosperity through Competition* (note 35) pp. 16, 20–21.
80. P. Cagan, 'The Monetary Dynamics of Hyperinflation', in M. Friedman (ed.) *Studies in the Quantity Theory of Money* (Chicago: University of Chicago Press, 1956) Table 1, p. 26.
81. Ibid. pp. 29–37.
82. M. Friedman, 'The Quantity Theory of Money – A Restatement', in M. Friedman (ed.) *Studies in the Quantity Theory of Money* (Chicago: University of Chicago Press, 1956) pp. 3–4.
83. D. Patinkin, 'The Chicago Tradition, the Quantity Theory, and Friedman', in his *Essays on and in the Chicago Tradition* (Durham, NC: Duke University Press, 1981) p. 247 (reprint of article originally published 1969).
84. Ibid. p. 245.
85. Or which have been recycled as new orthodoxies, but this does not alter the problem of historical understanding.
86. See, e.g., D. Laidler, 'Hawtrey, Harvard, and the Origins of the Chicago Tradition', *Journal of Political Economy*, 101 (1993) 1068–1103.

Comment

Horst Tomann

In this scholarly written paper, Dr Tribe highlights the historical background of the German currency reform in order to find 'implications for our understanding of its significance' (p. xx). The paper consists of four sections which pose an array of questions concerning the genesis of the reform (section 2), the history of German financial policies, covering the second quarter of this century and, in particular, war finance (section 3), the economists' debate in Germany during the war as to the requirements of a currency reform (section 4), and the experience of other currency reforms in post war Europe with a reference to reforms in earlier eras (section 5). By going through all this, Tribe challenges the customary thesis that the currency reform was the inaugural moment of the social market economy (SME) and stood at the inception of the German Economic Miracle. Based on a profound historical analysis, he argues against this thesis:

- The currency reform was prepared and enacted by the Allied forces. German experts played only a minor, subordinated role. That is well known (Benz, 1984).
- The German reform was only one in a series of post war currency reforms, and it was distinguished only insofar as it was delayed, mainly due to disagreements among the Allied forces. The long delay of the Reform 'contributed to the shock effect of its announcement' (p. xx).
- The conversion rate was based on incorrect and obsolete data of the money stock and national income. Taking correct data into account, the British proposal of a lower conversion rate would have been more adequate.

For those reasons, the author concludes, it is open to question whether the Reform's 'actual terms and conditions were important in stimulating activity' (p. xx). That is all, indeed, he can say from an historian's methodological point of view. But Tribe adds theoretical considerations to his conclusions which I should like to comment in more detail.

The case for a radical reduction of the money supply, Tribe argues, was deducted from a simple quantity theory of money, which looks remote today. A more detailed study of monetary thought of the time, he suggests, would reveal that American and German orthodoxy during the 1940s did not differ substantially. Consequently, 'the economic content of Ordoliberalism, the foundation of the Social Market Economy, is nothing more than a version of a neoclassical orthodoxy elsewhere eclipsed in the course of the 1950s' (p. xx). In a recent paper, Tribe is more precise about his critique of neoclassical orthodoxy: '[The Currency Reform] was a distinctly inegalitarian measure seemingly removed from the "social" credentials of the policies listed by Müller-Armack.' (Tribe, 1998, p. 25), and '. . . the Currency Reform has more in common with neoliberal structural adjustment policy than the kind of egalitarian policy which Maynard Keynes espoused' (Tribe, 1998, p. 27).

In this view, it seems evident that a radical currency reform does not comply with the concept of a social market economy. This requires to be clarified in order to avoid a misinterpretation of the SME concept.

First, we have to understand that the label 'social' in the concept of SME is a programmatic label. Müller-Armack as well as Ludwig Erhard were not only economists but also politicians who were eager to contrast their concept as sharply as possible against the German state socialism. Social objectives had been captured and put into the service of an inhumane, facist regime. Against this background it was of utmost importance to contrast the market economy as being a social institution quite different from what Hayek had called the road to serfdom.

Apart from programmatic aspects, however, the misinterpretation of the SME concept has theoretical reasons. The key to clarify this question lies in the way economic uncertainty and the formation of expectations is treated in the ordoliberal approach. Roughly, the idea of establishing an 'order', that is rules and conventions, is a response to economic uncertainty; in this sense, ordoliberalism is a concept similar to the classical political economy. By contrast, neoclassical orthodoxy lacks an adequate concept of uncertainty. Economic uncertainty is transformed into (seemingly objective) probabilities, a concept which opens the way to model 'rational expectations'. But it is neutral as to the role of institutions in society. The most striking evidence for this difference is the ordoliberal principle of the primacy of a stable money. This principle stresses the importance of how expectations are formed and the importance of credible monetary institutions. It provides the theoretical underpinning of a radical currency reform. But it cannot be deducted in a neoclassical framework.

To reveal the classical roots of ordoliberalism, let us consider the 'douceur of commerce' thesis (Hirschman, 1977) which governs the debate on enlightenment. A market society, to use Hirschman's (1992) terminology, can be attested a civilizing feature. The reason was most clearly stated by David Hume: 'I suppose a person to have lent me a sum of money, on condition that it be restor'd in a few days; and also suppose, that after the expiration of the term agreed on, he demands the sum: I ask, *What reason or motive have I to restore the money?*' (Hume, 1978, p. 479).

The key to this question is self-interest. It is in my interest to give the money back since my own property rights can only be secure if I do not question the property rights of others. The government has to comply to this basic idea of a contrat social in pursuing measures of economic policy and at the same time has to provide the framework which guarantees the viability of private property rights. In particular, the governments' committments not to cheat their citizens is constituent for a civil society. It is from this classical principle that the primacy of a stable money follows.

Against this background, social policy issues have to be treated in a coherent way. The theoretical foundation provided by Walter Eucken in his *Grundsätze der Wirtschaftspolitik* was that social objectives cannot be pursued independent of the Lenkungsproblem. Social issues are part of the overall constitution of economic policy. In the present time, we would treat these problems of social entitlements in terms of institutional economics. It is, in my view, a striking evidence that Keynes could stress the egalitarian objectives on the background of a macroeconomic model for a closed economy, whereas Eucken and his colleagues stressed the openness of markets and, in particular, the primacy of a stable money as being the constituents of a competitive order of economic policy. Social issues had to be interpreted differently in those different theoretical frameworks.

To be more specific, why does a currency reform and a tight monetary policy pursue social objectives? The basic idea is, and it is a modern idea, that governments commit themselves not to manipulate the value of their moneys. They tye their hands and dispense of inflationary strategies to reduce the burden of public debt. This creates credibility. In this view, credibility of the government is an endogenous issue, whereas Keynes could model egalitarian strategies of demand management without questioning the government's credibility.

Taking a long-term perspective, the existence of a stable money is a precondition for equity between generations. Samuelson (1958) has shown in a famous article that one of the basic problems in a market society is to ensure that the younger generations will pay for the elderly when these are not more in a position to make their own living. In an exchange economy, this problem is intractable since capital goods are not durable.

The resolution of this problem in a market economy requires the establisment of a monetary regime which provides for a stable money. Only this provides for time consistency of private plans.

To conclude, the social market economy is a classical concept, and it stands in sharp contrast to the 'neoclassical orthodoxy' assumed by Tribe. Nonetheless, the paper provides an excellent analysis of the history of German financial policy, covering the second quarter of this century. Tribe's purpose to sharpen our appreciation of the 1948 Currency Reform leads him to an intriguing comparative study of different methods 'to pay for the war'. Looking into the mirror of German and European history, we have the opportunity to test our own judgements.

Bibliography

Benz, W. *Die Gründung der Bundesrepublik. Von der Bizone zum souveränen Staat.* (Munich: dtv, 1984).

Eucken, W. *Grundsätze der Wirtschaftspolitik* (Tübingen, 1959).

Hirschman, A. O. *The Passions and the Interests. Political Arguments for Capitalism before Its Triumph* (Princeton, NJ: Princeton University Press, 1977).

Hirschman, A. O. *Rival Views of Market Society* (Cambridge, MA: Haward University Press 1992).

Hume, D. *A Treatise of Human Nature* [1739–40] 2nd edn. (Oxford: Clarendon Press, 1978).

Samuelson, P. A. 'An exact consumption-loan model of interest with or without the social contrivance of money', *Journal of Political Economy*, LXVI 467 (1958) 82.

Tribe, K. *The Economic Origins of the Social Market Economy.* Discussion Paper, Institute for German Studies, University of Birmingham, 1998.

4
Paradigm Changes of German Monetary Policy

Reiner König

Introduction

There is actually nothing to add if a proven expert on German monetary policy such as Stephen F. Frowen and his co-author Karakitsos arrive at the conclusion that 'The German policymakers have been very systematic and very pragmatic in their conduct of monetary policy. Their priorities between inflation and growth have remained time invariant ...' (Frowen and Karakitsos, 1997, p. 527). The salient feature of German monetary policy is indeed its striking continuity, rather than frequent 'paradigm changes'.

That applies first and foremost to its stability orientation. In the 50 years of the Deutsche Mark's existence, Germany has achieved a high degree of price stability. In that respect, the last 50 years have been in distinct contrast to the monetary upheavals of the first half of the twentieth century with their calamitous political and social consequences. A comparison with inflationary developments in other countries during the past 50 years also testifies to how deeply stability awareness is anchored in Germany – something which is undoubtedly due to its specific past experience. The average annual rate of inflation in the United Kingdom over the past five decades – based on a broad index of consumer prices – has been 6.4 per cent, for example. By contrast, the corresponding German rate has been 2.8 per cent. Even countries with a traditionally stronger anti-inflationary orientation, such as Switzerland and the United States, have recorded higher average rates of monetary erosion than Germany – at 3 per cent and 4.1 per cent, respectively.

In the implementation of monetary policy, continuity has undoubtedly been less pronounced, since the German central bank has repeatedly had to adjust to changes in the underlying conditions. Even so, the DM's stability lead over other major currencies has been accompanied by striking consistency in its fundamental monetary policy strategies and in the deployment of central bank policy instruments. By international standards, too, paradigm changes in German monetary policy tend to be rare occurrences; they have mainly been responses to secular developments in the international monetary system. Adjustments to changes in the domestic economy have been less pressing and have tended to take place gradually; it has been possible to avoid shock-like adjustments. Even German unification did not force a paradigm change in monetary policy.

The stability record of the DM and the relative continuity of monetary policy naturally give rise to the question of how far a correlation exists between those two factors. In order to shed further light on this issue – to identify not only the constants, but also the changes, in German monetary policy – I shall start by giving a brief outline of postwar monetary history. In doing so, one must distinguish – on account of the external conditions – between two major periods of roughly equal length.

1948–1973: Increasing tensions between domestic and external value of the German currency

Given the status quo in 1948, a reform of the monetary system was inevitable: the Reichsmark was virtually worthless and obviously no longer capable of performing essential monetary functions.[1] As early as March of that year, the institutional framework for that reform has been put in place by the establishment of a two-tier central banking system – comprising the existing Land central banks and the Bank deutscher Länder as its central office. The monetary 'break' in June meant that the existing monetary overhang could be removed and thus a fresh start made.[2] In several major respects, this implied a radical reorientation for German monetary policy. From the very start this included, as fundamental principles, the clear orientation towards monetary stability and the independence of the decision makers from political instructions – including those of the federal government, which had been in office since September 1949.[3]

The framework within which German monetary policy operated in the first 25 years of the DM's existence was marked out mainly by its external integration in the postwar international monetary system. The Bretton Woods exchange rate system was designed as a regime of fundamentally fixed exchange rates based on agreed gold parities with the dollar as the key currency, even though the possibility of exchange rate adjustments was not ruled out *a priori*.

In this preordained external framework, German monetary policy had to start from scratch in 1948: western Germany then had virtually no currency reserves and the external position was, moreover, characterized by an unfavourable balance of payments. To that extent, it is not surprising that the DM first appeared on the international stage as a weak currency.

To begin with, exchange rate pegging was not seen as a constraint on monetary policy. Instead, in the initial period following the 1948 Currency Reform, the view prevailed among the monetary policy makers in Germany that the internal and external stability of the DM should and could go hand in hand.

It was only gradually that the looming conflict between a strict exchange rate orientation and a monetary policy geared to domestic price stability emerged.[4] After overcoming a few teething problems – for which the Korea crisis may serve as an example – the DM developed into a comparatively strong currency within the international system. Growing foreign trade supluses and expanding financial assets of foreign investors in Germany caused the Bundesbank's foreign exchange reserves to increase while the exchange rates were formally fixed. Besides bank liquidity, the amount of money held by non-banks rose. In the 1960s, the dilemma in which the Bundesbank found itself became ever more manifest. If it wanted to combat the emerging inflationary trends by raising interest rates, it risked even higher capital inflows, which, in turn, undermined its efforts to achieve stability. In the final phase, the Bretton Woods system had become a 'perfect inflation machine' (Emminger, 1978, p. 7).

At the strategic level, the Bundesbank attempted to influence the banks' lending by manipulating the banks' free liquid reserves – those were short-term assets which could be sold to the Bundesbank at any time and free refinancing facilities – in such a way that resources in the real economy were not overstrained and inflationary trends did not emerge. Although the Bundesbank was able to rely on a stable relationship between the free liquid reserves and the banks' supply of credit up to around the mid-1960s, thereafter this relationship became looser and looser – not only with the inflowing deluge of foreign exchange but also with the growing market orientation on the part of the banks, which placed more emphasis on their overall liquidity and not merely on their recourse to the central bank. The commitment to exchange rate stability was an obstacle to the development of new strategic approaches. In the late 1960s and early 1970s, German monetary policy makers tried – with varying success – to engage in pragmatic damage limitation; their focus shifted increasingly away from the goal of defending the exchange rate at all costs, towards combating domestic inflationary trends.

At the instrumental level, the fresh start in 1948 was a comparatively modest break with the past. With the currency reform, the traditional refinancing policy options of discount and lombard policy and the option of operations in the open market were joined for the first time by an active minimum reserve policy. The array of monetary policy instruments available initially to the Bank deutscher Länder, and later to the Bundesbank, and their deployment therefore have to be regarded as due to historical circumstances in major respects, and likewise took account of the conditions in the German capital market – which were characterized in the early years of the Federal Republic of Germany by the fact that securities for open market operations were available only on an extremely limited scale.

Throughout the first 25 years of German monetary policy, the entire range of possible monetary policy instruments was of little significance for the practical implementation of monetary policy. Following an initial phase, the German central bank was essentially faced with the necessity of having to mop up inflowing liquidity. The purchase of foreign exchange often led to an excessive expansion of central bank money creation. That may be illustrated by the fact that the discount rate, as the cheapest refinancing facility at the German central bank, sometimes formed the ceiling of the day-to-day money market rate, and that the existing rediscount quotas were utilized only to a limited extent.

The monetary policy makers' hands were tied in that situation. The exchange rate orientation had reached its limits. Unless the domestic objective of price stability was abandoned, a radical change in the international monetary policy system had to take place. Only then could the necessary paradigm change in German monetary policy be effected in concrete terms. Even before that, however, the 'renaissance' of monetarism had already prepared the intellectual ground for such a change.

1974–1998: The monetary targeting policy of the Deutsche Bundesbank

The changeover to a floating exchange rate *vis-à-vis* the US dollar undoubtedly opened up new scope for German monetary policy and thus marked the start of the second major phase of postwar monetary history. The Bundesbank was no longer compelled to create central bank money involuntarily by buying foreign exchange. Lifting the intervention obligation had a liberating impact on monetary policy. The

Bundesbank no longer had to react passively to inflows of foreign currency, but again became master of its own money creation.

At the strategic level, this expanded scope of action confronted the Bundesbank not only with the option but also with the necessity, of redefining its stance. By announcing a monetary target for the first time for 1975, the Bundesbank – as the first central bank worldwide – decided on a course which was already mapped out by recent theoretical findings. In particular, the perception that excessive price rises always have to be accommodated monetarily in the medium term – and are, indeed, often sparked off by such accommodation – had again been placed at the centre of academic discussion by the monetarist school closely associated with the name of Milton Friedman.[5] Furthermore, the adverse experience of the late 1960s and the early 1970s had led to a loss of confidence in monetary policy being able to make a meaningful contribution to a short-term management of macroeconomic developments.

Although the strategy of pre-announced monetary targets tended to have an experimental character to begin with, it has by and large proved its worth over the past 25 years, and has been retained by the Bundesbank – despite some modifications – up to the present.[6] There have been – and still are – a number of good reasons for this: in the short run, monetary policy is unable to exert a direct influence on the price level. Instead, it is faced with the problem of long and variable time-lags. Given uncertainties of this kind, gearing to an intermediate target can enable the central bank to respond in good time to potential undesirable trends. In this respect, the above-mentioned relationship between price movements and monetary expansion in the medium term makes the money stock, as it were, the 'natural' intermediate target of a monetary policy geared to price stability. Furthermore, a pre-announced monetary target helps monetary policy to provide a better response to excessive demands placed on it from outside.

Above all, however, the advance announcement of a monetary target signifies self-commitment on the part of the central bank. Once the expectations of the general public had entered into the theoretical economic debate, what had meanwhile become an extensive literature again took up the old controversy between compliance with rules and discretion in monetary policy.[7] Here, it has proved to be undisputed that a credible precommitment is a *sine qua non* of successful monetary policy. It is only if the general public has no cause to fear that a pre-announced monetary policy stance might be subject to revision and thus be time-inconsistent that such a policy can be pursued effectively. The lasting achievement of low rates of monetary erosion on a sustained basis is predicated on the central bank's ability to convince the general public of its intention to do so.

Certainly, the Bundesbank's monetary policy strategy – which is often also referred to as 'pragmatic monetarism' – is not a precommitment in the sense of a strict unconditional precept for action. In the course of the last 25 years, departures from the pre-announced monetary target have been witnessed on several occasions.[8] But the published monetary targets do compel the Bundesbank to account for its actions and thus retain their significance for German monetary policy, even in the event of departures which have to be well explained.

What is crucial for the successful implementation of a monetary policy strategy is, first, the central bank's ability to manage its monetary target aggregate – in the case of the Bundesbank: the broad aggregate M3 – over the medium term. Second, there should be a stable medium-term relationship between the relevant monetary aggregate and the general price level. This is confirmed not only by external studies but also by internal studies undertaken by the Bundesbank.[9] The empirical foundations for monetary targeting may therefore be regarded as continuing to obtain in Germany.

The practical implementation of German monetary policy was likewise subject to a fundamental change after a time-lag compared with its strategic reorientation at the beginning of the 1970s.[10] Incidentally, the fact that it was possible to accomplish the changeover to a development of the instruments that is more closely in line with market conditions without formal amendments to the Bundesbank Act testifies to the remarkable farsightedness of the legislature.

The fact that it has largely ceased to be necessary continuously to mop up inflowing liquidity since 1973 did not initially involve a reorientation in the deployment of the instruments. It was possible to continue money market management with the aid of commercial banks' traditional refinancing facilities at the German central bank. Only the existing special refinancing facilities – such as those for foreign trade deals – were dismantled comparatively quickly.

In the mid-1980s, the German financial centre's increasing integration in the international markets made a change in the interaction between the Bundesbank and credit institutions appear necessary. Securities repurchase agreements became ever more important, leading to the vast majority of central bank money nowadays being made available to the credit institutions through this flexible and market-related instrument. In parallel with this, repurchase rates determine the German market for day-to-day money. The remaining discount business is mainly for the purpose of providing longer-term central bank money; its low interest rates particularly benefit small and medium-sized enterprises. Lombard credit, as a comparatively expensive form of refinancing, essentially performs the function of an upward safety valve.

The minimum reserve instrument, too, has undergone a radical change over the past 25 years, compared with the period of the Bretton Woods system of fixed exchange rates. Whereas, in situations of inflowing liquidity, changes in the reserve ratios were an important means of warding off excessive liquidity in the banking sector – and occurred with corresponding frequency – it is nowadays the steadying effect of the minimum reserves, their buffer function in the money market, which is in the forefront. Above and beyond that, they ensure a sufficiently stable demand for central bank money. For that reason, they are indispensable in the Bundesbank's view. In line with their changed functional pattern, the Bundesbank has not only reduced the differences in the reserve ratios as far as possible but has also significantly lowered the rates at the same time – not least in view of the possibility of this instrument exercising a distorting effect on competition. The present volume of the banking system's minimum reserve liabilities to the Bundesbank is consequently likely to be only marginally higher than its working balances.

During this second major phase of its life, the DM was more than able to maintain the stability lead over other currencies which it had previously achieved. Whereas, up to the collapse of the Bretton Woods system, price movements in Germany had ultimately been forced to follow international inflationary trends – even if at a lower level – after the exchange rate *vis-à-vis* the US dollar had been floated, a decoupling from global exigencies became possible.

Constants of German monetary policy

Both the above-described monetary policy changes at the strategic level – the transition to the monetary targeting strategy may be regarded as the main paradigm change in German monetary policy – and the practical implementation of monetary policy were embedded in a number of major constants. These included both continuity at the level of the final goal and a consistent institutional framework; both made a crucial contribution to the success recorded in anti-inflation policy over the past 50 years.

The clear orientation towards safeguarding monetary stability, which is now enshrined in section 3 of the Bundesbank Act, already applied to the Bank deutscher Länder. This assignment of responsibility – which was undoubtedly originally rooted in the special twofold German experience of hyperinflation – rests on a secure theoretical and empirical foundation.

The costs associated with a sustained process of monetary erosion are immense: even in the event of a correctly predicted inflationary process, the general public is compelled to devote resources to protecting itself adequately. As an illustration, I will mention no more than the tying-up of management capacity. The costs associated with monetary erosion are far more alarming, however, in the more realistic event of inflation coming as a surprise. Besides far-reaching effects on the distribution of prosperity within the economy as a whole (as a result of, say, a tax system which is not neutral in terms of inflation) there are also allocative effects to bear in mind: in particular, the price system is able to perform its due function in a market economy only inadequately in a situation of price uncertainty.[11]

The costs of inflation are not accompanied by any corresponding benefits. Instead, including the expectations of a critical public in macroeconomic theory has resulted in a radical rethinking in this context, too. First, it is nowadays uncontested that, at the most, only an inflation which comes as a surprise, and is thus associated with correspondingly high costs, can have any impact at all on the real economy. Given rational expectations on the part of the general public and flexible markets, not even that is true. Second, these growth gains and the associated gains in employment are only temporary. The existence of a relationship between employment and inflation that is lastingly exploitable in monetary policy terms in the sense of the Phillips curve debate must be denied. The permanent costs of monetary erosion can scarcely be offset by any transitory benefits which may accompany them. Hence, monetary policy serves economic prosperity best if it assumes the responsibility for stable underlying conditions.

Bearing that in mind, it appears astonishing that an animated debate, emanating from the United States, has recently sprung up in academic circles on identifying an 'optimum inflation rate'. The arguments put forward by the proponents of a (stable) basic level of inflation which differs from zero are primarily concerned with the labour market conditions obtaining in most industrial countries. Given nominal wage rigidities, it is claimed that price stability impedes adjustments of real wages that may be necessary; a permanently higher level of unemployment, it is said, is the inevitable alternative.[12]

These arguments are not persuasive, however, and scarcely stand up to critical scrutiny. A completely different picture readily emerges if the supposed costs of disinflation to a state of price stability are confronted with its benefits – in other words, if the above-mentioned costs even of a moderate inflation rate, which would no longer exist with price stability, are included in the calculation.[13] Moreover, the approach described fails to take account of the process of adjustment to a durably price-stable environment, which should lead to a reduction in price rigidities and thus also to greater flexibility on the labour market.

In addition to the unambiguous assignment of tasks that has obtained for the past 50 years, the underlying institutional conditions in the broader sense form the second constant of German monetary policy. First of all, reference should be made in this context not only to the policy arrangements, which immediately concern the Deutsche Bundesbank and its predecessor, but also, of course, to the overall financial system within which monetary policy operates.

(a) Neither the Bank deutscher Länder nor the Bundesbank has been subject to instructions from other domestic areas of policy. Within the frame of reference set by the mandate assigned to them by parliament to safeguard price stability, they have been able to deploy their arsenal of instruments freely and on their own responsibility. This independence of the German central bank – unlike that, say, of the Bank of England – is not recent, but has been in existence for all of the past half a century. From the very beginning, it was protected by a prohibition of central bank lending to finance government budgetary deficits.

Independence is certainly one – if not *the* crucial – precondition for the stability success that has been achieved; it has put the German central bank in a position to perform the role assigned to it by parliament without distractions.[14] The deeper-seated theoretical reason for this is once again to be seen in the potential time-inconsistency problem of monetary policy. In this respect, the independence of monetary policy can make a major contribution to its credibility.[15]

The fact that a considerable number of central banks have been made independent fairly recently means that the question of greater accountability has become more topical, precisely for an independent monetary policy. What is the guarantee that a central bank will act within the frame of reference of its mandate? How is democratic authority to be defined if part of the executive is independent?

The Bundesbank – like its predecessor – is not subject to any kind of obligation to report regularly to parliament, for example. Nor do the contractual terms under which the monetary policy makers operate in Germany provide for any kind of sanctions in the event of a low rate of inflation not being achieved. Nevertheless, German monetary policy makers have always regarded independence and accountability as 'two sides of the same coin' during the past 50 years; they are closely interconnected.

At all times, the Bundesbank has made use of many channels of communication in order to give the general public detailed information on its ongoing monetary policy measures, its monetary policy strategy and, above all, the degree to which its final goal has been achieved – by which it must ultimately be judged. Not least with the aid of its 'Monthly Reports', the Bundesbank is nowadays in a position to reach a comparatively wide audience and provide an in-depth account of its monetary policy intentions. Allow me to mention in passing that, as long ago as 1959, the British Radcliffe Report favourably highlighted the German central bank's publications and, moreover, recommended them to the Bank of England as an example.[16]

In particular, the chosen monetary policy strategy must be transparent for enterprises, trade unions and the public authorities; it must be underpinned by the broad approval of the general public. From the Bundesbank's point of view, an intermediate monetary target which is derived from a small number of components is especially suited to that purpose. Bearing in mind the German people's historical experience, the relationship between inflation and the money stock is well known. A monetary target documents the central bank's special responsibility for monetary transmission channels and is easily verifiable.

(b) Just as the basic principles of independence, transparency and accountability to the general public have accompanied the German central bank over the past 50 years, the financial system within which it has operated has been characterized by conspicuous stability. This is revealed most clearly perhaps by the continuing predominant position of the 'universal bank' in the German financial system, which also owes something to behaviour on the part of non-banks, which tends to be conservative, and a related, comparatively long-term orientation of financial relationships.[17]

Additionally, the regulatory framework – in contrast, above all, to the Anglo- Saxon countries – has been characterized by liberalisation and deregulation constituting part of a continuous, gradual process rather than taking place as a series of financial shocks. Moreover, the impetus for this trend was provided at an early stage – not only by the DM being made fully convertible in 1958 and the early liberalization of capital movements, but also by the complete decontrolling of bank interest rates in 1967.

Finally, monetary policy has also played its part in the steady development of the financial system. The comparatively high degree of price stability has undoubtedly contributed to the comparatively modest demand in Germany for some financial instruments which are widely used in other countries.

Conclusions and outlook for European Monetary Union

All in all, major changes have occurred in German monetary policy over the last 50 years. However, these have materialized with due regard to important constants, particularly in terms of the institutional framework and the defined objective of the central bank's policy. But for the strategic reorientation at the beginning of the 1970s, paradigm changes have remained the exception. By contrast, the salient feature of German monetary policy is continuity. Bearing in mind the positive experience which the Bundesbank has gained in this situation, it is possible only to warn against all-too-frequent changes of policy. This is the conviction arrived at, not least, by Frowen and Karakitsos, too, when they conclude in a comparative study of British and German monetary policy that, 'This frequent change of the monetary regime has contributed to a persistant inflation differential with Germany ...' (Frowen and Karakitsos, 1997, p. 529). Germany's experience of monetary policy during the past 50 years has been incorporated in the design of European monetary union. Safeguarding price stability is the key task of the future European System of Central Banks (ESCB). In order to achieve this, it has been made largely independent of both the national governments and the Community's institutions. It will now be important to invest the Treaty with life and to establish a tradition of credible action. I conclude by quoting from the Introduction by Stephen Frowen and Robert Pringle to *Inside the Bundesbank*. (Frowen and Pringle, 1998, p. xxi).

> It is deeply ironic that now, with its prestige riding high, and its gospel of central bank independence spreading around the world, the Bundesbank is due to make the ultimate sacrifice: its immolation on the altar of European integration. By the terms of the Maastricht Treaty it stands under sentence of death. If, with its last breath, it can pass on the torch of monetary stability to a new European System of Central Banks, the sacrifice will have been worthwhile.

Notes

1. See, e.g., Möller (1976) for a comprehensive overview of the preparations for, and implementation of, the 1948 Currency Reform.
2. Emminger (1986) points out on p. 26 that the currency conversion of 1948 was already basically a monetarist action.
3. This statement has to be qualified by noting that, although the Bank deutscher Länder was independent of German political decision makers, it was bound by the instructions of the Allied Banking Commission up to 1951.
4. See Oberhauser (1976) and Kloten (1976) for a detailed account of the historical development of the conflict between the domestic and external value of the DM.
5. See, e.g., Friedman (1963).
6. See, e.g., Schmid (1995) on the technical modifications which the Bundesbank's monetary targets have undergone over the years.
7. Major staging posts in the advance of economic theory on this subject were Kydland and Prescott (1977) and Barro and Gordon (1983).
8. Some problems for monetary targeting temporarily occurred most recently, e.g., in connection with the consequences of monetary union with eastern Germany. See, for instance, König und Willeke (1995).
9. See, e.g., Deutsche Bundesbank (1997a) and Deutsche Bundesbank (1997b).
10. See Schmid and Asche (1997) for a detailed account of the Bundesbank's arsenal of monetary policy instruments and its deployment.
11. See Driffill *et al.* (1990) on the allocative effects of inflation.
12. Estimates of this for the United States may be found in Akerlof *et al.* (1996).
13. Groshen and Schweizer (1997) for example, analyse the costs and benefits of moderate inflation for conditions on the labour market without arriving at a clear conclusion. At the macroeconomic level, however, the totality of the permanent losses of prosperity associated with inflation is likely distinctly to outweigh its supposed benefits. Estimates on this for the United States may be found in Feldstein (1996) for the United Kingdom in Bakshi *et al.* (1997) and for Germany in Tödter and Ziebarth (1997).
14. See Issing (1993).
15. The positive relationship between the central bank's independence and price stability is additionally confirmed by a number of empirical studies on different countries. See, for instance, Alesina and Summers (1993).
16. Emminger (1986) refers to this on p. 28.
17. See Deutsche Bundesbank (1998) on the position of the banks in Germany.

Bibliography

Akerlof, G. A., Dickens, W. T. and Perry, G. L. *The Macroeconomics of Low Inflation* (Brookings Papers on Economic Activity, no. 1, pp. 1–76, 1996).

Alesina, A. and Summers, L. H. 'Central Bank Independence and Macroeconomic Performance: Some Comparative Evidence'. *Journal of Money, Credit and Banking*, 25/2 (1993) 151–62.

Bakhshi, H., Haldane, A. G. and Hatch, N. 'Quantifying some benefits of price stability'. *Bank of England Quarterly Bulletin*, 37/3 (1997), 274–84.

Barro, R. J. 'Inflation and Economic Growth', *Bank of England Quarterly Bulletin*, 35/2, (1995), 166–75.

Barro, R. J. and Gordon, D. B. 'Rules, Discretion and Reputation in a Model of Monetary Policy', *Journal of Monetary Economics*, 12/1 (1983), 101–21.

Deutsche Bundesbank (1997a). 'Überprüfung des Geldmengenziels. Anhang 1: Zur Stabilität der Geldnachfrage'. *Monatsberichte der Deutschen Bundesbank*, 49/8 (1997), 27–9.

Deutsche Bundesbank (1997b). 'Überprüfung des Geldmengenziels. Anhang 2: Vorlaufeigenschaften der Geldmenge'. *Monatsberichte der Deutschen Bundesbank*, 49/8 (1997), 29–32.

Deutsche Bundesbank. 'Strukturveränderungen am deutschen Kapitalmarkt', *Monatsberichte der Deutschen Bundesbank*, 50/4 (1998), 55–70.

Driffill, J., Mizon, G. E. and Ulph, A. 'Costs of Inflation', in: B. M. Friedman, and F. H. Hahn (eds) *Handbook of Monetary Economics*. (Amsterdam: North Holland 1990) 1013–66.

Emminger, O. '30 Jahre Deutsche Mark'. *Monatsberichte der Deutschen Bundesbank*, 30/6 (1978), 5–12.

Emminger, O. *D-Mark, Dollar, Währungskrisen: Memories of a former Bundesbank President* (Stuttgart: Deutsche Verlags-Anstalt, 1986).

Feldstein, M. 'The Costs and Benefits of Going from Low Inflation to Price Stability' (*NBER Working Paper* No. 5469, 1996).

Friedman, M. *Inflation – Causes and Consequences* (New York: Asia Publishing House, 1963).

Frowen, S. F. and Karakitsos, E. 'An Evaluation of Inflation Targeting in Germany and the UK', *Kredit und Kapital*, 30/4 (1997) 501–32.

Frowen, S. F. and Pringle, R. Introduction of 'Understanding the Bundesbank', Special Issue of Central Banking, 6/1 (1995), 19–20.

Frowen, S. F. and Pringle, R. (eds.) *Inside the Bundesbank* (London: Macmillan; New York: St. Martin's Press, 1998).

Groshen, E. L. and Schweitzer, M. E. 'Identifying Inflation's Grease and Sand Effects in the Labor Market' (*NBER Working Paper* No. 6061, 1997).

Issing, O. 'Unabhängigkeit der Notenbank und Geldwertstabilität', *Abhandlungen der Akademie der Wissenschaften und der Literatur, Geistes- und Sozialwissenschaftliche Klasse*, No. 1 (1993).

Kloten, N. 'Erfolg und Mißerfolg der Stabilisierungspolitik', in Deutsche Bundesbank (ed.), *Währung und Wirtschaft in Deutschland 1876–1975* (Frankfurt: Knapp, (1976), 643–90.

König, R. and Willeke, C. 'German Monetary Unification', *Central Banking*, 6/1 (1995), 29–39. Revised and updated version in S. F. Frowen and R. Pringle (eds) *Inside the Bundesbank* (London: Macmillan; New York: St. Martin's Press, 1998), pp. 20–31.

Kydland, F. E. and Prescott, E. C. 'Rules rather than discretion: The inconsistency of optimal plans', *Journal of Political Economy*, 85/3, (1977), 473–91.

Möller, H. 'Die westdeutsche Währungsreform von 1948', in Deutsche Bundesbank (ed.), *Währung und Wirtschaft in Deutschland 1876–1975* (Frankfurt: Knapp, (1976), 433–83.

Oberhauser, A. 'Geld- und Kreditpolitik bei weitgehender Vollbeschäftigung und mäßigem Preisanstieg (1958–1968)', in Deutsche Bundesbank (ed.), *Währung und Wirtschaft in Deutschland 1876–1975* (Frankfurt: Knapp, (1976) 609–42.

Schmid, P. 'Monetary Policy: Targets and Instruments', *Central Banking*, 6/1 (1995), 40–51. Revised and updated version in S. F. Frowen and R. Pringle (eds.) *Inside the Bundesbank* (London: Macmillan; New York: St. Martin's Press, 1998), 32–44.

Schmid, P. and Asche, H. 'Monetary policy instruments and procedures in Germany; evolution, deployment and effects', in Bank for International Settlements (ed.), 'Implementation and Tactics of Monetary Policy', *Conference Papers*, 71–95 (1997), p. 3.

Tödter, K.-H. and Ziebarth, G. 'Preisstabilität oder geringe Inflation für Deutschland?', *Diskussionspapier 3/97* (Volkswirtschaftliche Forschungsgruppe der Deutschen Bundesbank 1997).

Comment

Andy Mullineux

Contradicting its title, the thesis of Reiner König's excellent paper, is that there have been no significant paradigm changes in German monetary policy over the last 50 years and nor should there have been, for it has done a remarkable job in maintaining price stability.

Its concluding remarks urge the (now) newly formed European Central Bank, which has been modelled in its most important institutional aspects on the Bundesbank, to continue with Bundesbank policies. I am sure that its first decisions, to eschew inflation targeting in favour or intermediate monetary targeting, to select M3 as the appropriate monetary aggregate, and utilize minimum (bank) reserve requirements as one of its instruments will meet with Reiner (and Stephen Frowen's) approval (just as the dispute, and its resolution, over the term of the first President will have been frowned upon).

Such views are not uncontroversial. Acceptance of the view that the Bundesbank's policy was right for Germany over the last 50 years (although this has become more questionable in the last few years, a point to which I will return), does not necessarily mean acceptance of the view that a similar policy pursued by the ECB will be beneficial for 'Euroland' in the future. Personally, I remain agnostic on this issue. I will thus explore some of the issues with a view to stimulating further discussion.

A fundamental question that needs to be answered is: Why has the Bundesbank been so successful? Is it simply the result of an appropriate institutional structure (that is, central bank independence coupled with a well defined constitutional goal, essentially price stability) operated by adroit central bankers pursuing a 'pragmatic' monetary policy using the appropriate intermediate target (M3 growth) and instruments (minimum reserve requirements and latterly government securities repurchase agreements ('repos'))? Alternatively, was its success derived from Germany's historical experience of hyperinflation which engendered a widespread fear of inflation, making the public predisposed to accepting a monetary constitution with an institutional structure designed to prevent the inflationary financing of government deficits?

Further, just to be sure that there was no conflict between fiscal and monetary policy, the electorate only voted into power fiscally conservative governments. But, would the consensus against inflation have survived a period of sustained high unemployment (which also has a negative resonance in the populace's consciousness)? Would the increasingly dominant younger generations of voters, who have no first hand experience of hyper-inflation, but have instead first hand experience of widespread unemployment, have continued to support the Bundesbank and fiscal conservatism? Despite the best efforts of neoclassically orientated economists to argue and demonstrate empirically that there is no trade-off between inflation and unemployment (at least in the long run) – and also that 'guest workers' do not take jobs from 'proper Germans' – there is a widespread belief to the contrary.

As an aside, inflation is perhaps best regarded as a tax. It is undoubtedly distortionary, but then so too are most of the commonly levied taxes. There seems to have been a worldwide shift on the part of electorates towards supporting governments that levy non- inflationary taxes (and that contain government expenditure and therefore tax burdens in general). Electorates have also shown support for governments willing to reinforce these preferences by establishing independent central banks and/or balanced budget laws. What appears to have been the right monetary policy for Germany in the last 50 years, may not have been right for Germany, let alone Euroland, in the next 50 years. A paradigm shift may indeed have already become necessary in Germany as a result of the rise in the fiscal deficit that followed 'unification', the recent, seemingly structural, rise in unemployment, and the problem of 'unfunded' future pension liabilities. Further, is the Euroland electorate (and their elected representatives) really ready to submit to the monetary strictures of an independent central bank with seemingly limited accountability?

Less generally, is the European Central Bank (ECB) correct to opt for intermediate monetary targeting, rather than direct targeting of its ultimate goal, inflation? This begs a couple of other 'big questions' – should the ECB have been given the goal of pursuing price stability alone, or should it have a wider ranging mandate, such as that of the US Federal Reserve System; which also has obligations with regard to unemployment? And, what does 'price stability' really mean anyway? The Bundesbank seems to assume it means inflation of 0 to 2 per cent. It should be noted, however, that prices have never been absolutely stable for long. Even under the gold standard, prices were only stable on average over a number of years. In periods of rapid technical change (as at present) the concept of price stability is even more problematic since most price indices are base-date weighted and hence inflation as measured by the growth in price indices may be overestimated. Recent estimates for Germany suggest that the consumer price index overstates true inflation by 0.75 per cent (*Financial Times*, 16 June 1998). Hence price stability should perhaps be regarded as CPI inflation of 1 to 2 or 3 per cent instead. Contrary to Reiner, I also have some sympathy with the view that nominal wages (and other prices) display downward rigidity and so some inflation may help 'oil the wheels' of growth by making relative price (including real wage) adjustment easier. Incidentally, taken as a whole, the empirical evidence is much less supportive of the benefits for economic growth of lower average inflation; than the benefits for inflation of central bank independence.

To pose the question another way, why did the UK (and other countries, including the US) witness the collapse of seemingly well established relationships between the growth of broad money aggregates and inflation in the 1980s? The countries in which the relationship has been most disturbed tend to be those that have experienced the most rapid financial innovation. This has marked distortionary effects on broad (simple-sum) money aggregates, leading many, including myself, to question their usefulness and to propose alternative monetary indices (based on Divisia index numbers). We cannot pursue this here, but suffice it to say that central banks which have abandoned intermediate monetary targeting in favour of inflation targeting utilize a range of indicators of inflation (including simple sum and Divisia monetary indices in the case of the Bank of England), while those, like the Bundesbank, that have stuck to monetary targeting, pragmatists as they are, feel that they should stick to targeting a broad money aggregate (that is, M3) however flawed, that the public understands. It is also worth re-stressing that correlation does not imply causality and that the causality debate (monetary growth causes inflation or vice versa) remains a live one.

Reiner König correctly argues that Germany, having operated with a universal banking system throughout the postwar period, and having liberalized interest rates and removed exchange controls by 1967, has, at least until recent years, not been significantly affected by financial liberalization. More recent evidence suggests that this may no longer be the case. Minimum reserve requirements have had to be reduced in order to reduce 'taxes' on banks to levels closer to those levied in Luxemburg and London. Equity financing has begun to grow in importance relative to bank debt financing. Numerous changes are being brought about as a result of the formation of a single European financial market and such changes can be expected to accelerate under a common European currency. Germany will no longer remain aloof from the ongoing financial revolution. It would increasingly have become evident that the 'money stock' was not the 'natural' intermediate target of a monetary policy geared to price stability in Germany. Further, removal of implicit (for example, pension investment restrictions) exchange controls would have increasingly exposed Germany to inflows and outflows of capital, adding to the complexity of monetary policy making.

Intermediate monetary targeting is even less likely to be the 'natural' or appropriate choice for Euroland. The importance of the various components of M3 vary significantly across the member countries and anyway the very concept of what is money (and thus how it should be measured) is being challenged by financial innovation and the development of electronic money. The chosen intermediate target (M3) is unlikely to be the appropriate one, and intermediate targeting itself is probably an outmoded concept. Inflation targeting using monetary aggregates and indices along with other indicators of inflation may well have become the most appropriate approach.

What is clear is that interest rates have become the most important monetary instrument in the UK, Germany, the US and elsewhere and that changes in 'repo rates' are increasingly the key signals of changes in monetary policy stance in Europe. Minimum reserve requirements appear to have been declining in importance in Germany and are likely to be of minor importance in Euroland once the ECB has got the hang of controlling interest rates through open market operations in the various European financial centres.

Before finishing, it is worth commenting that Reiner's paper highlights another highly topical issue pertaining to the recent troubles in Pacific and South East Asia. This is the conflict between fixed exchange rate regimes and monetary policy independence. For a period, as anti-inflationary credibility is being established, fixed exchange rates, by serving as a 'nominal anchor', can be helpful. Once political and economic stability has been achieved, a 'capital inflow problem' can emerge. Such a problem was developing in Germany in the late 1960s and early 1970s and was being contained, with increasing difficulty, through 'sterilization' (bond sales to soak up liquidity). The Deutsche Mark was not ultimately forced to revalue unilaterally, for the Bretton Woods system collapsed first in 1973. The problem experienced by Thailand in May 1997 was different to the extent that a devaluation was clearly required, but was not executed in a timely manner (unlike the Czech Republic at about the same time). If the Bretton Woods system had not collapsed, Germany may well have been forced into a regime change. The relevance of these considerations depends on the exchange rate policy adopted by Euroland.

The ECB monetary policy committee will have much less independence with regard to interest rate policy if the Euro is pegged to the dollar and/or the yen. Will the exchange rate policy in Euroland be set by the politicians or the central bankers?

5

Is the European Central Bank too Independent?[1]

Geoffrey E. Wood

Lacking the perspectives and concerns of an earlier period, we too easily impose the perceptions of a later time and misunderstand the reasons for earlier policies. (Philip Cagan, 1979, p. vii)

Introduction

Central bank independence is now widely regarded as desirable. It is associated with low inflation, and low and predictable inflation appears to have effects on growth rates which, although modest year by year, build up to having significant beneficial effects on national income over longer periods (Barro, 1995). The idea that a central bank might be 'too independent' – quite aside from whether independence is a concept admitting of various 'degrees' – therefore may seem bizarre.

Nevertheless the question is worth pursuing. Doing so raises questions about the stability of the structure of the European Central Bank (ECB) and its relations with the European Parliament and national governments; and these questions in turn raise concerns about future economic performance in the European Monetary Union (EMU) area.

This paper proceeds in the following stages. First there is a review of what can be meant by independence. Next there is discussion of the relationship between central bank independence and inflation, focusing on direction of causality, some exceptions to the general rule, and some questions raised by the history of the Bank of England.

There is then an examination of accountability and transparency, two matters given considerable attention in Great Britain and New Zealand, both countries where the central bank has recently been given independence in a particular sense of the term.

The paper concludes with a consideration, in view of the preceding discussion, of whether the ECB structure is likely to remain unchanged and of whether it is one which is likely to deliver stable prices over a period of some years.

Concepts of independence

Most recent work on the connection between central bank–government relations and inflation proceeds on the basis that the meaning of 'independence' is obvious. The implicit assumption is that it means simply that the government of the day has no formal means of influencing central bank decisions over monetary policy. Ways in which such formal influence might be exerted are then examined, and banks ranked in independence according to the number of such channels.

One study has, however, considered what independence can mean – an essay by Milton Friedman, first published in 1962 (reprinted in 1968: page references are to the reprint). The starting point of his discussion was the question: '... What kind of arrangements should a free society set up for the control of monetary policy?' Control over money, to quote Friedman again, is 'a potent tool for controlling and shaping the economy'. How can power be dispersed, as it should be to preserve freedom, in control over money? According to Friedman (1968, p. 174):

> The problem is to establish institutional arrangements that will enable government to exercise responsibility for money, yet will at the same time limit the power given to government and prevent the power from being used in ways that will tend to weaken rather than strengthen a free society.

It was in the context of addressing that problem that Friedman considered the concept of independence. There is, he suggested, a 'trivial meaning' of the word 'independence' – when, within an agency of government, monetary policy is entrusted to some separate organization which is subject to the head of that agency. Friedman then goes on to suggest 'a more basic meaning', which is that the central bank should be 'an independent branch of government, co-ordinate with the legislative, executive and judicial branches' (Friedman, 1968, p. 179). It would, that is to say, have a mandate, analogous to the mandate given to the judiciary. It would carry out a law or laws passed by the government, and its operations could be interfered with by government only if the law – its mandate – were changed. This describes well the present situation of, for example, the Bank of England. Friedman goes on to suggest several grounds for doubting the efficacy of such a proposal, and to argue that a monetary rule is likely to be more effective.

Whether the Bank of England delivered low inflation, sometimes even stable prices, before its 1946 nationalization because it was independent or because it pursued a rule is considered below.

Independence and performance

A pioneering analysis of the relationship between inflation performance and a measure of central bank independence was that by Bade and Parkin (1987). They consider central banks from twelve countries and their average inflation rates over the floating exchange rate period of 1973–86. The central banks are classified into four groups depending on the level of government influence. The classifications are based on two aspects, namely 'financial type' and 'policy type'. Financial type refers to the level of government influence in selecting board members, their salaries, budgets, and the distribution of profits. Policy type refers to the level of government influence in board meetings and whether government or board decides the final policy. The statistical procedure employed to determine the relationship between central bank type and inflation was to estimate a first order autoregression for each country.

Another classification of central banks was produced by Masciandaro and Tabellini (1988). Central banks from five 'Pacific basin' countries (Australia, Canada, Japan, New Zealand, and the US) are classified according to their 'dependency'. The classifications are based on government influence in the appointment of the board and the conduct of monetary policy. Although the study is primarily concerned with the relationship between central bank dependency and the fiscal deficit, it nevertheless considers the relationship with inflation. Average inflation rates for the period 1970–74, 1975–79 and 1980–85 are calculated for each of the five countries, and considered against the respective degree of dependency of the central bank. Some other studies considering the relationship between central bank dependency and inflation have employed the classifications carried out by earlier authors. Alesina (1988 and 1989) ranks central banks according to their dependency, based on classifications carried out by Bade and Parkin. Again average inflation rates are calculated over the period 1973–86 for each of the countries and considered against degree of dependency of the respective central bank. Capie, Mills and Wood (1993) provide a further classification based on factors considered by both Bade and Parkin (1987) and Masciandaro and

Tabellini (1988), and in addition to these considered the ownership of the bank and whether it had the sole right to issue notes and coins. (The last was important because some central banks only relatively recently received this privilege.)

Table 5.1 shows for the record the rankings produced by the various studies. By any of the measures used in these studies the ECB has considerable freedom. It chooses its own target. Board members are appointed from existing, already independent in some measure, central banks. Budgetary control over it ultimately rests with the European Parliament, a weak institution; and in any event its costs are likely to be covered by deposits placed with it by commercial banks. And, strikingly, it chooses its own target for inflation.

These are crucial characteristics. For when examining studies of the kind of 'independence' that produces low inflation, what Bade and Parkin (1987) called 'policy-type' independence was central.

Table 5.1 Classification of central bank dependency 1973–86

Central bank ranking*	Alesina's classification[2]	Reclassification of Alesina[2]	Masciandaro and Tabellini's classification[3]	Capie and Wood classification[1]
1	Spain (2)	Spain (2)	New Zealand (1)	Brazil (2)
2	New Zealand (3)	Japan (14)	Japan (5)	Argentina (1)
3	Australia (6)	New Zealand (2)	Australia (2)	India (8)
4	Italy (1)	Canada (11)	Canada (3)	Spain (3)
5	UK (4)	Australia (6)	USA (4)	Japan (11)
6	Finland (5)	Italy (1)		New Zealand (4)
7	France (7)	France (7)		Canada (9)
8	Denmark (8)	UK (4)		Austria (12)
9	Sweden (9)	Finland (5)		France (6)
10	Norway (10)	Denmark (8)		UK (5)
11	Canada (11)	Sweden (9)		Sweden (7)
12	Belgium (12)	Norway (10)		USA (10)
13	Holland (15)	Belgium (12)		W. Germany (13)
14	USA (13)	Holland (15)		
15	Japan (14)	USA (13)		
16	Switerland (16)	Switerland (16)		
17	W. Germany (17)	W. Germany (17)		

Notes

* 1 Refers to the most dependent central bank and 17 to the least dependent.

[1] In the study Belgium and Italy are unclassified.

[2] Central bank dependency ranking and infaltion rates from Alesina (1989).

[3] Central bank dependency ranking and inflation rates from Masciandaro and Tabellini (1988).

Figures in brackets relate to the ranking of inflation rates.

Summarizing this section, then, it is clear first that the concept of degrees of independence has meaning; and second, that the ECB is by any ranking procedure so far devised an extremely independent central bank. But will it stay that way, and if it does, is low inflation in the Euro-area guaranteed, as the evidence reviewed above would seem to suggest?

Causality, history and exceptions

In examining how institutions work, it is usually a mistake to ignore the factors which led to those institutions being created. That is certainly the case when discussing central bank independence. There are several reasons. First are the circumstances in which a good few central banks were granted their independence. Examination of the background to the 1989 Reserve Bank Act in New Zealand and the 1998 Bank of England Act will clarify this point.

The 1989 Reserve Bank Act was part of a major reform of the New Zealand Public Sector. Before setting out the main part of the Act, the economic background to these reforms and the reforms themselves must be sketched – the context of the 1989 Act is important.

Throughout the postwar period, New Zealand's growth rate was below – indeed less than half – the OECD average. New Zealand GDP grew at 1.4 per cent per annum; the OECD average was 2.9 per cent from 1950 to 1985. There was persistently low productivity growth; growth in factor inputs contributed over two-thirds to the growth of national income in New Zealand over that period, but less than one half in the UK, the US, Japan, Germany, or France (Smith and Grimes, 1990).

The economy was one of the most highly protected in the OECD area. Effective tax rates were high, and the government (by way of its control over monetary policy) regularly accommodated external shocks, so that inflation was both high (by OECD standards) and variable. New Zealand became what has been described as a 'cost plus economy' (OECD, 1993).

Monetary policy regularly switched between objectives – from the reduction of inflation to the lowering of (nominal) interest rates so as to encourage 'growth'. Policy relied increasingly on direct controls of a regulatory nature. There were both interest rate and exchange controls. The main financial institutions were constrained by reserve asset ratios, public sector debt requirements, and lending ceilings. These had their counterparts in other areas of economic policy. There were incomes policies, price controls (at a very detailed level), quantitative import restrictions, and so forth.[2]

By mid 1984, a crisis was believed to have arrived. (Knight (1991) writes of '... a disastrous outcome for the New Zealand economy by the mid 1980s'.) Following the change of government, there was widespread acceptance of the need to change both the nature and the direction of economic policy. Markets were to be relied on increasingly. Longer-term objectives were not to be sacrificed for immediate ones. It was accepted that economic problems had to be viewed together rather than tackled piecemeal regardless of their interconnections. A sustained programme of reform, affecting the institutions which designed and implemented policy as well as the policies themselves, was launched.[3]

There was deregulation of finance, communications, and transport; there were cuts in agricultural subsidies and in export assistance, border protection was lowered and free trade with Australia was established in all goods and most services. Government involvement in commercial activities was privatized or corporatized (made independent of government management, accountable only on a profit or loss basis). The tax system was simplified, with the base being broadened, rates reduced and exemptions removed. To quote the OECD, 'These reforms created one of the least distorting tax systems in the OECD area, the lowest OECD producer subsidy equivalent in agriculture, substantial trade liberalisation, and a more efficient public sector'. (OECD, 1993) On the financial reforms, Knight (1991) wrote, 'The whole financial system was thus remodelled in a remarkably short time, perhaps illustrating that you do not have to have a crisis to bring about major economic reforms, but it certainly helps.' (p. 141). (Cukierman (1992, pp 454–5) lists several other cases which support this conjecture.)

As part of these reforms of policy, the 'mechanics' of the public sector itself were reformed. Clear objectives were established for public sector organizations; clear accountability for the attainment of the objectives was assigned; performance-based contracts were given to the chief executives[4] of the organizations; and they were given much increased management and financial freedom within a framework of agreed policies and total budgets.

The Reserve Bank Act reforms readily fit into that framework; but before showing that, it should be pointed out that the conduct of monetary policy changed even before the Act. In 1984–85, monetary policy was directed explicitly at the objective of reducing inflation over the medium term. The operation of policy ceased to be through direct controls. In a period of nine months, interest rate controls, credit ceilings, exchange controls, and reserve requirements were removed, and the exchange rate floated. The government adopted a policy of 'full funding' – that is, ensuring that in the course of every financial year any deficit would be financed by the sale of debt, (by tender), in the market. There was no debt finance by money creation.

With all that done, why was any more necessary? Why was the Reserve Bank Act (1989) passed? There were actually two different kinds reasons; the 'economic' reasons, and the precedent of other public sector reforms.[5]

These are set out in order before describing the 'Contract' between bank and government.[6]

Monetary policy had been notably politicized and notably short term in New Zealand. There was concern that even though this had changed, the changes were dependent for remaining in place on political whim. This was thought undesirable. Interest rates would remain high in real terms (because of a risk premium),[7] and wage and price setters would not expect inflation to fall, and might expect, as had occurred in the past, accommodation of external shocks. These latter would raise unemployment unnecessarily as inflation fell and impart unnecessary volatility to employment in the future. The government was seeking ways of improving the credibility of its monetary commitment.

Almost simultaneously, some theoretical literature (noted above) was directing attention to the constitutional position of monetary policy decision makers. The literature led to the conclusion that inflation would be lowered by taking monetary policy out of the hands of politicians and was thus readily consistent with the course that was chosen for other parts of the public sector. Accordingly, a revision of the Reserve Bank Act was undertaken.[8]

After some detailed study of central banks which had been more successful than average in delivering low and steady inflation, the Act was drafted, passed with bipartisan support in December 1989, and became effective on 1 February 1990.

The Reserve Bank was given a clear statutory objective: 'The primary function of the Bank is to formulate and implement monetary policy directed to the economic objective of achieving and maintaining stability in the general level of prices' (Reserve Bank Act 1989, s8).[9]

That is the primary, not the only, function. But it is the only *macroeconomic* function. The Bank also has some regulatory and supervisory responsibilities. This single responsibility was assigned for a number of reasons. It was recognized that in the long run money influences only prices; that determined the objective. It was recognized that monetary policy, a single instrument, could have only a single objective. It was feared that having several objectives would lead to conflicts over what to do, and thus undermine credibility. Further, multiple objectives would require co-ordination with whoever else was trying to achieve these objectives, and could thus reinstate day-to-day government control of the central bank and, in addition, reduce the 'transparency' of monetary policy as failure to achieve one objective might be explained by reference to another.[10] (There was some discussion of a subsidiary macroeconomic objective – for example price stability subject to real growth being above a certain minimum. This was rejected on the grounds that it is no different from a multiple objective, and therefore flawed for the same reasons.)

The Act therefore assigns to the Bank authority to implement monetary policy consistent with its price stability objective. The Bank's discretion is limited, however; it is limited by its statutory objective (see above) and by the requirement under the 1989 Act for the Governor and the Minister of Finance to negotiate *and publish* a 'Policy Targets Agreement' (PTA).[11] The measure of the inflation rate used in the PTA is the consumer price index. This was chosen not because it was thought to be better in some sense than various other indices, but because it is the most widely known. The above zero range specified for inflation was chosen in the light of a '... judgement ... (that) 1 per cent inflation is consistent with stability in the general level of prices' (Archer, 1992). The factors leading to this judgement were index number problems, the survey method used, and the difficulties of adjusting for new goods and quality improvements to existing ones.

The PTA can be overridden by government. This can be done, however, only by an Order in Council, which must be tabled in Parliament, and which can last for a maximum of one year. This provision was underpinned, like the decision to introduce the Act, by both 'political' and 'economic' reasoning. The 'political' reasoning was that it ensured that monetary policy was ultimately a government responsibility, rather than that of unelected officials. The 'economic' was the belief that by allowing explicitly for an over ride, *long-run* credibility could be enhanced. This latter possibility existed because without such a provision, a bank–government conflict could lead to the Act itself being changed, perhaps after a Governor's resignation. (The precedent of Canada in 1967 was in mind here.)[12]

What of the exchange rate? Exchange rate and monetary policies are two sides of the same coin (a sometimes-made criticism of the Delors proposals for a European Central Bank – see Wood (1990)). New Zealand has a floating dollar – it was floated by the government which introduced the Act. There are provisions for the Bank to intervene in the foreign exchange market – but such intervention must be on the basis of a written and published directive. If there is a conflict between such a directive and the objective agreed in the PTA, the Governor is obliged to notify the Minister of Finance of this, and is not required to implement the directive unless the PTA is amended to ensure consistency.

Also in parallel with other public sector reforms, it was decided that once policy was delegated there should be clear mechanisms for monitoring performance. These mechanisms comprise the PTA; formal six-monthly monetary policy statements; the Bank's annual report; external performance audits which the Minister can commission at any time; and the Bank's board of directors. The Governor is personally accountable for policy, and may be dismissed if the target of the PTA is not achieved.

The board of the Bank has an explicit role in the monitoring process; it acts as the agent of the government in monitoring the performance of the Governor. It is *not* a policy making board – in contrast to, say, that of either the Bundesbank or the Federal Reserve Bank.

This was the result of a desire to have clear personal accountability for policy. The board can have between seven and ten members. It comprises the Governor as chairman, one (or two) deputy governors, and between four and seven non-executives. The non-executives have to be in a majority at board meetings, where decisions are by majority vote. There is no requirement to balance regional or sectional interests among non-executives. Members of Parliament are prohibited from being directors, and the Secretary of Treasury is no longer ex-officio a board member, as he was under previous legislation.

The PTA does not specify simply an inflation target: there are exemptions for certain events, which can cause shocks to the price level. These shocks comprise changes to the terms of trade (very important for a small open economy such as New Zealand) and changes in taxes which affect the price level. The rationale behind allowing exemptions is that as the price level is not perfectly flexible, a shock which changes *relative* prices can initially affect also the price level, and thus the measured rate of inflation over some time period. Because of price stickiness, an attempt to prevent this effect on inflation would (if the shock were positive) cause recession; and if it were negative lead to a boom which might well be hard to stop. The PTA aims to allow accommodation of the impact of the shock, but non-accommodation of any subsequent round effects.

The UK background was, although in some respects less dramatic, certainly very similar. Britain had experienced unsatisfactory inflation performance, and various changes to how monetary policy was conducted were implemented in an attempt to produce improvement.

(A vivid and detailed record can be found in Pepper (1997) a brief summary follows.) The first Thatcher government (of 1979) adopted money supply targets. These proved distinctly misleading, at least in part because of reforms carried out to the structure of the banking system. Various other experiments were then attempted, including several versions of exchange-rate targeting. Eventually (in 1990) Britain joined the ERM. The policy worked for some time. Inflation fell; but unemployment rose, and in 1992, just after German reunification, when a rate rise was appropriate for Germany it was clear that not only was it economically inappropriate for Britain, but also that the British government did not have the stomach for one, and sterling was evicted from the ERM.

There were desperate efforts to find a new anchor for monetary policy, not least for fear of how financial markets would react were one not found. Norman Lamont, then Chancellor of the Exchequer, allowed the Bank (by way of the 'Inflation Report') to comment publicly on inflation performance, and publicized the meetings between the Governor and the Chancellor. His successor, Kenneth Clark, while retaining final say over interest rates, published the record of these meetings. Gordon Brown took the next step, and adopted a model very close to the New Zealand one, with the Bank choosing interest rates to achieve a government-chosen target. All these changes were responses to problems. Lamont had the greatest problem; Clark was replacing a predecessor who had made way reluctantly; and Brown was Chancellor in the first Labour government for 18 years, and from a party whose reputation for economic policy was (in some respects unfairly) rather low.

The fact that these changes were responses to crises gave both central banks a breathing space – they were sure to be left alone to get on with things for a time.[13] The ECB will not have that initial advantage. Certain other contrasts between the ECB and these two central banks are drawn out below.

But a concern of perhaps greater importance, and also highlighted by these narratives, is what is the *direction of causality* between central bank structure and inflation performance?

There is a fairly clear cut relationship between low inflation and central bank independence. But which way does causality actually run? Does independence bring low inflation; or low inflation independence? Or is causality bi-directional? This question was raised by Cukierman (1992, pp. 448–9). He makes two points. The first is that inflation erodes independence. His evidence for this is two fold. Inflation increases the turnover rate of central bank governors. (One measure of independence may be their security of tenure.) Second, the rate of growth of central bank credit to the public sector rises with inflation. The latter would seem itself to raise questions over the direction of causation; has inflation eroded independence, or started through lack of it? But the former seems both plausible and straightforward.

Cukierman also argues, on the basis of interwar and post war German experience, that independence by itself can not reduce hyperinflation, but that once inflation is down it is a bulwark against it. Do the New Zealand and UK experiences strengthen or weaken these points, and does it in combination with them tell us anything about causality? In New Zealand the Governor was reconfirmed after a successful first contract period – suggesting that low inflation increases independence. Second, as discussed above the granting of independence was a *political* initiative to achieve the *consolidation* of low inflation. Independence did not bring low inflation. (It may serve in that consolidating purpose when fear of the harms of inflation has faded, as the Bundesbank has in Germany. For evidence on that we must wait.)

So far, the New Zealand example helps confirm that successful low inflation achievement reinforces if it does not bring independence; and that independence may sustain, but is not necessary to achieving, low inflation. It also, of course, shows that independence, low inflation, and better fiscal policy may be due to a third factor – past experience of monetary and fiscal irresponsibility.[14] In the UK the evidence is remarkably similar. Inflation had fallen even before Norman Lamont's changes; and it has fallen little since. Certainly it is hard, in view of the lags of policy, as yet to ascribe much effect on inflation to Gordon Brown's reforms.

There is a similar argument over whether low inflation brings independence, or whether the relationship is the other way round. An item of evidence in favour of the latter being important is that three attempts to change the Bundesbank's constitution, the latest being Helmut Schmidt's threat in 1978–79, all did not even get as far as being formally presented to the Bundestag.[15]

Still further complexity is introduced, along with the importance of a rule, by looking further back in history.

The Bank of England was privately owned until 1946, when it was the first nationalization by the then newly elected Labour government. It is not clear, however, how 'independent' it was before then. Throughout most of its history (the Bank was founded in 1694) it operated under a constraint imposed by the government. This constraint was the gold standard. Apart from suspension in times of war (the Napoleonic wars and the First World War) and the time it took to get back to the standard after the war had ended, the Bank was until 1931 obliged to conduct interest rate policy so as always to be able to exchange gold for notes at a fixed rate of exchange, and it had to do so whether notes were presented by a British resident or from abroad. That standard did not deliver a constant price level; prices rose and fell.

But what was different between then and the years after 1931 is that prices rose *and fell*; prices did not rise continually year after year. The main reason was that over a long period of years the supply of gold grew roughly in line with the economy, so that the money supply also did. It was not the independence that brought that result, but the rule that gold convertibility should be maintained. 'Independence' was not an issue.

An additional complexity in the independence–inflation link emerges when it is noted independence is certainly not *necessary* for low inflation. This is illustrated in the case of Sweden; the Riksbank over a long run of years performed about as well as the 'independents', while not really independent. A still further problem is raised by comparison of Belgium and Italy. Both countries' central banks had until recently somewhat ambiguous status; but Belgium had relatively low inflation and Italy relatively high (Capie, Mills and Wood, 1993).

This section, then, has somewhat complex implications. Independence is often a product of crisis, which brings anti-inflationary will. Some countries are low inflation regardless of the central bank's status. Some countries have widely different inflation performance despite similar central bank degrees of independence. And for at least one episode, and a substantial one, Britain from 1694 to 1931, what mattered may well have been not the central bank status but choice of an appropriate monetary rule. This may suggest that independence is not enough, or, an alternative way of looking at the same set of facts, that independence does not matter. It certainly does indicate that the ECB lacks the appropriate historical context to be confident of low inflation; it draws attention to the fact that it is based on a mixture of 'low-inflation' and 'high inflation' cultures; and that it is not constrained by a rule. What this means for the ECB's future structure is considered below.

Accountability and transparency

Accountability legitimizes a central bank's freedom to act independently of political control.[16] Transparency in economic policy making helps to enhance the credibility and effectivenes of policy. In terms of the 'time consistency' literature, one advantage of transparency is that it makes it more difficult to spring inflation surprises. In the literature, the preferred solution is to commit oneself to a monetary rule. But if one is not sure what the optimal rule is, transparency is an alternative. For if agents understand what actions are being taken and why, they can adjust their inflation expectations accordingly. This reduces the short-run output benefit from unexpected inflation, and so reduces the time inconsitency problem. King (1997) says that instead of 'unfettered discretion', transparent monetary policy arrangements mean that the authorities have to act with 'constrained discretion'.[17] Briault *et al.* (1996) argue that transparency can serve as a partial substitute for a good track record. 'Reputation amounts to revealing information by "deeds". Transparency, or de facto accountability, can be thought to do it by "words"'.

It is arguable how much of a substitute for reputation transparency can be, but it is nevertheless indubitably important for a new regime or a country with a relatively poor inflation history.[18]

Two further arguments for transparency are as follows. It allows well-informed debate and builds up a constituency for stability orientated policies and low inflation. Economic policy goals often take a long time to achieve, and so de-politicizing some aspects of policy making, such as interest rate decisions, can bring long-term benefits. And transparency reduces risk of policy being manipulated behind the scenes by powerful lobby groups. It may also make policy and the effects of policy more predictable. Clear signals about the basis of policy decisions help markets to function effectively and can help to reduce inflation expectations.

In the current British format, the Monetary Policy Committee (MPC) is accountable to the Court of the Bank. It is also accountable to the Chancellor of the Exchequer for its performance against its inflation remit. And it is accountable to Parliament, through scrutiny by the Treasury Committee and through debate of the Bank's annual report in the House of Commons. Finally, the MPC is accountable to the public at large through public reported discussion of what it considered and how each member voted. Having a clear and simple target, and the transparency of the policy process, both greatly facilitate this.

There are of course some complications. There may be instances when it will be appropriate to allow inflation to deviate from the target. It will be up to the MPC to ensure that when such deviations occur, the explanation of its policy is convincing. For example, suppose a commodity price shock causes on upward jump in measured inflation. The MPC might decide that this is a shock to the price level which will have only a short-lived effect on inflation as measured by the retail price index (RPI). If they can persuade the markets and the public that this is what will happen then inflation expectations should be unchanged. If there are doubts, then inflation expectations would rise and the MPC would need to consider tightening monetary policy. Openness would facilitate the conduct of policy.

The process of decision making in the UK is very open – 'transparent', in the term often used in New Zealand debates. The minutes of the MPC meeting are published a week after the next meeting, along with a note of the votes of individual MPC members. The minutes also include a summary of the information presented to the MPC by the Bank's staff.

All decisions, including no change, are announced at a fixed time soon after the MPC meetings finish, the dates of MPC meetings are announced well in advance, and the *Inflation Report* gives the Bank's forecasts for inflation and output along with key underlying assumptions (e.g. about exchange rates).

Given that interest rate decisions are determined by a committee, rather than a single individual, publication of the voting is important. The fact that individuals' votes are published means that individuals can be held to account. The voting record can provide the basis for assessing individuals' track records when the Chancellor has to decide on reappointments.[19] Where there are different opinions the minutes set out the different arguments. This helps to demonstrate that the committee's deliberations cover a wide range of views, important in persuading various groups that they are being taken account of, and thus in building support for the policy.

The parlimentary process gives the MPC further opportunity to set out the thinking underlying decisions. Perhaps more important, it is a chance for Parliament to scrutinize the MPC's actions. This scrutiny is important in monitoring procedures, requesting further information and in giving monetary policy democratic legitimacy.

The Treasury Committee plans to have at least two sessions a year dedicated to monetary policy, following two of the four *Inflation Report*s. The Treasury Committee is expected to take evidence on the Bank's annual report and the House of Commons will debate this within a month of the Treasury Committee taking evidence.

The Treasury Committee can also call on the Chancellor and the Governor to appear around the time of the Budget to comment on the inflation target. The Committee has said that in the absence of statutory provisions for confirmatory hearings it will instigate its own hearings and make reports to Parliament.

The Governor must send an 'open letter' to the Chancellor if inflation is more than one percentage point above or below the inflation target. This will inform the public as to why the divergence has occurred, the policy action being taken to deal with it, the period within which inflation is expected to return to the target, and how this approach meets the government's monetary policy objectives.

The Treasury Committee can reinforce this mechanism by taking evidence from the Governor when an open letter is sent. The open letter system provides an additional level of accountability and transparency when there are 'large' deviations of inflation from the target. Smaller deviations will still have to be accounted for through the other mechanisms (e.g. minutes, *Inflation Reports*, parliamentary scrutiny). The open letter system gives the MPC the opportunity to explain in full, and in a very public way, why the overshoot or undershoot has occurred and what it intends to do about it. (King (1997) notes: '... one of the main purposes of the open letter is to explain why, in some circumstances, it would be wrong to try to bring inflation back to target too quickly'.)

The framework makes clear that when the MPC allows a deviation of inflation from the target, they must act to ensure that the long-term commitment to price stability is maintained. An open letter does not automatically imply censure. As noted above, there may from time to time be good reasons for missing the target.[20]

The transparency of the process also makes the 'fear of failure' sanction very powerful. Lord Kingsdown (a former Governor of the Bank of England) observed in 1997.

> 'I believe the transparency of the process will be its own sanction. I can say from experience that there are few more powerful sanctions than the prospect of an uncomfortable hearing in front of the (Treasury) Committee.

The government determines three parts of the framework. It sets the inflation target, decides on whether to enforce the override mechanism, and appoints the members of the MPC. Opinions differ on whether the government or central bank should set the monetary policy target. The Roll Committee (1993) argued '... we believe that UK monetary policy needs greater independence than can be achieved through any system in which ministers have operational responsibility for framing targets'.

But Bean (1997) maintained:

> The latter (goal independence) may make sense in countries where the people's trust of the government is weak (such as Germany after the war, when the statutes of the Bundesbank were drawn up), but is less suitable for countries like the UK with more established and trusted democratic structures. In this case the model of instrument

> independence is more suitable, as by giving the central bank a clear remit against which it can be held accountable, democratic legitimacy can be maintained.

The Treasury and Civil Service Committee's report (1993) also favoured the instrument independence model. In his Mais Lecture (1997), the Governor of the Bank noted that even where the government sets the target the degree of latitude in that choice would be limited 'by the need to maintain the credibility of the commitment to price stability'. He also argued (again in the Mais Lecture) that having the government set the target 'may provide reassurance, and help to secure greater acceptance of the policy'.

The ECB was established 1 July 1998. Some aspects of how it will operate are set out in the Maastricht Treaty. For instance, the monetary policy target will be set by the central bank and heads of government of member states appoint the Governor. However, it is still unclear how transparent the decision-making process will be. For instance, although the ECB is obliged to publish reports it is not stated what should be included. This means that the practice of the ECB early on is likely to set important precedents.

Comparisons

With regard to accountability and transparency, what views have been expressed are, certainly from a perspective broadly approving of the New Zealand Reserve Bank Act and its close relative, the 1998 Bank of England Act, distinctly alarming.

It is perhaps understandable that Wim Duisenberg, about to be the first President of the ECB, was not particularly comfortable with the prospect of outside influence on the ECB after he was told at the 1 May Brussels summit that he had volunteered for early retirement in view of his age and infirmity in four years time. Nevertheless, with allowance for this, his views on accountability and transparency still appear far from the above-noted examples. They were set out in his evidence before the European Parliament on Thursday 7 May 1998.

The crucial points are as follows. The ECB will have both an inflation and a monetary target. He admitted this would make policy more complicated to explain. It could be argued it will make it opaque. Mr Duisenberg is willing to appear before the (powerless) European Parliament, but not before the (still powerful) national parliaments. It is, he said, the task of national central banks (in practice without jobs to do after the ECB is formed) to appear before national parliaments. He also said the ECB should publish records of its discussion after 16 years. This was because individual MPC votes in the UK had been exposed, and this made it difficult for members to change their vote without loss of face. It is worth considering these contrasts with the New Zealand and UK frameworks in a little detail, as they have interesting implications.

The ECB may inherit some credibility. To quote Dr Hans Tietmeyer (1998):

> Credibility normally develops, gradually, on account of one's own track record. To that extent, it seems to be a privilege to be able to inherit credibility from the national central banks. In this context, the Bundesbank, as the guardian of the DM (the long-standing anchor currency of the EMS) naturally plays an important part.

That quotation raises the question of whether credibility can be inherited: replacing one central bank with another is a bigger change than, for example, replacing one Chairman of the Board of Governors of the Federal Reserve System with another but preserving the same institutional framework. But suppose credibility can be passed on through at least one generation of central banks. How much credibility is there to pass on? The DM was indeed the anchor of the system. The Bundesbank is the only central bank which has credibility in *running* an anti-inflationary policy, as opposed to having the political will to import one through a pegged exchange rate.

This may suggest that inherited credibility will need to be boosted – in which case transparency, usually urged as a substitute for credibility, is singularly absent. Lacking, too, is the political legitimacy which comes from the government setting the inflation target.[21] This lack may be important because there has been no 'crisis' to give the new central bank a period of unquestioning acceptance. Another, and related, problem arises over which price index the ECB will aim to control. In both New Zealand and the UK, it was considered important that the index be widely understood and accepted. There is no such Europe-wide-index.

Publishing votes (or in the New Zealand context, there being only one vote) is a way of ensuring accountability. If no votes are published, this diminishes accountability, as, too, does reporting only to the European Parliament. But from another perspective these two weaknesses become strengths. For it can be argued that they prevent the members of the governing body, who inevitably come from different nations, being seen as representatives of those nation's individual interests. Without such protection, discontent might develop if one country found it was being overruled, and having monetary policy tightened (for example) despite the vote of its 'representative' or perhaps inappropriately for its own circumstances. This fear might diminish as there were repeated rounds of voting, and it was seen that the problem affected all countries at different times; but in view of the length of the business cycle, this process could take many years.

That there is a 'regional balance' of board members conflicts with both the New Zealand and UK models. The lack of such balance is a deliberate feature of the New Zealand Bank, as the designers of the Act were aware that the great geographical diversity of New Zealand might otherwise give rise to 'regional' pressures. For similar reasons the proposal that there be a 'Scottish representative' on the MPC was rejected by the government during the debate on the Bank of England Bill. Their argument was the entirely correct one that monetary policy has to be made for the entire monetary area, and that so far as monetary policy goes regions matter only so far as they affect the whole monetary area's inflation rate. It may turn out that chosing the ECB's council from national central banks, although a most natural way of finding experts in the conduct of monetary policy, has the consquence of producing great political tensions in the EMU area.

All these comments, of course, stem from viewing the objective of the ECB as the production of a stable currency; that is the point of comparing it with other central bank structures which seem to deliver that goal. But if one views it differently, as an institution whose primary purpose is the political one of rapidly turning Europe into a single country, then its lack of accountability to national governments and lack of transparency in its procedures may be viewed rather differently.

Conclusions

The main conclusion of this paper is that the present structure of the ECB is not well supported. Most central banks granted independence in recent years were freed because of past unsatisfactory monetary performance – of a crisis, in the cases of New Zealand and the UK. Such a crisis gives the new institution some measure of popular support, and time to build up its reputation. No such crisis occurred in the Euro area. It has been argued that accountability and transparency are important adjuncts of independence. They help give the institution political legitimacy. The ECB has no clear channels through which it is accountable, and while it has yet to develop any procedures of its own, most of its constituents come from environments where transparency is absent. Nor does it have any clear, albeit perhaps incomplete rule – such as the gold standard – to guide its conduct and constrain its critics. Further, as recent disputes over who will head the Bank show, it is not an institution over which politicians have sworn an ordnance of non-influence. And unlike the Reserve Bank of New Zealand, the ECB is not embedded in a set of institutions with similar constitutions and which can by their existence provide some protection against challenge. In the New Zealand context it would now seen bizarre to change the constitution of the central bank without changing the entire framework of government. What is crucial so far as producing a stable Euro is concerned is how the ECB evolves. There appear to be three possibilities. Given a lot of luck, a period of economic prosperity and tranquillity might enable it to build up reputation – to become a new Bundesbank. It might rapidly become politicized. Or it might rapidly develop transparency and propose a framework for accountability. This last is probably the most desirable, but how feasible is it? To which body would the ECB be accountable? That is a question which the ECB can not solve, but thinking about it tends to reinforce the view, which is usually based simply on the history of monetary unions (Chada and Hudson, forthcoming) that no monetary union has survived without becoming a nation state. That of course takes us back to whether it may perhaps be better to view the ECB not as an institution designed to produce price stability, but one intended to further the building of Europe into a nation.

But, starting from an economic viewpoint, the idea that because the ECB is independent we will have low inflation and all will be well is a mistake. It results from ignoring the historical context in which currently established and successful central banks were set up. Those who ignore history are not necessarily condemed to repeat it; but they will certainly make serious and avoidable mistakes.

Notes

1. I am indebted for comments on this paper to Andrew Haldane, Michael Lyon, and the participants in the conference in honour of Stephen Frowen at which this paper was presented.
2. A detailed and lively account of these is contained in Prebble (1993).
3. See Douglas and Carrol (1987) for a vivid account of the political background to the changes, written by a leading participant in them.
4. Note that they became chief executives, instead of 'permanent secretaries', the former term, and that term is still in use in the UK.
5. Dalziel (1993) ascribes this and previous changes to the Act exclusively to changes in the climate of economic opinion. He does not explain why New Zealand was peculiarly sensitive to these changes, nor does he consider why

economic opinion was so influential over monetary policy while completely ignored over trade policy. (The latter is examined in Wooding (1993)).

6. Strictly speaking, between Governor (representing the former) and Minister of Finance (representing the latter).
7. There was particular concern over interest rates because New Zealand had a large external debt.
8. So far as I can discover, no reference was made in the course of the reforms to Friedman's (1962) paper, in which he discussed various concepts of central bank independence and set out explicitly what has become the 'New Zealand Model' – one where the central bank has a clear mandate to carry out, free of parliamentary interference, an explicit instruction of parliament.
9. Support for the single objective of price stability was widespread among the public. One difference is, however, worth noting: farmers supported it while manufacturers did not. Does this reflect the fact that in the case of the farmers's products any increase in the NZ$ price above the world price can not be passed on without a collapse of sales?
10. 'Transparency' is a term which has become very important in New Zealand's policy making. Policies should be 'transparent' in the sense that both the objective and the methods should be clear. This is intended to help enforce accountability, and to make as clear as possible signals which may encourage the desired private sector response. This transparency, in conjunction with the inflation objective, would seem to rule out the use of information 'private' to the central bank so as to conduct a covert stabilization policy by producing inflationary surprises. There can in this framework be no private information about a change in the objectives of policy. In principle there could be private information about shocks – to the natural rate of unemployment, or to the money demand function, for example. But given that stabilization of anything other than the price level is ruled out, it is hard to see why such information should be kept private, and hard to see why it should matter if it were. For a review of models which discuss the exploitation by the policy maker of private information, see Cukierman (1992) ch. 8, and the references therein. As will emerge below, transparency has also been important in the UK.
11. The agreement is published by the Minister in the *New Zealand Gazette* and presented to the House of Representatives.
12. Note that it is government and not Parliament which negotiates the PTA and which can use the override. This is parallel with the constitutional division of responsibilities in other areas. The governing party has in New Zealand always had a majority in Parliament. This may change, however, as New Zealand is moving towards a proportional representation system. The workings of the Act under coalition governments might well be an interesting area of study. Although the Act allows explicit political overrides, it can not prevent covert attempts to exert pressure. So far such attempt have not been a problem.
13. The same is certainly true also of the founding of the Bundesbank. The currency it managed, the DM, replaced a currency so eroded in value that Germany had almost reverted to Barter, with cigarettes often serving as currency.
14. Posen (1993) argues that low inflation is associated with central bank independence as a result of yet another factor. His explanation is that low inflation is produced when there is a powerful coalition of interests wishing

low inflation, and capable of preserving the central bank's independence. Countries where financial sectors are most opposed to inflation are, he maintains, also those most eager for their central bank to be independent. Universal systems with their greater reliance on lending than on securities trading, are more likely to be aware of the costs of inflation, and more likely to want low inflation. Hence the low inflation records of Germany and Switzerland. New Zealand would appear to be a counter example; but its past experience may weaken this claim.

15. I am indebted to Professor Norbert Kloten for discussion of these episodes.
16. Mr Christoph Lindemann of the Bundesbank has pointed out to me that the German word into which accountability is translated, 'Rechenpflicht' and which is translated into English as accountability, actually has an implication not necessarily present in the English word. A full English translation of it would convey that if called to account and found wanting one could be dismissed. This raises the question of what accountable actually means. In the New Zealand case it is made explicit in the Reserve Bank Act that the Governor of the Bank can be dismissed for unsatisfactory performance. But 'accountability' by itself leaves the sanctions undefined.
17. Like the judiciary, to use Milton Friedman's analogy (1962).
18. Bean (1998) and Blinder (1997) question the relevance of the time inconsistency problem when the operational reponsibility for monetary policy is delegated to the central bank. Their point is that it is hard to undertand why the central bank would want to produce an inflation surprise.
19. The US FOMC minutes are published without a record of how each member voted. But they do give an even more detailed account of the Fed's thinking than do the MPC minutes' and further, there was no need in the case of the Fed to find a quick substitute for reputation in the form of transparency.
20. A point to note about the thresholds is that they are symmetrical. While low inflation is better than high inflation, achieving low inflation by excessive deflation and a period of slow growth would be undersirable. As deviations from the target are treated symmetrically the MPC does not have an incentive to set interest rates too high in order to keep inflation below the target.
21. Of course, the ECB may have been allowed to set it (following Bean's argument) because the European government which drew up its statutes know that their citizens do not trust them.

Bibliography

Alesina, A. 'Macroeconomics and Politics', in *NBER Macroeconomic Annual 1988* (Cambridge, MA: MIT Press, 1988).

Alesina, A. 'Politics and Business Cycles in Industrial Democracies', *Economic Policy* (April 1989) 55–98.

Archer, D. J. *Organising a Central Bank to Control Inflation: the Case of New Zealand* (unpublished manuscript, 1992).

Bade, R. and Parkin, M. *Central Bank Laws and Monetary Policy* (University of Western Ontario, Department of Economics discussion paper, 1987).

Barro, R. J. 'Inflation and Economic Growth', *Bank of England Quarterly Bulletin* (May 1995).

Bean, C. The New UK Monteray Arrangements: A View from the Literature (HM Treasury Academic Panel 1998).

Bean, C. Memorandum submitted to the Treasury Committee. Treasury Committees Report (Oct. 1997), Appendix 12.

Blinder, A. 'What Central Bankers can Learn from Academia and Vice-Versa?', *Journal of Economic Perspectives* (Spring 1997) 3–19.

Briault, C., Haldane, A. and King, M. 'Central Bank Accountability and Independence: Theory and Evidence', *Bank of England Quarterly Bulletin* (1996). Vol. 36, 63–8.

Cagan, P. *Persistent Inflation: Historical and Policy Essays* (New York: Columbia University Press, 1979).

Capie, F. H., Mills, T. C. and Wood, G. E. 'Central Bank Independence: An Exploratory Analysis of Historical Data', in P. Siklos (ed.) *Varieties of Monetary Reform* (Kluwer, 1993).

Capie, F. H. and Wood, G. E. 'The Structure and Stability of Banking in Europe: Some Lessons from History', in N. Thygessen (ed.), *Financial Institutions in Europe under New Competitive Conditions* (Kluwer-Nijhoff, 1991).

Chada, J. and Hudson, S. *Historial Experience with Monetary Unions* (forthcoming).

Cukierman, A. *Central Bank Strategy, Credibility and Independence: Theory and Evidence* (Cambridge, MA, and London: MIT Press, 1992).

Dalziel, P. 'The Reserve Bank Act: Reflecting Changing Relationships between State and Economy in the Twentieth Century', In B. Roper and C. Rudd (eds), *State and Economy in New Zealand* Auckland: (OUP Press, 1993).

Douglas, R. and Carrol L. *Toward Prosperity* Auckland: (David Bateman, 1987).

Friedman, M. 'Should There be an Independent Monetary Authority?', in L. B. Yeager (ed.) *In Search of a Monetary Constitution* (Boston: Harvard University Press 1962; reprinted in M. Friedman *Dollars and Deficits*. Englewood Cliffs, NJ: Prentice-Hall, 1968).

Governor of the Bank of England, Mais Lecture – City University Business School. Reproduced in *Bank of England Quarterly Bulletin* (Aug. 1997).

King, M. The Inflation Target Five Years On. *Bank of England Quarterly Bulletin* (Nov. 1997).

Kingsdown, Lord. Memorandum Submitted to the Treasury Committee by Lord Kingsdown. *Treasury Committee Report* (Oct. 1997), Appendix 8.

Knight, R. L. 'Central Bank Independence in New Zealand', in Downes, L. and Vaez-Zadeh, R. *The Evolving Role of Central Banks* (Washington: IMF, 1991).

Masciandero, D. and Tabellini, G. 'Monetary Regimes and Fiscal Deficits: A Comparative Analysis', In A. F. Cheng, (ed), *Monetary Policy in the Pacific Basin Countries* (Dordrecht: Kluwer Academic, 1988).

OECD. *Economic Survey: New Zealand* (Paris: OECD, 1993).

Pepper, G. *Inside Thatcher's Monetarist Revolution* (London: Macmillan, 1997).

Posen, A. 'Why Central Bank independence does not cause low inflation: there is no institutional fix for politicians', in *Finance and the International Economy. Prize winning essays from the Amex Bank Review Essay Competition* (Oxford: Oxford University Press, 1993).

Prebble, M. *Economic Reform in New Zealand.* (London: Institute of Directors, 1998).

Roll Committee. *Independent and Accountable: A New Mandate for the Bank of England* (London: CEPR, 1993).

Smith, R. and Grimes, A. 'Sources of Economic Growth', *Reserve Bank of New Zealand Bulletin*, 53, 2 (1990).
Tietmeyer, H. *Financial and Monetary Integration: Benefits, Opportunities and Pitfalls* (Mais Lecture, City University Business School, London, 1998).
Treasury and Civil Service Committee. *The Role of the Bank of England* (1993).
Wood, G. E. 'One Money for Europe?', *Journal of Monetary Economics*, 25 (1990), 1–10.
Wooding, P. 'New Zealand in the International Economy', in Roper and Rudd (eds), *State and Economy in New Zealand* (Oxford: Oxford University Press, 1993).

Comment

Anke Jacobsen

One of the central questions in the discussion concerning the foundation of the European Central Bank refers to the ECB's possibility to achieve a low inflation performance – even in the first years of the beginning of European Monetary Union. Geoffrey E. Wood analyses institutional factors which could help to achieve credibility for a central bank and by that, to facilitate carrying out price stability.

In the first step of Wood's analysis, he describes several meanings of independence and discusses the relationship between central bank independence and inflation with a special focus on the direction of causality. Going back to 1962, Wood finds several concepts of independence in the theoretical discussion. Taking these concepts, he tries to find out the direction of causality between central bank independence and low inflation performance by analysing special cases of changing central banks' statutes in the past. The author takes examples of the central banks of New Zealand and the UK and tries to show that the introduction of a new institution like an independent central bank, '... is often a product of crisis, which brings anti-inflationary will' (p. xx). Wood concludes that these two cases of the central banks show that low inflation is not necessarily linked with independence. In my view, the appearance of a crisis in advance of the establishment of an independent central bank can not be interpreted as a presumption for a successful monetary policy of price stability, but just as a stylized fact in these country cases. Moreover, one can find the real advantage of an independent central bank in the separation of monetary policy from the control of national governments' decisions with short-term horizon. Carrying out an anti-inflationary will is not a problem of monetary policy, but could be one of fiscal policy referring to national indebtedness. Being confronted today with near perfectly mobile international capital, central banks are forced to achieve price stability in order to sustain international competition.

Following Wood's argument, institutional independence of a central bank is not a crucial point in carrying out a monetary policy of price stability. He proposes that a new regime that chooses its monetary policy goal independently and that can not look back to an inflation history, should substitute the lack of reputation by transparency and accountability in its monetary policy strategy. The British Labour government in May 1997 chose this strategy instead of establishing a formal goal independence. This transparency and accountability should be generated by offering a so-called open letter.

These letters could help to reduce inflation expectations and therefore, would thus facilitate the conduct of policy. Seeing the experiences of New Zealand and the UK, young monetary regimes should have a democratic legitimacy basis in order to strengthen their credibility. This could be achieved by involving Parliament in the process of decisionmaking of the central bank. He argues that if Parliament takes the decision concerning the inflation goal, the young central bank will achieve further transparency in its monetary policy because of this kind of supervision. But supervision by Parliament will just be necessary, if we assume that it is Parliament that has the stronger anti-inflationary will compared to the attitude of the central bank.

However, Wood cites a paper of Bean (1997) in which it is said that, '... in countries where the people's trust of the government is weak (such as Germany after the war, when the statutes of the Bundesbank were drawn up) ...' (p. xx) – goal independence makes sense. From this example, one can draw a comparison to the European Union where the people's trust of the European Commission, of the European Parliament and of the national European governments is strongly limited. In this case, it could make sense to grant a European Central Bank independence rather than introducing an open letter policy that tries to substitute for goal independence. In the case of the UK with its democratic tradition, this strategy of offering open letters is perhaps preferable, but looking at the European Union it should be decided for a perfectly independently acting European Central Bank. Achieving credibility is not just a strategy of tying one's hands, but also includes the opportunity to react flexibly. An open letter system with a limited independence would restrict such possibilities in a drastic way and by that, would cut further steps in reaching credibility in a prospective EMU. A formal independence of the central bank signals policy change from a regime of full employment guarantee to a regime of price stability. Independence is crucial for achieving credibility for the ECB. Especially, national fiscal policies in the EMU could undermine monetary policy if the 'no bailing-out' clause is not credible. So, the important question is not, if the European Central Bank is too independent, but if there are political decisions outside the ECB that could impede the monetary policy strategy of price stability.

6
The Euro: Implications for Germany and Europe

Norbert Kloten

Despite my understanding concerning the reluctant attitude of the UK towards joining the euro, I have myself come to the firm conclusion that only a United Europe will be able to achieve fully Europe's economic and cultural aims, and that for its realization the European Economic and Monetary Union with its single currency will be an effective catalyst. (Frowen, 2000, p. 119, translated from the German).

A backward look on Germany

Prevailing opinions

Since the establishment of the European Coal and Steel Community in 1951, Germany has been split into two rival camps. The one regarded European integration by way of the creation of common European institutions as an historical option that was in accordance with European realities and prospects. The other camp rejected the idea of establishing communities with specific organizational patterns. It advocated an economic integration of Europe propelled by market forces. Ludwig Erhard, a man with wider ideas, favoured a free trade area – of course an all-embracing one, not the realized small one.

Over several decades German economists had nurtured a detached attitude towards the European Economic Community (EEC) and the European Monetary System (EMS). European Monetary Union (EMU) was regarded as justified only if previously established converging processes led towards an optimal currency area (the so-called 'coronation theory'). They considered that adequate built-in prerequisites of a stable money policy, guaranteed by a firm statute of the European System of Central Banks (ESCB), should be supported by binding regulations of a stability pact limiting the scope of fiscal policy, which were still to remain under national regimes, and the new stage of economic integration should be matched by political integration.

Reservations against both economic and political integration and doubts about the sincerity and ability of European authorities to implement these schemes caused the Academic Council to the German Federal Ministry of Economics – which is, by the way, the prototype of the external advisory bodies in Germany, founded as early as January 1948 – to be split in antagonistic factions and in 1997 proved itself unable to draft an urgently needed report about the pros and cons of German entry into the final stage of European Economic and Monetary Union (EEMU). In February 1998, 155 German-speaking economics professors, including Stephen Frowen, published a last-minute open letter in the *Frankfurter Allgemeine Zeitung* and in the *Financial Times*, advocating a postponement of German entry. The time was regarded as not yet being ripe to justify European Monetary Union. They contended that the still obvious lack of convergence and the not yet truly existing 'stability culture' in Europe would most probably lead to a disaster. In January 1998, two university professors (an economist and a lawyer) applied, together with a former president of a Land central bank (branch of the Deutsche Bundesbank) and a former high ranking official of the federal ministry of economics and subsequently president of a Landesbank (top level bank of the German saving banks organization) before the Federal Constitutional Court (Bundesverfassungsgericht – BVG) for an injunction to stop the start of EMU (Hankel *et al.*, 1998). The plaintiffs argued that the proposed single European currency would not be compatible with people's basic rights (*Grundrecht*) in respect of the established stable currency – the Deutsche Mark. Euro currency – as it was argued – could not become a stable currency since the necessary requirements for it were not safeguarded. The plaintiffs referred to a decision of the Federal Constitutional Court in October 1993 (BVG, 1993), in which the court justified EMU as a common European goal. But the court limited the federal government's competence to take a final decision without prior approval by the German legislative bodies, that is the Bundestag and the Bundesrat. Both institutions were obliged to respect the mandatory prerequisites of economic and monetary stability. In its decision, the court rejected the request of a wide section of the German population for a referendum on the issue of joining a European Monetary Union. Again it was confirmed that political decision-making in Germany is a privilege of the constitutional bodies (based on the principle of indirect representation introduced in the Basic Law

(*Grundgesetz*) of 1949 as a result of the disastrous experiences during the Weimar Republic.

The official Germany, the Federal Government, the governments of the Bundesländer and the vast majority of the members of the Bundestag, the commercial federations and the labour unions had already approved in principle the entry into the third stage of EMU, but they as well as the general public were waiting for a report from the Deutsche Bundesbank, requested by the Federal Government, and not least for the decision of the Federal Constitutional Court. Most German citizens at that time still opposed the introduction of the Euro, being concerned about the loss of their highly esteemed Deutsche Mark.

Steps towards participation in EMU

The Deutsche Bundesbank presented its 'Report on Convergence' on 27 March 1998, two days after the official delivery of the 'Report on Convergence in Europe' by the European Monetary Institute (EMI) in Frankfurt. After debating the text of the Bundesbank Report for approximately fourteen hours, the Central Bank Council as the decision-making body of the Deutsche Bundesbank, appreciating the success of *monetary* convergence achieved, declared that a participation of Germany in EMU would be 'justifiable from the stability policy point of view'. This positive vote was overshadowed, however, by a harsh critical judgement about fiscal convergence in Europe. In plain words the Council stated that Belgium and Italy still have to accept 'substantial obligations' in their fiscal policy 'to meet serious concerns' in respect of their debt ratio and budgetary deficits. Other countries, such as Germany, France, the Netherlands, Austria, Portugal, Sweden and Spain should feel obliged, according to the Stability and Growth Pact (30 April 1998) to realize the necessity for additional measures concerning budgetary consolidation, a decline of the quota of public expenditures (related to their GDP) and reforms of their social security schemes. The Central Bank Council expressed firmly its belief that 'the selection of participants' depends on a 'political decision'. Clear words, but no definite conclusion. The public was disappointed – not with the analysis but with the vote.

The Federal Government felt entitled on the same day (27 March) to declare its willingness to participate in EMU and to vote on 2 May in favour of Germany's entry into the third stage of EMU on 1 January 1999, with altogether eleven member states as proposed by the European Commission. The decision got its blessing indirectly from the Federal Constitutional Court which on 2 April rejected the petition of the four plaintiffs. It simply declared the petition as 'clearly unfounded'

(BVG, 1998). The responsibility for German entry into membership of EMU would rest with the Federal Government and both the Bundestag and Bundesrat – not with jurisdiction. The Maastricht Treaty had given them the competence to decide on entry and terms. Immediately after the court's decision, the Bundestag approved a law on the introduction of the Euro, substituting the Deutsche Mark. On 23–24 April, the Bundestag and Bundesrat authorized the Federal Government with an overwelming majority (Bundestag: 575 in favour with 35 against and 5 abstentions; Bundesrat: unanimously in favour, with one abstention) to vote in Brussels as intended. The evident second thoughts on EMU membership in the report of the Deutsche Bundesbank were not taken into consideration, and neither were the former assurances of the Federal Government and Bundestag to stick to the convergence criteria of the Maastricht Treaty 'without any cuts'.

The Euro ahead: an accepted fact

The final decision about the realization of EMU on 2 May in Brussels made in accordance with a recommendation of Ecofin took its course as expected. The Bundestag – apart from a small group of opponents – celebrated the historical date. What provoked emotions was solely the quarrel within the European Council concerning the candidates for the first presidency of the European Central Bank (ECB). Doubtless, Wim Duisenberg was the best choice. Critical reproaches carping at the role of Chancellor Kohl in this debate were unfounded. Generally, the opponents of EMU had lost the battle. Since then they have been virtually eliminated from the political stage. Immediately after the Brussels breakthrough, there were still 65 to 70 per cent of the German population who preferred retention of the Deutsche Mark but about 55 per cent were aware that an intensified European integration would not be possible without a common currency. Since then the Euro has been more widely accepted by the German public – if even for the most part still with some uneasiness (Issing, 1999), not least stimulated by the long-lasting decline of the Euro's external value until the latter part of 2000.

Implications of the Euro

What implications?

In the final stage of the pro-Euro crusade, the advocates argued primarily on the basis of lower transaction costs. In so-called Euro-acceptance campaigns, naive calculations were presented, being largely based on the *ceteris-paribus* clause reminding us of those in the ill-fated

Cecchini Report. The really hard-hitting and far-reaching implications to be expected from the implementation of European Economic and Monetary Union were put in the background. They were at least not defined properly. But they have to be borne in mind. They are – seen from today's perspective – the basic elements of any evaluation of moving to the third stage of EMU, and they, as well as the impact of EMU experience, will constitute the basis for a final judgement of this historical experiment. The implications are

- that an integrated Europe will become a community totally together economically as well as politically and far beyond the already existing binding forces in the Europe of today;
- that EMU provides the participating European countries with a single currency controlled by an independent central bank, thereby fundamentally changing the pattern of monetary data and the spectre of European economic policy;
- that competition in goods and financial markets will be intensified, and together with ongoing globalization, there will be adjustment processes of all kinds in not yet experienced dimensions;
- there will be increased competition between institutional systems, at a national and a European level;
- that EMU will enlarge the problems to be solved before the EU can be extended, possibly changing intended patterns of integration;
- that with the Euro, much of Europe will be changed at an international level and foremost in this connection will be the role Europe has to play in settling monetary and financial changes.

Europe: a community of fate?

The Bundesbank's Central Bank Council was asked in February 1992 by the German Federal Government to evaluate the Maastricht Treaty and in response emphasized that EMU would lead beyond the given contractual constraints to an indissoluble community of countries forced into solidarity in good and bad times ('Solidargemeinschaft auf Verdeih und Verderb'). This would demand a political integration equivalent in dimension to the economic integration marked by EMU and should be realized before entry into the third stage. I personally – at that time still a member of the Central Bank Council – did not entirely share that view. European integration has to be regarded as a process characterized by almost dialectically interconnected political and economic steps towards a unified Europe. This is true of the realities of European integration policy from the early 1950s with the establishment of the Coal and Steel Community and the Treaty of Rome (1957) right through to the Single European Act (1987) and the Treaty of Maastricht (1992). In that Treaty, the already scheduled 'Succession Conference' about additional conventions for the sake of political integration fell short of what was hoped for with the Treaty of Amsterdam in October 1997 ('Maastricht II'). The steps towards economic integration had been well prepared since the Delors Report (1987) by a profound debate at all levels and in academic circles. The political procurements of integration lacked a solid intellectual preparation. They took shape in a process known as 'European compromising'. They are simply the fallout of a vague process of reasoning and negotiating. Amsterdam and also the Berlin meeting of the European Council (1999) with its again comparatively poor achievements, made this perfectly clear.

But today's state of affairs regarding political integration must not contribute to any possible failures of EMU. The statute of EMU puts the European monetary authorities, independent of political directives as they are, in a strong position. The policy of the ECB will be burdened considerably by any deficiencies in economic convergence and might even be endangered by an inability to co-ordinate the different spheres of economic policies, that could lead to undue political pressure on the ECB. But in principle EMU has to be regarded as an effective lever to push forward political integration, thus becoming a dynamizing force of European unification. The Euro is the first element of a common factor in European daily life and one with which Europeans can identify. European monetary policy concerns everybody and will be observed by everybody and by all media on a day-to-day basis. And the data set by the ECB will influence the room for manoeuvre for other economic policies. Seen in this way, the realization of EMU has indeed to be evaluated as a fundamental decision, pushing forward economic and political integration and as a constituent element of both (Academic Advisory Council, 1994). It ultimately implies a union of fate.

Single monetary policy prepared properly?

As a result of EMU, monetary policy will be Europeanized. Cushioning anti-shock mechanisms such as exchange-rate adjustments will no longer exist (Ehrmann, 1998). Divergent monetary data for member states and regions set by ECB and national central banks are not compatible with the rationale of EMU. In other words, they are ruled out. Under the auspices of an efficient monetary policy, unified monetary data generate real converging processes to an extent that reflects the given divergencies in countries concerned. To take reasonable precautions against this undisputed nexus of a unified monetary policy, the Maastricht Treaty established the European Monetary Institute (EMI), situated in Frankfurt. From 1994 onward, EMI had to co-ordinate monetary policy activities of the still 'independent' national central banks and to prepare technically, organizationally and conceptually the entry into the third stage of EMU.

Convergence criteria were thought to inform about the spread between the given and the desired degree of convergence in monetary and fiscal affairs as well as with regard to interest rates and exchange rates. Furthermore, the convergence criteria defined the threshold for joining EMU. In principle, this implies that the entry date should have been determined by the convergence data. But this date had already been fixed twice in the Maastricht Treaty. The dates (1 January 1997 and alternatively 1 January 1999) testify the inclination of politicians to underrate time requirements of economic adjustment processes as well as the probable negative consequences of the fixing of incorrect deadlines. The first date was a non-starter from the very beginning, the second forced EU member countries to make every effort to match the convergence criteria, whether this was seen as justifiable or not viewed from other angles. Doubtless, the arbitrary setting of a time limit gave the politics of convergence in Europe a special momentum. With the exception of Greece, all other countries met before the Brussels final decision regarding the requirements of the monetary convergence criteria: Inflation rates were on an historical low with only small spreads. The same was true of long-term interest rates, which signalled the anticipation of stable currency. The exchange rates barely varied. To achieve all this would not have been possible without the much criticized hegemonial role of the Deutsche Mark and the Deutsche Bundesbank (Kloten, 1995) in the European Currency System (ECS), but it also reflected the preparedness of member countries to accept the German monetary prerogatives.

It is a well-known fact that the financial convergence criteria were not properly met by most countries. Only Denmark, Finland, Ireland and Luxembourg enjoyed consolidated public finances. All other countries offended and still offend especially against the debt level criterion (60 per cent of GDP). And they all manipulated realities in one way or another to prove progress in consolidating. I referred above to the findings of the Deutsche Bundesbank in its report. No convergence criteria were defined to measure the state of affairs of real convergence. No doubt, remarkable real convergence processes took place in the 1990s on all goods and financial markets, concerning the main bulk of products, the organizational patterns of marketing and supply, the schemes of financial transfers and the flows of capital and – to a far lesser degree – labour. The adjustments speeded up when the start of the third stage of EMU became likely. But structural differences of all kinds and divergences at all levels of economic activities, not least in the per capita GDP, are still evident. The critics of a fixed entry date certainly had arguments on their side, when they stated that the European Union was not prepared to start the Monetary Union on the data available.[1] But as European realities and plans had been taking shape since 1997, the more convincing arguments were in favour of the implementation of the prefixed (second and final) date. Any postponement would have had far greater political risks as had been conceded by many opponents.

The preparations on the part of EMI and hence of the community of national central banks had been appropriate. They were well in line with the monumental task of introducing a common European currency, the Euro. One has to acknowledge that almost all technical, organizational and conceptional procurements fitted well into the whole scheme. The national central banks, led by the Deutsche Bundesbank, secured a smooth transition – based on agreements within the already active European Central Bank Council. Minor irritations did not matter. The first Directory of the ECB convened and international financial markets seemed inclined to trust the new European monetary policy institution, despite the Euro's loss of value against the US dollar. In the meantime the ECB has adopted a slightly different approach. In December 2000 for the first time an inflation rate projection was published, provided by the Governing Council's staff as well as other projections of macroeconomic variables, thought as a useful source of information for the Council's decision-making, not as a sort of an intermediary target as in the context of direct inflation targeting.

Since January 1999 the ECB Council and the ECB Board have acted prudently (Duisenberg, 1999b). The monetary policy assignment: a quantitative money reference figure used as main indicator and an unpublished inflation rate as a supporting indicator, corresponded to the requirements of the European state of affairs (Issing, 1999).

The public will be kept fully informed by means of a press conference after each meeting of the ECB Council and by statements and regular publications, thus avoiding the abysses of published protocols covering

1 This concession is not concerned with the demand of many economists for the establishment of an 'optimal currency area' prior to EMU getting its starting license. A true currency area can only be shaped by EMU itself. To aim with vigour at such an area was and is a justified concern.

internal debates. In addition, President Wim Duisenberg will report regularly to the European Parliament (e.g. Duisenberg, 1999b) Moreover, the ECB is prepared to discuss frankly any aspects of common concern with the Euro-X Group, but made clear its refusal to accept any interference in its own decision-making. It is indeed the task of the ECB to care for a currency which is 'depoliticized' in the sense, that monetary decision-making should be determined solely by the deliberations of the ECB Council to secure a stable currency. All action taken so far can be regarded as a sound foundation for a European stable currency policy. It is, however, no guarantee of that. There are some weak elements in the statute of the ESCB. It is a two-staged system, composed of the ECB as the steering entity and the national central banks (NCBs) as executive units.

The latter's presidents are still appointed by the corresponding governments and whether they like it or not, they will be confronted with the expectations of their respective national political authorities. Political pressures are to be foreseen coming from national political groups, from informal border-crossing coalitions or even as a result of decision-making processes at the European level. Driving forces behind such conflicts can be (a) an inadequate performance of policies which have remained in the hands of national authorities, (b) coercions stemming from adjustments determined by market forces, (c) constraints imposed by competitive systems within Europe and between Europe and the rest of the world, and (d) the impact of exogenous shocks.

Risks for monetary policy?

A stable currency policy and the macroeconomics state of affairs have to be compatible (Jochimsen, 1999a). The same applies to fiscal policy, social security policy, labour market policy, structural policy, etc. Data prepared by them and political interferences in market processes can lead to developments which are not consistent with the foremost target of stabilizing economic growth at a suitable level combined with a stable purchasing power, a low unemployment rate and external balance (Remsperger, 1999).

Deviations from the intended economic development either dampen the propensity to invest in real capital or shift investment capital into foreign countries. The dynamics of growth will slow down and the number of unemployed will tend to increase. If monetary policy adheres to its stable money concept it incurs the risk of being blamed for any shortcomings brought about by other policies. The intention of blaming monetary policy is especially common in case of ideological fixations, or if the fundamental role of stable money to enable undistorted relations between the elements of real economic development and to secure social justice is not acknowledged, or finally if the opinions about adequate political behaviour simply divert (Dornbusch *et al.*, 1998). Monetary policy will then be pressed to achieve the desired effects by way of easy money, but it cannot achieve what are regarded the primary goals of other policies. Stable currency is a principal economic target, but it is more than that since it is a necessary prerequisite for achieving any of the other main objectives of a sustainable economic policy (Tietmeyer, 1999b). But to realize these goals requires a harmonisation of all relevant policies (Jochimsen, 1999b).

In case of defective economic developments, it needs effective well-balanced measures assigned for an appropriate timespan to correct the given biases and to approximate an economic equilibrium. Under the auspices of globalization, the application of monetary policy is becoming increasingly complex (Duisenberg, 1999c; Padua-Schioppa, 1999; Tietmeyer, 1999b). And the implications of EMU as I see them will lead to stronger political pressures on the ECB to aim at an easy rather than tight monetary policy.

The biggest risk arises from data set by fiscal policy which divert substantially from an unwavering stable money policy (Issing, 1999b). This is the rationale of the Stability and Growth Pact, which perpetuates the adherence to fiscal convergence criteria and puts national budget policies under European scrutiny. The pact and the regulations of the Maastricht Treaty, for example sanctions in case of failure, limit the budget competences of national parliaments. This, of course, reduces the potential for conflicts between monetary and fiscal policy behaviour – at least in principle.

Intensified market competition

The most obvious implications of EMU within Europe relate to adjustment processes, generated by the new monetary policy environment. They are the substratum of intensified competition. These processes, initiated or accelerated by EMU, change the patterns more or less of all markets and in the long run the regional distribution of economic activity within the EU. The adjustments will be enforced by given differences in prices, qualities in productivity and the real cost per unit of output. Financial resources, ready to be invested in real capital stock will follow the comparative best margins of return. The labour force will migrate to places were real wages and working conditions are attractive. The intensified competition will stimulate market-product and processing innovations, new marketing strategies, entrepreneurial alliances, and mutual and joint ventures. There will be winners and losers and that affects not only market participants, but also the markets themselves, regional developments and the economies concerned.

Many economists believe that since the early 1990s, the main bulk of adjustment processes had already taken place, anticipating the impact of EMU. Indeed, what has been achieved impresses, even if much or the greater part of it should be attributed to the impact of globalization. But the adjustments are still going on and might gain momentum. There are many signs to support this view. One example is that European banking is almost in turmoil. The pace of mergers and acquisitions has accelerated. The segmented markets of bank services (typical for Europe) are almost in dissolution or at least ticking-over. Even the savings banks and the co-operative banks are thinking in new dimensions, considering the abolition of traditional patterns.

The challenges and risks which accompany the adjustment processes correlate with an enormous potential of growth opportunities. The country, the region, the branch or the company that makes best use of them will be in the front line among competitors. The opposite of the coin will be the collapse of many companies with certain locations being eliminated. Many white- and blue-collar workers will lose their jobs, others will be forced to orientate themselves anew. Labour markets and organizational representations of the labour force and entrepreneurs will have to adapt.

Competition of systems intensified

To what extent and in what way the European economies will be affected in the long run depends to a large extent on how they will respond to these new challenges. Member countries of EMU, now linked by a single currency, can easily be compared. That is obvious in a situation where market prices and items as assets in nominal terms exist. But it will also be easier to evaluate the activities of public sectors within EMU, the repercussions of tax and/or social security schemes etc. Whether regulations in these fields are compatible with the requirements of efficient market performance and whether they contribute to economic dynamics can be detected and judged more precisely than in a world of multiple national currencies.

This situation will encourage a special kind of competition, a competition between national systems of regulation and economic institutions, between constituent elements and driving forces of national politics, and even between the complex states of mind of social groups. All these facts and performances contribute to social welfare and help to shape the framework of private economic activities. Competition of systems is a common phenomenon, but under EMU it gets a new and strong momentum. In the near future the new features connected with EMU and with the enlargement of the European Union will – with the impact of globalization in the background – force the countries involved to scrutinize their institutions and their patterns of regulation. Countries seen from an economic point of view, with less efficient systems, will lose ground. Their locations of economic activities will lose their attractions. To stem the tide means to stay further behind in this competitive process. To avoid being misunderstood, it must be stressed that in future, too, there will be a wide range of societal divergencies of all kinds, as for example demonstrated in the various parts of Switzerland. Negative economic implications might be compensated by social advantages, which could in the long run strengthen the overall performance of the economy. Yet, under new European realities the competitive advantages and disadvantages of 'systems' will no doubt play a more intrinsic role. Successful 'systems' in one country will force countries with inferior 'systems' to react. This means as a matter of fact that under the new auspices their scope for considerations about their 'systems' has changed its quality. The impact of an increasing competition of systems and the thus provoked restraints on political room for manoeuvre – exerted by a persistent stable currency policy – constitute the most penetrating challenge for the politicians in the EU (whether they are members of EMU or not yet). How should they respond to it?

According to the philosophy of EMU, all fields of politics are expected not to endanger the effectiveness of monetary policy but rather to accept the maxim of compatibility in action. That refers to social and public authorities, to entrepreneurial organizations and to trade unions. But that they all perform adequately cannot be taken for granted. The given systems and the applied rules of conduct may be of an adverse, or at least of a partly counterproductive nature. If that is the case, the percussive power of a competition of systems first has to shape correspondingly the organizational patterns of home systems and to induce a suitable change on behaviour. Expected implications may already have led to anticipating actions. The reviewing of systems can thus be instrumentalized as a parameter in strengthening one's own position (economically as well as politically) compared with other economies or societies. Initiatives of this kind have their own dimensions. One has to bear in mind the basic political conceptions, possible conflicts with the realities of income distribution and taxation, with the handed-down schemes in social securities and state subsidies, with the facts on the labour markets, with vested interests as well as with the given procedures of political decision-making. The pros have to be compared with the cons, and that includes inevitably some kind of arbitrary reasoning.

All kinds of responses are possible. What is desired is open-mindedness, a positive attitude towards a firm and consistent monetary policy, and a prudent consideration of all that is at stake. In contrast, there might be dominating ideological prejudices, the desire to make use of monetary policy for the benefit of growth and employment, or the inclination to preserve given structures, for example of subsidies and regulations. Positions can be held and actions be taken, going it alone or together with others – all accidentally happening or performed by intended alliances at whatever level and of whatever kind.

This leads to the question as to whether or not the competition of systems can be directed and controlled politically by agreements between national governments or by European institutions without blockading their preparedness to adjust. Putting that question means to open a box of pandora. Seen at least from the point of view of Friedrich A. von Hayek, the competition of systems generates, as any competitive constellation 'procedures of detection' with results that are not foreseeable (Streit, 1997; Vanberg, 1999). Thus political data setting in such a competitive state of affairs have to be regarded as probably counteracting interventions. Nevertheless the question is there and already on debate on the European scene.

Exogenous shocks

It is obvious that shocks stemming from outside the EU will effect the European countries under the regime of the ECB somewhat differently if compared with the previous situation. It is not up to me to discuss the divergences of the scenario involved neither in general nor in detail. I refer simply to the evaluations of the impact of the Asian crisis on Europe and the rest of the world (G-7, 1999).

Germany and the European Union put on test

Germany on test

Germany in the past was a main driving force towards European integration, jointly with France pushing forward the economic and – as far as feasible – the political unification of Europe. Germany did not hesitate to relinquish the DM, the hegemonial European currency and hence the by far most valuable and powerful asset in the German arsenal. German politicians pleaded at the European level – not always consistently – on behalf of market economy solutions. To ensure a stable monetary policy in EMU, it was primarily the German Minister of Finance Theo Waigel who demanded the Stability (and Growth) Pact that was finally accepted by all EU members; in most cases not because a fiscal policy straitjacket was desired, but rather as a concession to get Germany definitely into EMU and the Deutsche Bundesbank out of its unbeloved dominating position. For Germany enlargement of the EU was and is not questionable. The central and eastern European countries are regarded as historically, intellectually and economically belonging to Europe. But in crucial questions of institutional steps towards a politically integrated Europe, Germany as well as the other EU members hesitated and still hesitate to overcome their own objections. This is well demonstrated by the Amsterdam Agreement.

What type of policy would one expect from a country as European minded as Germany? A rational response to the new European realities certainly has to focus on a 'fitness' programme for the German economy and the German public sector to cope with intensified market competition, on a reasonable attitude towards a persistent competition of systems, and on strategical outlines concerning the co-operation with fellow governments in the case of questions of common concern. Such requirements are implied in the challenges which the Kohl administration already faced. For many years Germany has been in need of urgent fundamental reforms. During 1992–95 the German economy had to endure a persistent recession. It again gained momentum after harsh adjustments, which took place at the expense of higher unemployment. There were also increased shifts of economic activities in other European and overseas countries. German economic dynamism is still shocked by unwavering and high expectations of the Germans regarding social securities and the luxuries of life. Germany suffers badly from high tax burdens and unreasonable contributions to the social security system, from top wages and connected payments, from counterproductive regulations and subsidies, and from a preponderance of public consumption, etc. Hundreds of incentive programmes, primarily on behalf of eastern Germany, absorbed and are still absorbing billions of Deutsche Marks without leading properly to the expected results. The German model of social market economy has degenerated more or less to a propagandistic capsule. It has lost its policy-shaping power. Helmut Kohl and his government went two-thirds of the election period from 1994 to 1998 without signs of convincing efforts to initiate reforms.

What was on the agenda and what had to be done had been consistently outlined for many years by parlamentarians, advisory bodies and academics. But it seemed as if the creative vigour of the then ruling parties had been absorbed, even exhausted by German unification and its aftermath, as well as by the efforts of paving the way to EMU. It is true, initiatives of the Kohl government were blocked by the Federal Council (Bundesrat) which had been more and more dominated by the middle-left Land governments led by social democrats. However, equally important were the internal blockades within the yellow-black coalition, the propensity not to jeopardize traditional schemes, and the anxiety to run into uncalculated risks. Almost at the very last minute – under the auspices of the elections to the Federal Parliament in the autumn of 1997 – the Christian Democrats and the Liberals decided to reform taxation and social security regulations, for example by the increase of the age on which pension claims are based. This failed to convince the public. The measures were of an eclectical nature, not at all related to a well balanced reform programme, and they were certainly not popular.

The opposition then declared to abolish them in order to win support. The red-green government indeed kept its promise, which was applauded by those supposed to benefit. But they were unaware that what was cancelled were imperative elements of the true reform programme so badly needed. Leading figures of the now ruling Social Democrat and Green parties wanted to change the realities in Germany, to improve social justice and to realize environmental awareness. What Oskar Lafontaine and Jürgen Trittin, the exponents, had in mind was a change of political paradigms. The term 'social market economy' was regarded as a relic of the past period if even referred to in the 'Regierungserklärung.' Within the new coalition there prevailed a thinking and a pattern of behaviour brought about by the experiences and the wishes of the former opposition. That led and still leads to disastrous failures. The start of the new government laid bare after a very short while a tremendous lack of political competence, a disregard of legal provisions, divided opinions, and an almost unbelievable shortage of professional skill. The Greens, yearning for an environmental breakthrough, experienced a frustrating setback in the dispute about the future of nuclear energy. In addition, Lafontaine had mastered the negotiations between the coalition partners and commanded the most powerful ministry, the Federal Ministry of Finance – enlarged by the core of the formerly basic department of the Federal Ministry of Economics. This was provided with responsibility for macroeconomic policy. But after some rebounds, Lafontaine just threw in the towel. The way he vanished from the political scene reflects like nothing else the substance of his personality.

In the context of my deliberations I have to hint at the amateurish handling of vital European and international issues by leading members of the new German government (with some exceptions, for example Foreign Minister Joschka Fischer). It was quite incredible how Lafontaine and Trittin in particular, but also in the beginning Chancellor Schröder, confronted our partners in the EU with their political priorities and their belief in the virtues of a European coalition dominated by left-wing governments. It was simply naive to expect that German positions would be accepted without resistance. France and Britain did not hesitate to disillusion their German partner in the nuclear case. Neither were the Europeans willing to follow Lafontaine's attacks on the autonomy of the ECB. Furthermore, even France, which initially showed sympathies to identify with the German request for a harmonized European employment policy and for setting up uniform social standards, gave evidence of detached views. Lafontaine evaluated the competition of systems as basically unwanted and asked for an alliance considering its political implications. The German fiscal policy programme instigated by him tends to hurt core elements of the Stability and Growth Act. Chancellor Schröder had to learn that the presidency of the European Union requires an adequate style in arguing. It also limits the scope for pursuing national (in his case German) concerns. Most important, it is time that Germans acknowledge that with the Brussels decisions on 2 May 1998 they have lost, with the setting up of EMU, their exceptional former bargaining position based on the strength of the Deutsche Mark and the leading position of the Deutsche Bundesbank in European monetary affairs. With both at hand, Germany could enforce political concessions which would otherwise not be achievable. Since Germany, as well as the other member countries of EMU, relinquished the currency symbolic of national sovereignty, Germans have to define themselves and to make use of more subtle procedures of convincing reasoning and of winning allies for co-operative action.

On the whole the new government for a long time did almost nothing to bring the German economy back into shape in order to hold its stand in the new European environment or even to gain ground. On the contrary, Germany lost further in ranking. And that applied not only to its position on Europe. Worldwide it had been acknowledged that Germany advocated target zones for exchange rates, only to be shown the cold shoulder by the United States and the ECB (Graham, 1999; Tigges, 1999). Social Democrats and the Greens had to learn step by step that under the new monetary regime any government will have to proceed with the reforms already debated for years. They are simply a must, the question is only how and when they will be realized and under what circumstances. Despite remarkable positive elements in the tax reform put forward by the coalition, political leadership, distinguished by a conducive conceptual thinking and a sustainable way of action here and in other fields, is still asked for. And it is in the interest of German society that German authorities find the way back to the virtues of social market economy as outlined decades ago and to stand up for liberal solutions at the European level. Whether the red-green coalition is able to such a turnaround has still to be questioned. I fully acknowledge that the upright and determined stance of Chancellor Schröder in the Kosovo case as well as in the settling of quite a lot of irritating national affairs has provided the government with the reputation of skilful political proceedings. But for the time being the open questions foremost on the domestic front are still in urgent need of clear answers.

Europe on test

Europe is a community of states, bound more or less by treaties. The EU member countries have assigned additional competences to European institutions. All who have joined EMU – *cum grano salis*, that is even true for those who have remained onlookers – have principally to face the same challenges as Germany. But there are quite a lot of differences. These result from history, by divergencies in organizational patterns, by the given state of economic and political affairs, by systems of regulations, by dominant ideological maxims and so on. Almost all countries have seen themselves confronted with the hardships of accomplishing the convergence criteria. Doubtless not a few of the EU members are prepared to adhere strictly to the directives of the Stability and Growth Pact. Others seem to be inclined to interpret the rules permissively. Without referring to details, one can observe that so far it is not yet clear what course the EU countries will follow in future. Will they respect the statute and the political mandate of the ECB? (Dumas, 1999) Will they stay on the road of consolidated budget policy in case of political conflicts? Will they except probable consequences of the Single European Market and of EMU with regard to the labour market, the wage structure and the social security arrangements, or will they blockade them? Are they open-minded in respect of the competition of systems or will they try to mould it? The 1999 Berlin agreement on financing the EU-budget failed to reveal what we have to expect in future. The EU obviously is, even after the Agreement of Nice, still behind schedule with its technical and institutional preparations for enlargement. Crucial questions of a further political integration are not yet answered. What is at stake is still a path-finding process. By the way the Brussels crisis triggered by the charges of misconduct against some members of the European Commission can have its merits if used as an occasion to review the network between the European institutions and especially between the Commission and the European Parliament.

Concluding remarks

As conditions are in the EU it has to be regarded as an historically lucky chance that Maastricht provided the ECB with autonomy and political competence. Until now the performance of the ECB has been fully in accordance with its mandate. The Euro has after all good chances of becoming an internationally trusted currency.

Only political shortsightedness and internal quarrels, especially if they are caused by ideological stubbornness, can jeopardize the new European monetary regime. It might be regarded as a further historically lucky chance that EMU has to prove its strength in an environment marked by globalization. The impact of an intensified integrated network covering the whole world, and geared by market forces as well as by the economies in transition in central and eastern Europe have practically ruled out alternatives such as 'fortress Europe' or, on a global level, the 'Third Way'. No doubt the next decades will be as demanding as the past decades. Today the challenges will concern Europe as a whole far more than in the past. All who believe in the virtues of European integration should be prepared to contribute to the future of a united Europe.

Bibliography

Academic Advisory Council to the Federal Ministry of Economics. *A General Policy Orientation for the European Union*, Report no. 369 to the Federal Ministry of Economics, Bonn (Oct. 1994) pp. 1–73.

BVG – Bundesverfassungsgericht. 2 BvR 2134/92 und Urteil vom Okt. 2BvR 2159/92.

BVG – Bundesverfassungsgericht. Beschluß des Zweiten Senates vom 31. März, 2 BvR 1877/97 und 2 BvR 50/98.

Deutsche Bundesbank. *Stellungnahme des Zentralbankrates zur Konvergenzlage in der Europäischen Union im Hinblick auf die Dritte Stufe der Wirtschafts- und Währungsunion* (Frankfurt a.M.: 26 March 1998).

Dornbusch R., Favero, C. and Giavazi. F. *The Immediate Challenges for the European Central Bank* (*NBER Working Paper* No. 6369, 1998. 6369).

Duisenberg, Willem F. (1999a). *Hearing at the European Parliament's-Sub-Committee on Monetary Affairs on 18 January 1999*, reprinted in Deutsche Bundesbank *Auszüge aus Presseartikeln*, (20 Jan. 1999).

Duisenberg, Willem F. (1999b). *The Eurosystem's Strategy for the Euro*. Speech at a conference organized by *The Economist*, Rome, 12 March 1999, reprinted in Deutsche Bundesbank, *Auszüge aus Presseartikeln*, 17 (15 March 1999).

Duisenberg, Willem F. (1999c). *The Euro, the Dollar and National Economic Policies: What Room for Manoeuvre?* Speech at the Euro, J + 80 Conference, Paris, 25 March 1999, reprinted in Deutsche Bundesbank, *Auszüge aus Presseartikeln*, 20 (30 March 1999) pp. 7–10.

Dumas, Charles. 'Power struggle over EMU has only just begun', *The Times*, 24 March 1999.

Ehrmann, M. *Will GMN Generate Asymmetry 2 Compain, Monetary Policy Transmission Across European Countries*. Paper presented at the Banca d'Italia/IGIER Conference *Monetary Policy of the ESCB. Strategy and Implementation Issues*, Milan, (17 July 1998).

Europäische Union. *Vertrag von Amsterdam zur Änderung der Verträge zur Gründung der Europäischen Gemeinschaften sowie einiger damit zusammenhängender Rechtsakte vom 2. Oktober 1997*, Presse and Informationsamt der Bundesregierung, Bonn 1998: March (1997).

Europäisches Währungsinstitut. *Konvergenzbericht* (Frankfurt: March 1998) pp. I–VII, 1–382.

Frowen, S. F., 'Europäische Integration als Gestaltungsaufgabe: Die Verantwortung für die kommenden Generationen', in Eduard J. M. Kroker and Bruno Dechamps (eds.) *Das Menschenbild der freien Gesellschaft: Globalisierung und Europäische Integration* (Frankfurt: *Frankfurter Allgemeine* Buch, 2000), pp. 99–121.

G-7. *Communiqué of G-7 Finance Ministers and Central Bank Governors*, Petersberg, Bonn, 20 February 1999, reprinted in Deutsche Bundesbank, *Auszüge aus Presseartikeln*, 13 (26 Feb. 1999) pp. 7–10.

Graham, Robert. Mr. Euro-Zone. France's finance minister Dominique Strauss-Kahn wants to bridge the gap between Germany, which wants to forget zones for currencies, and the US, which doesn't, *Financial Times*, Frankfurt/London, 12 Feb. 1999.

Hankel, W., Mölling, W. N., Schachtschneider, K. A. and Starbatty, J. *Die Euro-Klage. Warum die Währungsunion scheitern muß* (Hamburg: rororo Rowoht 1998) pp. 1–303.

Issing, Otmar (1999a). *The Euro – Four Weeks after the Start*. Speech to the European-Atlantic Group, House of Commons, London, 28 Jan. 1999, reprinted in Deutsche Bundesbank *Auszüge aus Presseartikeln*, 25, 1999, p. 8–93.

Issing, Otmar (1999b). *Der Euro und seine Stabilität – Konsequenzen für die Finanzpolitik*. Rede anläßlich des Finanzpolitischen Kongresses 1999, veranstaltet von Goldman, Sachs & Co. OHG, Frankfurt, March 1999, reprinted in Deutsche Bundesbank, *Auszüge aus Presseartikeln*, 19, (25 March 1999) pp. 10–16.

Jochimsen, Reimut (1999a). *Die Europäische Wirtschafts- und Währungsunion nach dem Start*. Vortrag im Rahmen einer Vortragsreihe des Goethe-Instituts in der Universidad Complutense, Madrid, 25 March 1999, reprinted in Deutsche Bundesbank, *Auszüge aus Presseartikeln*, 23 (13 April 1999), pp. 13–19.

Jochimsen, Reimut (1999b). The Euro-Opportunities and Callenges. Statement at a Symposium of the German Ambassador to the U.N. and the Westdeutsche Landesbank of New York, New York, 15 March 1999, reprinted in Deutsche Bundesbank, Auszüge aus *Presseartikeln*, 25 (20 April 1999) pp. 5–11.

Kloten, Norbert. 'European Monetary Union: Sovereignty and Hegemony', in S. F. Frowen and F. P. McHugh (eds), *Financial Decision-Making and Moral Responsibility* (London: Macmillan; New York: St. Martin's Press, 1995) pp. 197–206.

Padua-Schioppa, Tommaso. *The External Representation of the Euro Area, Statement at the Int-Committee on Monetary Affairs*, European Parliament, Brussels, 17 March 1999, reprinted in Deutsche Bundesbank, *Auszüge aus Presseartikeln*, 18 (18–19 March 1999) pp. 7–10.

Remsperger, Hermann. *Europäische Geldpolitik und nationale Wirtschaftspolitik*, Vortrag anläßlich der Jahresversammlung der Gesellschaft für Angewandte

Wirtschaftsforschung, Stuttgart, 13 April 1999, reprinted in Deutsche Bundesbank, *Auszüge aus Presseartikeln*, 23 (13 April 1999) pp. 6–13.

Stark, Jürgen. *Regional Integration and Stability in the Context of Global Markets.* Speech at the Banco Central de la Republica Argentina, Buenos Aires, 24 March 1999, reprinted in Deutsche Bundesbank, *Auszüge aus Presseartikeln*, 19 (25 March 1999) pp. 5–10.

Streit, Manfred, E. 'Constitutional Ignorance, Spontaneous Order and Rule-Orientation: Hayekian Paradigms from a Policy Perspective, in Stephen F. Frowen, (ed.), *Hayek: Economist and Social Philosopher – A Critical Retrospect* (London: Macmillan; New York: St Martin's Press, 1997) pp. 37–58.

Tietmeyer, Hans (1999a). *International Cooperation and Coordination in the Area of Financial Market Supervision and Surveillance.* Report, Frankfurt, 11 Feb. 1999, reprinted in Deutsche Bundesbank, *Auszüge aus Presseartikeln*, 13 (26 Feb. 1999) pp. 1–4.

Tietmeyer, Hans (1999b). *The Eurosystem's Approach to Monetary Stability.* Lecture to the Swedish Economic Association, Stockholm, 12 April 1999, reprinted in: Deutsche Bundesbank, *Auszüge aus Presseartikeln*, 23 (13 April 1999) pp. 1–6.

Tigges, Claus. 'Zielzonen bedürfen der Aufgabe der geldpolitischen Selbständigkeit'. Ein Gespräch mit Michael Frenkel, in *Frankfurter Allgemeine Zeitung*, (17 Feb. 1999).

Vanberg, Viktor. 'Der Weg zur Freiheit. Der evolutionäre Liberalismus Friedrich August von Hayeks und sein Verhältnis zur Freiburger Schule', in *Frankfurter Allgemeine Zeitung* (8 May 1999).

Comment

David Cobham

Professor Kloten's paper offers us a wide range of insights on the past, present and future of EMU with special reference to Germany. His brief account of the political story of Germany's entry into EMU in the last few years will be particularly useful for non-German readers. As is widely recognized, Germany had the least to gain from EMU and its economists were for long as unenthusiastic about the Euro as British economists, although often with much better reasons (given the records of the Bundesbank and the pre-1997 UK monetary authorities). But German opinion at all levels moved eventually in favour, for reasons that are partly articulated later by Kloten's own arguments.

First, with regard to the call for increased political integration to accompany monetary integration, he argues that 'European integration has to be regarded as a process, characterized by almost dialectically interconnected political and economic steps . . .' (while the position of the ECB is strong enough for EMU to function satisfactorily in the meantime). This is surely a useful contrast to the economist's tendency to reason in comparative statics, that is in terms of a limited number of alternative equilibria which are alone considered to be internally consistent and hence viable. It must also be accurate as far as the past is concerned, and plausible for the future.

Second, Kloten acknowledges the force of the argument that it might have been better economically if EMU had come a little later, after yet more convergence. But he counters this with the observation that, as things developed, postponement beyond 1999 would have incurred much greater political risks. His point can be made more widely: the Delors–Maastricht strategy for European monetary integration represents a careful compromise between the traditional 'economist' (converge first, fix exchange rates later) and 'monetarist' (fix exchange rates first to impose convergence) views, a compromise which was necessary not just for political reasons but as the only strategy which could ensure both that EMU was attained and that an acceptable form of EMU was attained.

Kloten goes on to argue that the single currency will have major effects on the EU economies as a result of the significant increase in competitive pressures, both in goods and financial markets and between 'institutional systems'. Certainly the effects of competition should never be underestimated; in the UK, for example, the increase in competition brought about by the abolition of exchange controls in 1979 was responsible (over a period of up to ten years) for a comprehensive revolution in UK banking and financial markets. But at the same time the inertia of the real economy and the inertia of 'institutional systems' should not be underestimated.

Institutional arrangements that deserve the epithet of 'systems' are complexes of interconnecting institutions where the existence and operations of each type of institution depend on those of the others. Thus such systems clearly have multiple equilibria characteristics, and it is likely that the equilibria have strong local stability properties. This suggests that it may be many decades at least before some of the most deeply entrenched features of the different European economies are brought into any convergence. For example, the changes in financial markets which have been occurring in different countries (partly as the result of deregulation which is independent of European-level policy decisions) will have little immediate effect on the patterns of ownership and control of firms, particularly small and medium-sized firms. Indeed, in terms of the net sources of finance for firms there is as yet no evidence of significant movement of the French financial system towards the Anglo-Saxon model despite some 15 years of intensive financial innovation in France (Cobham and Serre, 2000).

Let me turn now to the situation in which EMU is being launched, and look both backwards and forwards, with respect first to economists, then to politicians, and then to European public opinion. Economists have learned a great deal from their involvement in the issue of monetary union, and they have contributed a great deal in the form of policy recommendations which have been incorporated into the actual arrangements (e.g. independence for the European Central Bank). One reason for both of these may be that European monetary integration is an attractive policy issue, but one which – at least until recently, and at least outside the UK – did not have standard left-right ideological connotations. At the same time, economists – in particular, many Anglo-Saxon economists – have often been wrong about EMU. In particular, they have repeatedly underestimated the chances of EMU being implemented, mainly because they have operated with an informal public choice theory perspective in which social and government preferences have been too narrowly specified and wider social and political attitudes have been undervalued, so that the strength of the political will behind EMU was underplayed.

One example of this can be found in the analysis of strategies of monetary unification due to Vaubel (1978), which was widely shared at that time in the profession. Vaubel criticized 'co-ordination strategies' such as the EMS for being too gradual, not sufficiently automatic, allowing too much discretion for politicians. But he – and we – failed to see that co-ordination strategies perform a quite different function, that of encouraging in electorates and politicians the willingness to make the essential commitment to monetary union when that commitment does not already exist. In this respect the EMS performed very well.

A second example is the reaction to the 1992–93 upheavals in the EMS. Many observers, particularly Anglo-Saxon, took the currency upheavals as the death-knell of the EMS and by extension of EMU also, and it is conventional to refer to the decision to widen the parities in August 1993 as the 'breakdown' of the EMS. This epithet could be justified only in terms of the legalities, since in practice (by contrast, for example, with the breakdown of the Bretton Woods system in 1972–73) the ERM countries continued to behave in much the same way. But even those economists who did not take this view worried about whether Europe should return to the old narrow exchange rate bands, which would have to be reinforced in some way to avoid a repeat of the turbulence, or about how, if the wider bands were retained, Europe could take some decisive steps to make sure that EMU was really attained. In the event, of course, Europe did neither: it retained the wider bands and reaffirmed but did not bolster its prior commitment to EMU, and in the end this did not matter.

Economists, then, have cause for humility. But so too have the politicians. They got many things right in the movement towards monetary union, in the sense that the basic design and construction of EMU are near to being as good as they could have been, partly because of the input of economists which has been accepted on this issue more than on some others. However, politicians also made a number of mistakes, two of which are worth drawing attention to.

The first was the German government's approach to the Maastricht deficit criterion – where the problem stemmed from earlier irresponsibility on the part of the politicians over the costs of German unification, in the form of an unwillingness to recognize the implications of unification for the public finances (comprehensively analysed in von Hagen and Strauch, 1999). The government at one point in the run-up to the 1998 decision on entry to EMU proposed to revalue the Bundesbank's gold and use the profits as a source of revenue, instead of acting on the balance between expenditure and taxation. This plan was not implemented, because of Bundesbank and general public opposition, but the episode suggests strongly that the German stability culture is an attribute of the German electorate rather than German politicians, and that German politicians are not unlike other politicians. This may be a useful lesson for electorates and politicians in other European countries; it is also consistent with the view that formal statutory independence for central banks makes a positive rather than a passive contribution to good monetary policy.

A second mistake was the French President's attempt to impose a Frenchman as President of the European Central Bank (ECB). The rationale for this was never clear, since the ECB is clearly independent and Jean-Claude Trichet's reputation is 'dry' rather than 'wet'; presumably President Chirac's action was designed mainly for domestic political consumption. The consensus hindsight view is that Chirac was justified in arguing for the ECB President to be appointed through a definite political choice by the heads of state (rather than his name emerging from the confabulations of EU central bank governors), but not justified in trying to impose a specific nationality on the post. What is interesting about the episode, however, is that Chirac's actions were instinctively opposed by much of public opinion in France, among which it cast further doubt on his political skills and political principles. French opinion was in that sense ahead of its politicians in understanding what is involved in and required for monetary union and central bank independence.

As this last example in particular suggests, there has in fact been an enormous amount of change in public attitudes over the two decades since the start of the EMS. One way of thinking about this is to refer to the familiar 'political economy' explanations of the Maastricht convergence criteria: the idea that the criteria cannot be justified on purely economic grounds (particularly if the proposal is to introduce a new common currency rather than just to lock exchange rates between the existing currencies), so that they must have been designed for one or more of the following purposes: to convince Germany that the other member countries were serious about monetary union with price stability; to fulfil Germany's own criteria for good monetary arrangements in order to ensure that Germany itself would join; and to enable the exclusion of countries which Germany might regard as 'unreliable'.

There were always many things wrong with this sort of explanation. Good behaviour pre-EMU does not guarantee good behaviour post-EMU. Past experience of inflation in different countries cannot be taken as indicating some deep-seated national preference. Explanation should be sought instead in the theory of time-inconsistency, on the one hand, and the range of empirical evidence available on the determinants of budget deficits, on the other hand. And the determinants these approaches emphasize are things which have been changing rapidly, in part because of the approach of EMU.

But in any case there is a lot of casual evidence of changes in popular attitudes in countries such as the UK and Italy, which experienced inflation rates of over 20 per cent in the 1970s or the early 1980s, and in countries such as France which experienced unsuccessful economic expansions (such as the Chirac expansion of 1975 and the Mitterrand policies of 1981–82). In particular, it is difficult to think of any major political party in an EU country which still espouses the view that full employment can be brought about simply by monetary or fiscal expansion, or which has not adopted price stability as an underlying objective (the first months of the SPD government in Germany, with Oskar Lafontaine as Minister of Finance, looked like an exception to this, but the rule was upheld). These changes in popular attitudes have been associated with the increasing informal independence over the 1980s of central banks in countries such as France and Italy (before the adoption of formal independence in 1993–94), and with the exemplary role played by many 'southern' European central banks in bringing down inflation since the early 1980s.

What these points suggest is that EMU started in a 'political economy' position which is very different from and much more favourable than that which existed in the 1970s and the early 1980s, and which continued to dominate the thinking of economists and perhaps politicians into the 1990s. As Professor Kloten has indicated there is a need for major changes of different kinds in the EU, but as he also suggests there are good grounds for optimism.

Bibliography

Cobham, D. and Serre, J.-M. (2000)[6] A characterisation of the French financial system' *Manchester School*, Vol. 68, pp. 44–67.

Vaubel, R. (1978) *Strategies for Currency Unification* (Tübingen: Mohr, 1978, pp. 44–67.

Von Hagen, J. and Strauch, R. (1999) 'Tumbling giant: Germany's experience with the Maastricht fiscal criteria', in D. Cobham and G. Zis (eds), *From EMS to EMU: 1979 to 1999 and beyond* (London: Macmillan, 1999).

7

The DM Undervaluation and West Germany's Economic Performance*

Jens Hölscher, Eric Owen Smith and Geoffrey Pugh

I Introduction

> *West Germany, a highly successful social market economy and one of the strongest economies of the West ... Her independent central bank, the Deutsche Bundesbank, totally in command of monetary policy, has secured one of the lowest inflation rates among Western industrial countries virtually throughout the post-war era* (Frowen, 1997, p. 2).

The hypothesis advanced in this paper is that the Bundesbank was fundamentally responsible for postwar economic growth in West Germany.[1] A monetary policy which targeted price stability produced an undervaluation of the Deutsche Mark. This was the basis for West Germany's export-driven accumulation. It is thus necessary to distinguish between the nominal and real exchange rates of the DM. The former became increasingly influenced by West Germany's international monetary commitments, whereas the latter was additionally derived from productivity gains. Qualitative factors also played a role in export growth. All these factors are, of course, difficult to disentangle:

> Such is the ubiquity and consistency of the Big Mac that *The Economist* has adopted it as a stable unit for the calculation of currency values. The Big Mac index establishes the relative over- and undervaluing of world

* In view of the extremely lively discussion which followed the delivery of the draft of this paper by Jens Hölscher and the original discussant's (Eric Owen Smith's) remarks, it was decided to provide a composite paper which embodied a more detailed account of the factors involved.

> currencies by converting them into the price of a Big Mac in each country and then comparing parities. This otherwise useful system is vulnerable to McDonald's promotions, however. On the first day of trading in the Euro, for example, Sterling appeared to lose 50 per cent of its value owing to a two-for-the-price-of-one deal. (*The Independent*, 10 June 1999)

The analytical difficulties are further compounded by the changes in the postwar trading regime. There was a gradual reduction in tariff barriers which facilitated an expansion of trade among industrialised countries; this trade expansion grew at a significantly more rapid rate than world output and GDP in industrial countries (Bhagwati, 1988, pp. 4–6). In this sense, free trade became the dominant method of determining the choice between trade and domestic production – in contradiction to mercantilism and its legitimation of autarkic policies (ibid.: pp. 24–5). Yet the notion that the Bundesbank in effect behaved in a 'mercantilist' manner and German industry participated in the 'neo-imperialist' dominance of world trade must explicitly and implicitly influence any meaningful analysis. This necessity will be borne in mind in this chapter. Moreover, Bhagwati (ibid.: pp. 9–15) notes the exceptions to free trade. Agriculture is a principal example – and German agriculture has historically been well protected. The agricultural sector also affords the best examples of literal free trade requiring deregulation and the consequent abolition of traceability. In such a regime, the British BSE crisis demonstrated that a blanket ban was the only conceivable response. Also central to the notion of free trade – given external trading opportunities – is that the mix of trade and domestic production is optimised at the margin. But this is subject to two critical assumptions (ibid.: pp. 25, 33). The price mechanism must work well enough to ensure that prices reflect true social costs; and if a country's trade share in a sector confers the monopoly power to affect price, a tariff will restrict trade but increase the gains from trade. Examples of avoiding unwanted social costs are the protection of infant industries and creating sufficient aggregate demand to minimize unemployment (Bhagwati, 1988, pp. 25, 32–4; 1991, p. 108). Finally, the nationalist and cosmopolitan theories of free trade must be carefully distinguished (ibid., 1988, p. 34). The latter rules out subsidies, protection and dumping.

The emergence of the basic market constellation is elaborated elsewhere (Hölscher, 1994). Similarly, the impact of intra-European exchange-rate variability on unemployment, employment and investment are analysed by Belke and Gros (1999). This analysis will rather critically review the current account debate in its second section. The underlying question of the section will be whether four decades of West German trade surpluses indicate a permanent mercantilist strategy of the Bundesbank to boost exports at the expense of domestic absorption or whether this external imbalance is a result of West Germany's superior position in the international division of labour. The third section will present four phases of DM undervaluation culminating in GEMSU, which placed further strains on the 'German model' (Owen Smith, 1998a). The conclusion will look at the transformation of the former currency undervaluation into a new German devaluation policy by wage policy within 'Euroland' and point to the danger of deflation.

II The current account debate

II.1 The background

West Germany's current account is largely driven by the trade balance, as Figure 7.1 clearly shows. (The contents of Figures 7.1–7.4 and 7.6 were calculated and plotted using background data from Dresdner Bank, 1999).

Even more specifically, the trends in the main components of the current balance of payments account reveal the importance of exports to the German economy. During the period 1950–98, the trade balance was in surplus in 47 out of the 49 years – the two deficits occurring in 1950 and 1951. Prior to GEMSU in 1990, each peak in the trade balance, as a percentage of GNP, exceeded the previous record. But the current account was in surplus in only 35 of these years. In particular, outlays on tourism

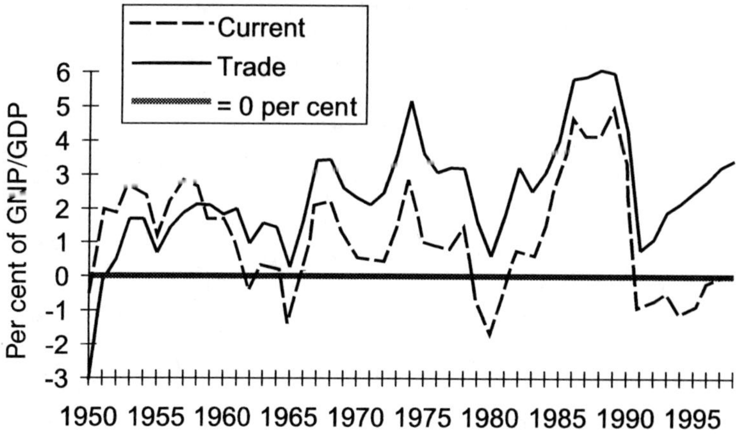

Figure 7.1 Current and trade balances

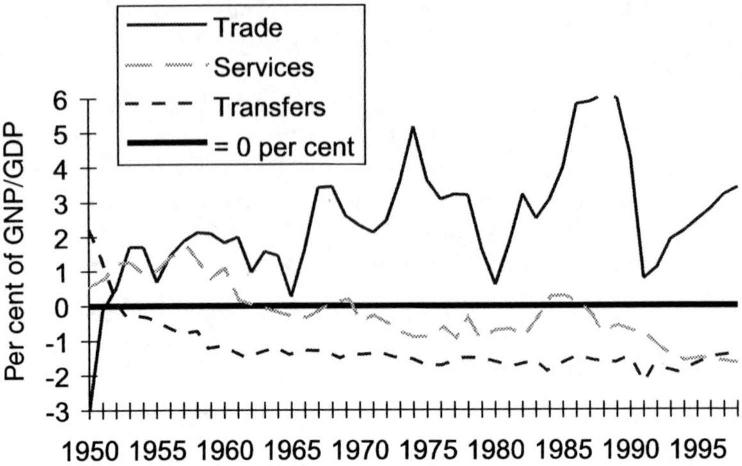

Figure 7.2 Visibles and invisibles

and transfers kept the current account balance on average below the extraordinary level of the 1950s. Nonetheless, prior to GEMSU, the overall picture of the current account is of an export-led surplus over four decades with relatively few deficits as a percentage of GNP.

However, services were in surplus on 19 occasions during the period 1950–98, with transfers in surplus on only three occasions (1950–52 inclusive). In Figure 7.2, the general worsening of these two current items is contrasted with the buoyant trade balance.

Within services, as already indicated, tourism was in surplus during only eight years between 1950 and 1957. The services' deficit grew dramatically in the 1990s, reaching DM 62bn in 1998 (1.6 per cent of united Germany's GDP). Transfers came down to a DM 53bn in deficit in 1998, the deficit having almost doubled in nominal terms earlier in the decade. A rising part of these transfers consists of payments resulting from German obligations, namely net retirement pensions and foreign workers' remittances (Schuller, 1998, p. 10). Net payments to the EU, on the other hand, are small relative to GDP but in principle inequitable when compared to other member states (ibid, pp. 11–12). In any case, 57 per cent of German exports go to other members of the EU. Critically, the rise in transfers during the early 1990s exacerbated a deterioration in other invisibles and initially coincided with smaller trade surpluses. From 1991, the consequent current-account deficits declined only after substantial improvements in the trade balance. GEMSU may have been responsible for a diversion of goods which would otherwise have been exported, but it was by no means responsible for the deterioration in invisibles. Net capital imports were necessary to offset the deficits on the current account, although on some estimates there will be a return to a current surplus early in the new millennium. Germany is then expected to return to being a net capital exporter.

II.2 The view from Kiel

A summary of the interpretation of the West German post war economic performance based on the analysis of scholars from the Kiel Institute for the World Economy (Giersch *et al.*, 1992) has to recognize that by and large the undervaluation of the DM is seen as a feature that promoted growth in the beginning, but prevented structural change in the long run. The paradigm is neoclassical with a Schumpeterian element. The line of the argument is as follows: due to an 'historical accident' after 1952 the DM was undervalued and the competitive advantage lead to a process of 'spontaneous growth'. The exchange rate is seen from the viewpoint of a real exchange economy. In terms of relative prices the undervaluation consequently means the subsidy of the production factor capital. As undervaluation continued over the decades, the West German economy became 'overcapitalized' and the miracle is fading away. Empirical evidence is found in the underdeveloped share of services within the shares of factor proportions in the German economy. Structural change was too slow to avoid the emergence of bottlenecks in the labour markets and the of the transformation of the supply side of the economy was restricted by rigidities and regulations, although the capital markets and anti-trust policies were not considered in any depth. The persisting surplus on current account throughout the 1980s came to be interpreted as 'indicator of unattractiveness for foreign capital' (Giersch *et al.*, 1992, p. 275) rather than as signpost for the competitiveness of German industry. Moreover, a trade surplus is evidence 'that a country saves more than it deems profitable to invest at home' (ibid. p. 246).

II.3 The view from Berlin

A summary of the interpretation of the West German postwar economic performance based on the analysis of scholars from Berlin's Free University would stress that the stability oriented undervaluation of the DM was the basis for Germany's growth and the development process of four decades The paradigm is 'monetary Keynesianism' and builds on Keynes' writings of the 1920s, the *Tract on Monetary Reform* and *The Treatise of Money* in particular, but – as with the Kiel view – it also contains a Schumpeterian element. In this view stabilization after 1952 was brought about by highly interventionist (although sometimes unplanned) measures, including protectionism, and substantial assistance from abroad, in particular the London Debt Agreement of 1953.[2] The undervalued DM generated windfall profits in the entrepreneurial sector, which led to confirmation of profit expectations and subsequently to investment acceleration. Undistributed profits and budget surpluses induced forced saving. For monetary policy the constellation became unsustainable when the DM grew into the position of a 'key currency' aside the US dollar. A 'key currency' would normally, like the £-sterling under the gold standard and the US dollar under the Bretton Woods system, tend to overvaluation. This position confronted the Bundesbank with the dilemma of external balance and internal stability. After GEMSU the decline of this 'German model' was threatened, when appreciable export surpluses disappeared and mass unemployment emerged in the east. Unemployment also remained a serious problem in the West.[3] Nevertheless German monetary policy remained tighter than that of its trade partners thereby improving the competitiveness of German industry. Aggregate demand is still therefore able to support a higher level of employment than would otherwise be the case.

II.4 The 'Melitz model' of DM hegemony

Melitz (1988) puts the traditional Barro-Gordon type of monetary policy model into an international setting. This approach includes the simplest possible assumptions about monetary policy, but leads Melitz to conclude that monetary policy co-operation within the European Monetary System had clear advantages for Germany due to its reserve currency status. In short, the German benefits are more secure than those derived by other members (Melitz, 1988, p. 51). The argument is similar to the Berlin view: the lower degree of inflation in Germany improves the competitiveness of German traded goods and forces the other EMS members into realignments, which remain lower than the inflation difference. In addition, the devaluations *vis-à-vis* the DM involved high political costs, as this was felt to be an embarrassment within the countries concerned. In his two-country model of France and Germany Melitz finds an optimal level of French inflation which permits Germany to achieve both zero inflation and the desired ratio of traded goods (Melitz, 1988, p. 66).

Figure 7.3 suggests that there may normally be something of a lagged response (the interest rate data are plotted from MRDB). In 1981 and 1992 relatively high annual average inflation rates by post war west German standards (6.3 and 5.1 per cent respectively) induced the Bundesbank policy makers to dramatically increase short-term interest rates. This could

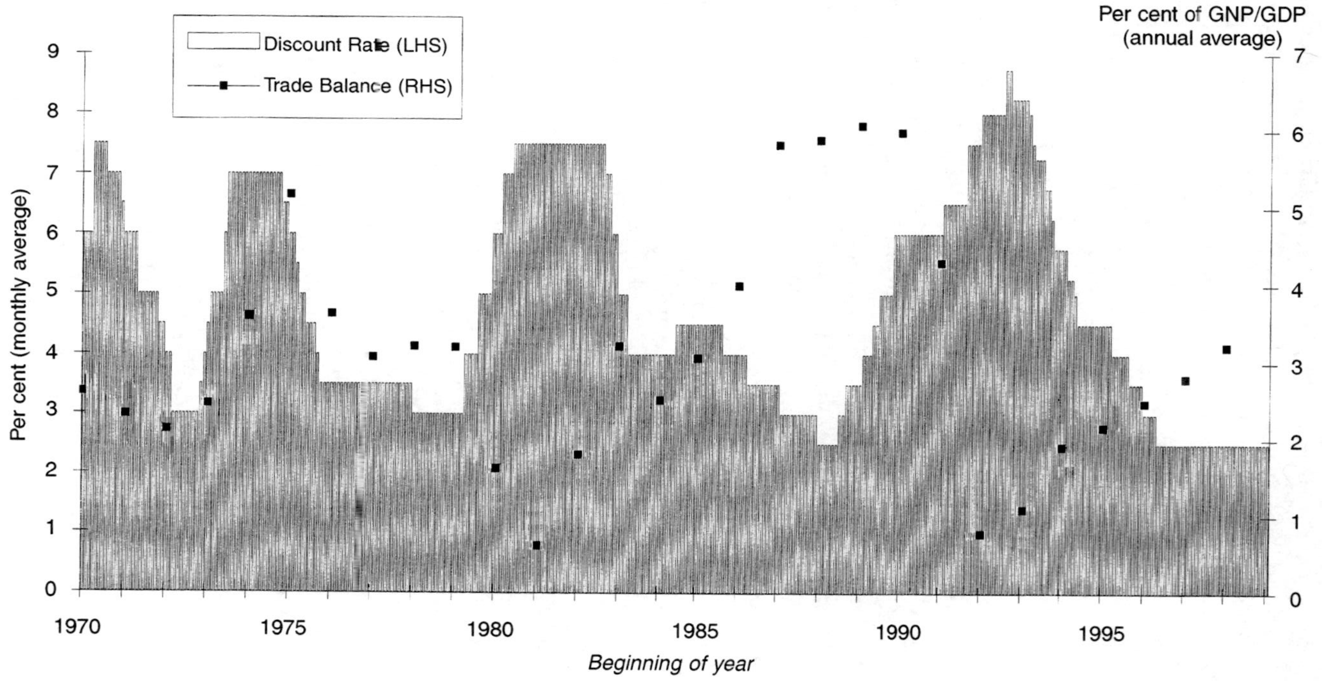

Figure 7.3 Interest rates and trade balances

be achieved because their target was domestic inflation, whereas other members of the ERM targeted the DM exchange rate. German interest rates were relaxed when domestic inflation reached rates acceptable to the Bundesbank Council. Meanwhile, exports had recovered. The first half of the 1970s is an obvious exception. Bretton Woods collapsed; the Bundesbank engineered recessionary conditions – falling real GDP – which were similar to the effects of the 1981 and 1992 deflations; yet exports atypically peaked in 1974; finally, the savings propensity unusually peaked in 1975, thus behaving in a *counter* cyclical manner and coinciding precisely with the *negative* trough in real GDP (Owen Smith, 1998c). Admittedly, there was a similar, though less pronounced, savings response to the second oil shock but by 1990 the well-behaved pro-cyclical relationship had been restored. The central hypothesis of this paper is thus supported: economic growth has been export-led in West Germany, thereby positively contributing, along with relatively high physical capital investment, to the determinants of GDP and compensating for the relatively lower consumption function (ibid.). However, in the 1990s domestic absorption, particularly consumption, grew at an unprecedented rate. More specifically, both fiscal transfers from West Germany to East Germany, along with the diversion of the west's exports to the east, above all supported eastern consumption (Hölscher and Stephan, 1998; Lange and Pugh, 1998, pp. 11, 17, 84; Owen Smith, 1994, pp. 128, 476). Hence the emphasis on the decline of exports and imports during the 1990s as *a percentage of GDP* in the discussion around Figure 7.6 below. Notwithstanding this powerful shock, the spectacular recovery of west Germany's exports after 1993 is added as a fifth phase to the conventional four-phase approach in the next section.

II.5 The technical background

Export price and income elasticities, as well as the all-important qualitative aspects of West German goods, are dealt with elsewhere (Owen Smith, 1994, pp. 508–9; Owen Smith, 1999). Here the emphasis is on exchange rates as such. Judgements that a currency is under- or overvalued presuppose some measure of its appropriate value in terms of other currencies. Accordingly, we begin by presenting a simple method of estimating the appropriate or equilibrium level of the exchange rate.[4]

We calculate equilibrium exchange rates as bilateral rates compatible with macroeconomic balance. Our method comprises two steps:

(1) We identify the most recent year in which the two economies were closest to macroeconomic balance. Our proxy for macroeconomic

balance combines output growth, inflation, unemployment, and the current account.

(2) Starting from this base year, we use time-series data to calculate the equilibrium exchange rate in each subsequent year. Two methods are used to perform these calculations.
   (a) The first takes into account the effects of inflation on the long-run equilibrium exchange rate in the manner suggested by the theory of relative purchasing power parity (PPP). In year t – the base year – we assume that the equilibrium (PPP) rate is given by the period average spot rate in this year. In each succeeding or preceding year – starting with year t + 1 or t – 1 – the PPP rate is calculated by adjusting the previous year's PPP rate to offset the effects of different inflation rates.
   (b) The second takes into account not only the effects of inflation on the equilibrium exchange rate but also the additional effects of differential productivity growth. This approach is suggested by a productivity-modified theory of relative PPP. After or before the base year, each year's modified PPP rate – starting with year t + 1 or t – 1 – is calculated by adjusting the previous or following year's modified PPP rate to offset the effects of both different inflation rates and different rates of productivity growth.

The choice of base year is critical. The market average rate in this year provides an initial value for the long-run equilibrium exchange rate. Accordingly, this initial value influences the level of all subsequent calculated values of the equilibrium exchange rate. The further one or both economies from macroeconomic balance in the base year, the further the market exchange rate in the base year is likely to be from equilibrium. And the less reliable the initial value, the less reliable the calculated rates for successive and preceding years as a guide to equilibrium values.

By assumption, in the base year the market-average nominal exchange rate gives the equilibrium exchange rate. To determine the year in which both economies were closest to macroeconomic balance, we establish a set of macroeconomic 'glee' indices for each economy. For the UK:German – sterling:DM – series, the period considered is 1950–89; for the US:German (dollar:DM) and French:German (FF:DM) series, 1960–89. The year with the optimum mix of the standard macroeconomic performance criteria during the period is assumed to be the year closest to 'macroeconomic balance'. The components of the indices are unemployment, inflation, annual GDP growth and the current account balance.[5] For all countries,

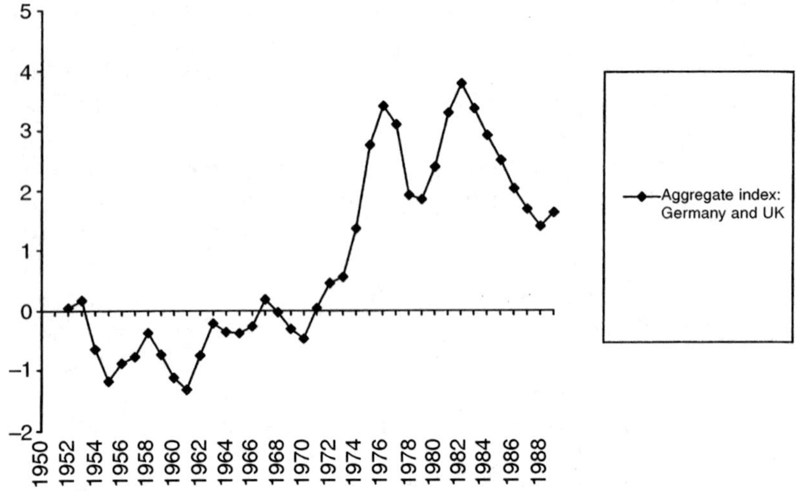

Note: * The lower, the closer to macroeconomic equilibrium in both countries.
Sources: Consumer price indices (CPI), *International Financial Statistics* (IMF); constant price GDP, ONS Databank (UK) and Maddison (1991) (Germany); unemployment, Maddison (1991); current price GDP and current account balance, ONS Databank (UK) and JG, 1976–77 and 1996 (Germany).

Figure 7.4 Mean macroeconomic index for Germany and the UK

the early 1960s emerged unambiguously as the era closest to the ideal of macroeconomic balance. For all countries, the early 1960s emerged unambiguously as the era closest to the ideal of macroeconomic balance. Figure plots the mean or bilateral index that establishes 1962 as the base year for the sterling: DM estimates – significantly one of the few years when the West German current account was in deficit. The same method also identifies 1962 for the FF:DM and 1964 for the $US:DM estimates.

We calculated equilibrium time paths for three bilateral DM exchange rates: PPP rates with respect to sterling (1950–95), the US dollar and the French franc (from the base year to 1995); and, in addition, a productivity-modified PPP rate with respect to sterling (1950–95). Finally, we compared these calculated equilibrium rates with the actual (market) period average bilateral nominal exchange rates in order to measure year by year the extent by which the DM was over- or undervalued. The results are displayed in Figure 7.5. In both cases, the precise level of under/overvaluation in each year *is less important than the overall character and direction of movement in successive periods.*

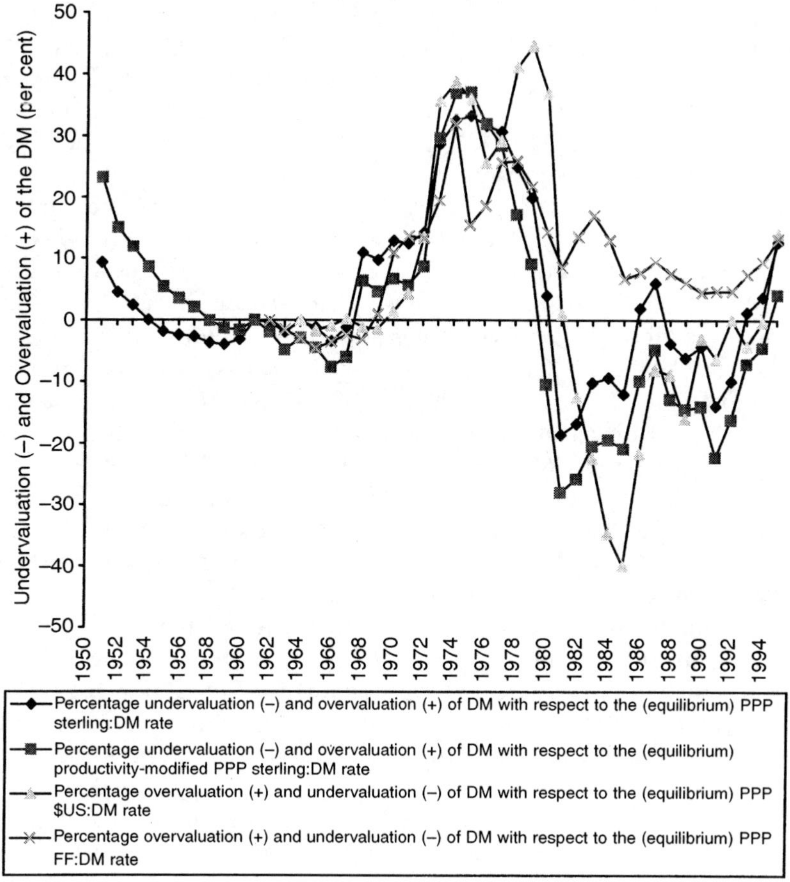

Sources: UK: Germany: CPI and period average (market) exchange rate, International Financial Statistics (IMF); productivity, for 1950–88, van Ark (1990) and, for 1989–95, Main Economic Indicators (OECD) and Labour Force Statistics (OECD) (1997). US: Germany and France: Germany: CPI series: Maddison (1991) and OECD, Main Economic Indicators (various issues); productivity (1960–88): van Ark (1990); productivity (1989–92): calculated from (a) manufacturing output: OECD, Main Economic Indicators (Various issues) and (b) employment in manufacturing and hours of work per week in manufacturing: International Labour Office, Year Book of Labour Statistics (various issues); market (nominal) exchange rate, annual average: Financial Statistics (CSO).

Figure 7.5 Percentage undervaluation (−) and overvaluation (+) of the DM against sterling (1951–95), the French franc (1962–95) and the US dollar (1964–95)

The four series in Figure 7.5 reveal similar patterns of DM under- and overvaluation. For the 1950s, we have only the evidence of the two sterling:DM series. However, there are two reasons for thinking that this bilateral series may be representative of the external value of the DM: first, bilateral rates move in much the same way as effective rates (Amitrano, de Grauwe and Tullio, 1997); and, secondly, from the 1960s, the evolution of the sterling:DM series is consistent with the USD:DM and FF:DM series. The two sterling:DM series suggest that the DM was overvalued in the early 1950s. However, in the presence of a fixed parity, low inflation and high productivity growth rapidly reduced and then reversed this overvaluation. Consequently, from the mid-1950s to the late 1960s, the DM was slightly but consistently undervalued. Again, lower inflation and/or higher productivity growth tended to increase German price competitiveness, while fixed exchange rates prevented an offsetting appreciation of the DM or depreciation of other currencies. Thus under the Bretton Woods system the DM was generally undervalued until, successively, sterling devalued (1967), the franc devalued (1968), and the US dollar floated (early 1970s). In the 1970s, floating exchange rates allowed Germany's inflation and productivity growth advantages to be more than offset by currency depreciation in the UK, US and France, causing the DM to be substantially overvalued with respect to their currencies.

The tightening of monetary policy at the turn of the decade, first in the UK and then in the US led to an appreciation of sterling and the US dollar sufficient to make the DM undervalued against both currencies. DM undervaluation against sterling reached its maximum in 1981, declined steadily until 1986, but then persisted as preparation for ERM entry and then actual membership precluded the UK government from offsetting the competitive effects of higher inflation with currency depreciation. Following exit from the ERM in 1992, DM undervaluation was reversed. By 1995, the DM was overvalued against sterling: by 13 per cent according to the PPP measure; and 4 per cent according to the productivity-modified measure.

In the case of the US dollar, speculation boosted its appreciation so that by 1985 the DM was 40 per cent undervalued. Most of this was reversed by 1987. The remaining undervaluation of the DM was eliminated by the aftermath of German reunification, with substantial overvaluation (14 per cent) appearing in 1995. In the case of the franc, from 1979 the Exchange Rate Mechanism (ERM) precluded higher French inflation being offset by overvaluation. From then on, and particularly with the onset of the 'strong franc' policy in 1983, the constraints of fixed exchange rates once again favoured relatively low-inflation Germany by reducing the overvaluation of the DM to less than 5 per cent during 1990–92. However, the

Table 7.1 Average percentage deviation of market rate from PPP rate (by period of under/over valuation)

	UK: Germany: PPP	UK Germany: Productivity-modified PPP	US: Germany PPP	France: Germany: PPP
1951–53	5.38	16.71		
1954–67 (US from 1964; France 1962)	–1.89	–0.85	–0.60	–2.63
1968–79	21.79	18.48	22.24	16.16
1980–92	–7.26	–16.92	–10.50	8.98
1980–95	–4.80	–14.22	–7.95	9.16

relaxing of ERM bands in 1993 allowed the DM to appreciate against the franc, steadily raising the degree of overvaluation from 7 per cent in 1993 to 13 per cent in 1995.[6] This overview of the evolution of the external value of the DM is summarized in Table 7.1.

Finally, we focus on the post-reunification changes in the value of the DM. Here, by the mid-1990s our results are indicative of a *tendency towards overvaluation*. We have analysed the three exchange rates that, respectively, determine the price competitiveness of German products with respect to its three major trading partners. In 1994, France accounted for 12 per cent of German exports and 11.1 per cent of imports, the UK for 8 per cent of exports and 6.2 per cent of imports, and the USA for 7.9 per cent of exports and 7.3 per cent of imports (JG, 1995, p. 64). In relation to these three economies, accounting for almost 30 per cent of total German exports and 25 per cent of total imports, we have found that in round terms the DM was overvalued by about 10 per cent (see Table 7.2).

Table 7.2 Changing value of the DM and its impact on German price competitiveness

	Over-/undervaluation of DM in relation to the £UK, $US and the FF (percentages); consequent changes in price competitiveness					
	Sterling (£UK)		Dolar ($US)		Franc (FF)	
	Productivity-modified PPP	PPP		PPP		PPP
1991	–22	–14	1989	–16	1990	+4
1995	+4	+13	1995	+14	1995	+13
Loss of price competitiveness	26	27		30		9

In assessing the competitive effect of DM overvaluation, we need to consider not only the extent of overvaluation but also the path by which the DM reached its value against the currencies of Germany's major trading partners. For the period since 1989 (the last complete year before Unification), Table 7.2 compares the maximum under- and overvaluation of the DM against the currencies of Germany's three major trading partners. Against sterling and the dollar, DM appreciation worsened the price competitiveness of German traded goods by about 25–30 per cent. In the case of the franc, the ERM constrained DM appreciation and loss of competitiveness to be only a third as extensive.

Figure 7.5 and Table 7.1 show that in the 1970s movements in the value of the DM were even more dramatic. However, we can surmise that loss of price competitiveness might be less tolerable now than in the 1970s. First, an increased number of rivals capable of supplying high-quality products has eroded quality differentials as a source of competitive advantage for German producers. Accordingly, as the offset of non-price competitiveness has declined so the loss of price competitiveness becomes more serious. Second, since the 1970s, outward foreign direct investment has increased the proportion of company earnings that are denominated in foreign currency and thus vulnerable to DM appreciation.[7] Against this background, the value of the DM must play a major part in any story about Germany's competitiveness. In the short run, overvaluation will not necessarily reduce Germany's trade surplus. This is because firms can defend market share by reducing profit margins (as in the mid-1990s; Barclays Economics Department, 1996, p. 9). In the long run, however, reduced profitability curtails investment which, in turn, undermines price and non-price competitiveness alike. Accordingly, long-term overvaluation is likely to intensify downward pressure on both wage and non-wage labour costs.

Summarizing, the *disaggregated* series of under/overvaluations in Figure 7.5 imply a remarkable run of good fortune as far as West German exports were concerned:

- By inference, the most important external factor for West German export success during the 1950s was the protection provided by the fixed exchange rate regime of the new Bretton Woods international monetary system. A fixed parity of DM 4.20 to the US dollar stimulated German exports for several years and at the same time it constrained foreign competition in domestic markets.
- During the 1960s, there was a period of normalization, when the German economy adjusted to international standards. A stable

exchange rate – fixed at DM 4 from 1961 – in combination with stability-orientated economic policies meant a steady improvement in German industry's international price competitiveness.

- Following another enforced revaluation of the DM in 1969, there was a general rise in protectionism in the form of non-tariff barriers during the 1970s. In 1974–75 and 1979–81, the world economy had to bear two severe recessions with rapidly rising unemployment rates. As the cause was the externally induced crude oil price shocks, import-competing firms demanded more protection on these grounds. Finally, the first half was unique (see above).
- Reaganomics stimulated German exports in the early 1980s. A mix of over-stimulative fiscal policies and tight monetary action drove up the dollar from a low of DM 1.72 in January 1980 to a peak of DM 3.31 in March 1985.
- By way of a happy coincidence for West Germany, the fall in her exports to the USA was compensated for by Europe's emergence from the slow growth of the 1970s and early 1980s. The increase in her exports to the then EC therefore immediately followed her success in the USA – despite France's fort FF policies.

III A four-phases stylization

III.1 Introductory remarks

At the first glance the stylization presented here might look like the exercise pursued by Giersch *et al.* (1992), but the difference lies in the detail. The exact punctuation and the characterization of the four phases of economic development are both different. A fifth phase can also now be added:

- The 'miracle' (*sic*): 1953–61
- 'Employment import' and capital export: 1962–68
- Transition to flexible exchange rates: 1969–73
- Within a tripolar world currency system: 1974–90
- The (under the circumstances) spectacular recovery of west Germany's exports after 1993

The spectacular rise in West Germany's trade in goods is illustrated in Figure 7.6.[8]

The secular improvement between 1950 and 1990 of export performance (as a percentage of GNP) can be immediately be seen. There were notable peaks at the time of the two crude oil price shocks in 1974 and 1981. Further peaks followed in 1985 and 1989. Expressed

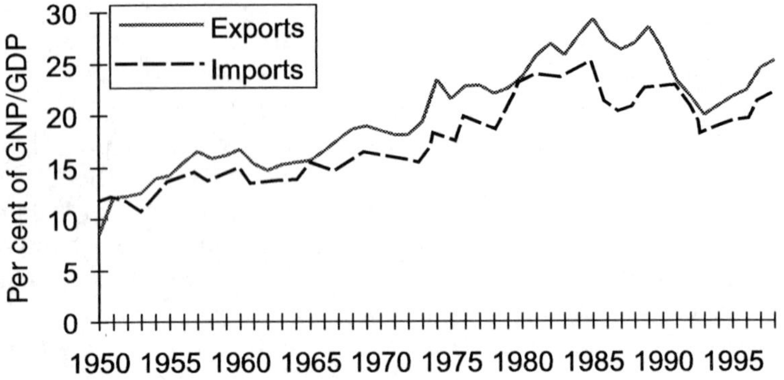

Figure 7.6 Growth of trade

in a different way, West Germany's export share in world trade over the same period (1950–90) rose from 3.5 per cent to 12.1 per cent, with two peaks of 12.9 and 12.6 per cent in 1973 and 1987 respectively. Moreover, from 1986 to 1990, with the exception of 1989, West Germany headed the international export league table, ahead of the US and Japan, with France and the UK in fourth and fifth position in 1990. It is equally important to note that West Germany's share of world imports consistently grew less than exports during 1951–90. In 1950, her share of imports was 4.6 per cent; by 1990 it was almost 10 per cent. Further, east Germany is included from 1991 in the data used in Figure 7.6, although exports and imports are now expressed as a percentage of GDP. Hence, the dramatic effect of GEMSU on the shares of visible exports and imports is illustrated in Figure 7.6. Crucially, the diversion of west German goods to east Germany was accompanied by a reduction in imports *as a percentage of GDP*. However, a recovery in both ratios took place after 1993. As a *percentage of world trade*, exports fell from 11.5 per cent in 1991 to 9 per cent in 1998, having initially staged a recovery after 1993. On the same basis, imports, having marginally increased in 1991, fell to 7.9 per cent in 1998.

What were the long-run effects on the current account of this export achievement? As already shown in Figures 7.1 and 7.2, the dominant role of the trade balance for much of the postwar period is immediately apparent. If the untypical years of 1949 (not shown in the figures), 1950 and 1951 are excluded, the trade balance has always been positive. However, a relatively small trade balance has resulted in West Germany's current account slipping occasionally into the red. But this happened only in 1962, 1965, 1979–81 and in the wholly different circumstances of

1991–98. Conversely, relatively large trade surpluses have produced correspondingly large current account surpluses. The second half of the 1980s are a particularly striking illustration of this factor – a part of *The Fading Miracle* in the terminology of Giersch *et al*. Indeed, the recovery in the trade balance after the 1980 record current account deficit soon led to steadily growing surpluses. The extent of the return to export-led growth during the 1980s should not be underestimated. At the beginning of the decade things looked very different:

> The world economy as a source of German vulnerability, as well as of strength, became apparent when the Federal Republic slipped within a matter of a few years from its usual position of export leader to that of export junkie and oil import addict. (Riemer, 1983, p. 4)

In 1991 about 50 per cent of employees were directly involved in export production. Export dependence, however, differs markedly among industries. The motorvehicle and machine-tool industries, which together account for more than one third of German exports, are especially dependent on world trade. Furthermore, the foreign direct investment by West German enterprises grew considerably in the 1980s, whereas foreign direct investors were generally less and less attracted to West Germany. In both 1990 and 1991 – when east Germany was attempting to attract foreign investment – net German foreign direct investment reached the record amount of over DM 25bn. Consequently, the stock of German overseas investment was DM 211bn in 1990; this was DM 71bn more than the stock of foreign investment in Germany. The USA was by far the largest host and donor country. Chemical, electrical and financial companies were the largest German direct investors overseas.[9] These few numbers show that Germany, on the one hand, has considerable effects on the world economy, while, on the other hand, foreign economic policy and growth linkages affect Germany.

The economy of East Germany was far less integrated into the international division of labour (Frowen, 1985). Her export ratio was about 22 per cent of GNP, while her world market share, including intra-German trade, was only 1.5 per cent. About half of her exports flowed to Western countries, the remainder to the other socialist countries in the east. In 1989, trade with the rest of the eastern bloc accounted for about 2 m of East German jobs. For a small industrialised country with only 16.4 m inhabitants this share was far smaller than in similar market economies such as, say, the Netherlands which had an export ratio of 58 per cent of GNP. East Germany's inferior position was in the main due to her borders being closed against the west and under specialization. Giersch *et al.* (1992, p. 259), for example, point out that the East German 'metal manufacturing industry' produced 65 per cent of the range of goods in this category in the world, whereas the much more specialized and bigger West Germany produced only 17 per cent of the range. This bias against a rational division of labour was partly the consequence of a deliberate policy aimed at almost full self-sufficiency in most products.

Quite clearly, then, the eastern part of postwar Germany has to emulate the more successful economy into which it has been incorporated. It will be an uphill struggle. More specifically, what were the conditions which led to the West Germany's superiority? An examination of the various phases in West Germany's international trade experience will afford a partial answer to this question. Of particular importance here are three widely debated issues. First, the future German competitiveness in the main export industries. Second, the related question of Germany's position in the global high-tech race. Third, the effects of German unification on international trade, although this is obviously a more recent strand in the debate. All three factors affect the German economy's potential to remain a leading exporter *and* international investor. They are well summarized by the German term for the debate (*Standort Deutschland*).

III.2 Phases in the development of trade

Following the war, the extent of the material damage done to the economy's productive potential was overestimated and there was still a substantially intact stock of human capital. A rapid expansion of trade was the best way for a country with a large population, dependent upon large imports of food after the war, and almost no natural resources to regain its position among the leading countries quickly. West Germany was soon in a position to take such a step. She therefore advocated a policy of trade liberalisation and took advantage of:

- the significant increase in world trade due to the Bretton Woods pegged exchange rate agreement of 1944,
- the successive GATT rounds after 1947 which led to worldwide tariff cuts, particularly for industrial products,
- (by implication) lower transport costs and improved telecommunications
- the beginning of European economic integration which removed custom barriers within Europe. (Bhagwati, 1988, pp. 1–9).

Economic development and integration into the world economy took place in West Germany with an unexpected dynamism. This self-reinforcing dynamism of real economic forces which led to the rapid recovery and reconstruction of West Germany was a result of a number of stimuli. Among these stimuli was the special situation in which West Germany found herself as the loser of the Second World War. Cost conditions were exceptionally favourable because of the very modest real wage demands of a highly motivated and productive labour force. Unions had probably underestimated the rate of improvement in productivity. Among other factors, this caused relatively moderate wage demands. It also meant that the scope of supply-side growth and the rapid reduction of unemployment were not diminished by extraordinarily high labour costs (Giersch *et al.*, 1992, p. 73). In other words, low social-policy costs and a very elastic supply of labour improved the situation still further by their productivity-enhancing effects. The shortage of capital due to the very limited capital market was overcome by high business profits favoured by tax concessions. These conditions led to low consumption and incentives to private-sector investors from abroad. The rapid growth of productive capacity with its increasing rate of utilisation during the reconstruction period improved the availability of goods and increased exports in the new economic world order with again new demand enhancing multiplier effects and incentives for further private investment. As a result of all these extremely favourable conditions, price inflation was low.

The most important external factor for the West German export success during the 1950s was the protection provided by the fixed exchange rate regime of the new Bretton Woods international monetary system. A fixed parity of DM 4.20 to the US dollar stimulated German exports for a number of years and at the same time it constrained foreign competition in domestic markets. Indeed, the most important factors for Germany's success on the export markets was this undervalued exchange rate, along with the relatively low average rate of price inflation in the 1950s. Other contributory factors were the Korean War – which enabled the strengthening German economy to fill gaps in international markets – the considerable restrictions on international capital transactions and the low level of foreign tourism until 1957–58. It resulted in export-led expansion above all in the capital-good industries:

> West Germany was transformed by a combination of good luck (high demand for capital goods) and policy (less inflation than abroad) into a country enjoying all the benefits of export-led growth. (Giersch *et al.*, 1992, p. 116)

In contrast, the other market economies had to face an accumulation of disadvantages in the postwar period. The victorious powers had to meet the cost of having financed the war mostly under existing market rules. They could not introduce a far-reaching currency reform, whereas West Germany largely eliminated the cost of financing the war in such a way. This laid a burden of considerable government debt on the other economies' shoulders. Another result of the war for the victorious European powers was a considerable debt to the USA which they had to settle under the fixed exchange rate system. Moreover, productive capacity which had been shifted largely to war production had to be reorganized for civil production. Where dismantling of obsolete plants in Germany took place, their reconstruction in the receiving countries as reparations did not enhance productivity as expected but only transferred obsolete technology. Much of the labour involved was thus tied up with work which did not achieve any innovative activity. Last not least, the victory over Germany had led the people of the other Western market economies to have unjustified expectations for the future which could only be disappointed during the phase of reconstruction. Economic growth in these countries was adversely affected by demands for too high real wage increases in comparison to productivity. Trends in costs and demand brought about a situation in which these countries required goods imported from Germany for their own reconstruction.

During the 1960s, there was a period of normalization, when the German economy adjusted to international standards. A stable exchange rate – fixed at DM 4 from 1961 – in combination with stability-orientated economic policies meant a steady improvement in German industry's international price competitiveness. The real undervaluation of the DM again fostered exports whereas imports did not grow in the same amount. This had two contradictory effects within the domestic economy:

- Persistent over employment and a strong influx of foreign labour which reduced the frictional costs of structural change and helped to maintain a fairly harmonious industrial climate; the labour force was reallocated to areas where the West German economy enjoyed long-term comparative advantages.
- Early structural change away from industry to the modern service sector was prevented; the effects were manifest as soon as prices and the exchange rate were adjusted (on the collapse of the Bretton Woods agreement), and the dynamics of European integration came to a temporary halt (Giersch *et al.*, 1992, pp. 126–39).

The increasing degree of undervaluation of the DM against the US dollar promoted exports without stimulating imports to the same extent. Such a situation was possible as long as the share of savings was high by international standards. This enabled the Bundesbank, in spite of the imbalance in the foreign trade sector, to achieve price stability. Because of the fixed exchange rate, however, an increasingly restrictive monetary policy was required to prevent the money supply being boosted by a growth in bank liquidity. External factors thus dominated policy making. Restrictive monetary policies were increasingly pursued due to threat of high current account surpluses being converted into DM bank balances. Even when the Bundesbank's tight credit policy caused the 1967 recession, a combination of Schiller's new approach to fiscal policy and an export boom brought about an economic recovery. Furthermore, the rapid integration into the world economy continued, although with a pronounced bias towards intra-European Community trade and heavy protectionism in agriculture and mining.

Several internal and external factors thus led to the persistent trade balance surpluses in Germany during the 1950s and 1960s. The internal factors in the embryonic economy were, firstly, a highly motivated, well qualified and plentiful supply of young, geographically and occupationally mobile labour. Secondly, the pragmatic approach to the SME in which Erhard played an important role. Erhard's policies stimulated corporate investment and labour productivity. External conditions also favoured German exports in the 1950s and 1960s. Stable exchange rates guaranteed by the Bretton Woods agreement favoured German international price competitiveness as much as the slower domestic cost increases due to the stability-orientated economic policies facilitated by a unique configuration of economic conditions. Tariff reductions, especially in industrial world trade, and the removal of customs barriers within Europe further enhanced the integration of world markets.

Writing in 1970, Frowen perceptively argued that the 1969 revaluation, like that of 1961, may well have strengthened West Germany's external position in the long run. The three years 1967–69 had been the most remarkable in West Germany's post-war balance of payments history (ibid.: p. 138): trade and current account surpluses, together with long-term capital account deficits – in contrast to 1962–66 when the visible trade surplus was insufficient to offset current account invisible items. Had it not been for the considerable long-term capital outflows, West Germany's current account surpluses would have been a much greater threat to the international monetary system (ibid.: p. 139; Owen Smith, 1994: p. 169). Trade surpluses, combined with the deflation of domestic demand, particularly in the monetary sphere, inevitably created hot money inflows in the anticipation of a revaluation (Frowen, 1970: pp. 138–40; Owen Smith 1994: pp. 122–23 and 193).

However, supply-side conditions deteriorated during the 1970s. With the collapse of the pegged exchange rate system, West German foreign trade was conducted in a more severe environment. Her ability to exploit an undervalued currency with revaluation potential was not as easy as during the 1960s and there was unrelenting upward pressure on the DM (Riemer, 1983, p. 99). Several other factors also undermined the international competitiveness of the German industry, above all a sharp rise in labour costs and two oil price hikes. Moreover, the tough monetary policy of the Bundesbank after the introduction of the floating exchange rate system prevented the unfavourable supply-side shocks from developing into accelerating price inflation. For West Germans the economic situation had deteriorated dramatically. The economy had stumbled into a severe recession and into a vicious circle of slow growth and high unemployment. In the short run, this scenario induced a lower level of aggregate demand and in the longer run a lack of investment. West Germany lost market shares to Japan, an economy which had become a new export power, particularly in the US market. In short, the competitive pressures from successful new exporters became more acute, especially as the high degree of the DM's undervaluation was removed. Foreign observers were not quite so pessimistic. West Germany stood out in comparative terms as an enclave of relative prosperity and stability (ibid., p. 41). With the exception of 1974 and 1975, GNRP grew at a respectable rate. Indeed, Riemer (ibid.: p. 99) referred to a 'the virtuous cycle of upward revaluation, enhanced stability and leeway for growth'.

The new successful exporters forced major traditional industries such as textiles, clothing, shipbuilding and iron and steel into further difficult adjustments due to an emerging new international division of labour. Newly industrializing countries, especially Hong Kong, Taiwan, Korea and Singapore possessed a comparative advantage in labour-intensive products as their labour unit costs are significantly lower. As a result, there was a partial rationalization of the West German industrial structure in accordance with the principle of comparative advantage, but there was also a partial revival of protectionism. Although GATT left little manoeuvre for international trade restrictions, a worldwide resurgence in protectionism followed the first oil crisis. Many governments and agents proved adept at building up non-tariff barriers such as technical and legal obstacles and import quotas to national markets. Like many other countries, West Germany simultaneously protected domestic industries by means of extensive subsidies. The clamour for protectionism consequently produced an elaborate response.

There were other reasons for the rise in protectionism. In 1974–75 and 1979–81, the world economy had to bear two severe recessions with rapidly rising unemployment rates. As the cause was the externally induced crude oil price shocks, import-competing firms also demanded more protection on these grounds. Furthermore, those economies which were able to register high growth rates during the 1950s and 1960s were unable to emulate their performance. It was decisively more difficult to overcome the steady structural changes of the economy without frictions. In other words, at growth rates of 1 or 2 per cent, employees displaced in the declining sectors had fewer alternative employment options than at a growth rate of 4 or 5 per cent. Accordingly, there was a higher demand for protection on these grounds, too. Finally, in addition to the support for traditional industries 'new industrial policy' and 'industrial targeting' came into vogue. Whether these latter policies promoted *Standort Deutschland* is a topic analysed elsewhere (Owen Smith, 1994, pp. 515–27). It can be concluded here that, in comparison to the 1950s and 1960s, protectionism during the 1970s damaged industry's flexibility. There was a consequent reduction in capital investment, employment and the pace of technological innovation. This catalogue of problems demonstrates the difficulties which faced Chancellor Schmidt when he was pressured to create the locomotive of international recovery.

Yet during the 1980s the West German trade surplus staged a dramatic recovery. In 1980 it had sunk in nominal terms to a level almost attained in 1966. Thereafter it increased 15-fold before it fell from a record high of DM 135 bn in 1989 to DM 92 bn in 1990. (If exports to East Germany before GEMSU are included, it increases the 1990 balance to DM 105 bn.) Some straightforward reasons for this impressive performance will be given shortly. Initially, however, it has to be regrettably indicated that there seems to be no clear-cut explanation of the economic and policy causes of this phenomenal recovery. The economic controversy is best summarized as follows. The early 1980s was a supply-led export expansion, that is deflationary policies in the domestic economy obliging manufacturers to seek markets abroad. Yet supply-side policies are designed to improve expectations and thus stimulate investment, rather than exports. The initial stimulus untypically came from the domestic economy. Export-led growth as a result of high export surpluses may have begun as late as 1986.

West Germany's export boom was, on the one hand, attributed to the real undervaluation of the DM which was in turn partially engineered by the distinctive role of institutional power and the intervention in the foreign-exchange markets by the Bundesbank. One possible result could be that the interests of the export sector were regarded as paramount by the Bundesbank and the DM exchange rate was kept deliberately low. Export-led growth would be the corollary. In addition, the real under-valuation of the DM was also due the refusal of other EMS countries to adjust the pegged exchange rates. In the run-up to a realignment, there were usually co-ordinating discussions between Bonn and Frankfurt to determine the German position. In these exchanges the Bundesbank was guided by the necessities of monetary stability. In order to avoid (destabilizing) speculative capital flows, the Bundesbank attached great importance to 'timely and silent' adjustments. In principle, the Federal Government supported this basic concept of the Bundesbank. But since France in particular considered a devaluation of its currency as a sign of weakness, the Federal Government sometimes had to weigh the economic against the political aspects of a realignment

On the other hand, others see the Bundesbank's currency policy as a balancing act between the longer-term requirements of low inflation and domestic monetary control with short-run pressing needs for co-ordinated exchange rate management and the promotion of internal demand growth.

But is there any evidence that the Bundesbank has been a party to boosting exports at the expense of domestic absorption? Such an employment policy came to be known as 'neomercantilist' (Riemer, 1983, p. 50). In a wider context, the maximisation of national wealth on the basis of persistently large and favourable trade balances which benefited exporters at the expense of overseas customers was known as 'mercantilism'. (Presumably the Bundesbank's accumulation of foreign exchange reserves are seen as the equivalent of the mercantilists' accumulation of gold.) In the later debate, the two terms were used interchangeably. It is true that there have been some periods when West Germany's monetary policy was guided by a *nominal* exchange rate target rather than by domestic price stability. Current account deficits in 1979–81 may also have contributed to the Bundesbank's deflationary policy. But its autonomy was in the main used to keep the domestic inflation rate almost always below the average of the other industrial countries. This endowed exporters with a competitive real exchange rate. It would require sufficient cynicism and access to unobtainable information to test whether this was a contrived or coincidental comparative advantage. Indeed, the orthodox view is that monetary policies favoured savers but were unfavourable to the immediate interests of West German industry.

For example, savers allied themselves with the SPD, the SVR and the Bundesbank in the revaluation controversy of 1969 – against the CDU and industry . More specifically, from the Bundesbank's point of view, the orientation of private banks and industrial clients toward exports is advantageous because it gives both sectors a stake in monetary stability. Low inflation rates keep German goods competitive.

There was, however, some policy concern about the system of concerted export promotion which dated from the 1950s, a system which was indeed dubbed 'neomercantilist' in the mid-1970s (Riemer, 1983, p. 50–51). As early as 1974, a robust free marketeer like Count Lambsdorff (FDP), at one stage the Federal Minister of Economics, expressed reservations about the export surpluses. He compared them to the winnings of a consistently successful card gambler during his days as a prisoner of war. Ultimately, the card games could only continue when this persistent winner had been robbed! Deficit countries would not permanently be content with their lot and, even if they were, they would eventually lose their creditworthiness. Hence, when West Germany's persistent current account surpluses led to deflationary tendencies in the deficit countries, West Germany was accused by the US and other EC countries of pursuing a beggar-my-neighbour policy at the cost of its trading partners. West Germany and Japan were urged in both the late 1970s and 1980s to act as 'locomotives' by the deficit countries. This illustrates one reaction to persistent trade surpluses. Yet the USA and the UK continued to run up sizable deficits. German unification disposed of the problem coincidentally in the sense that the current account surplus was dissipated and the demand for foreign goods increased. Relatively speaking, of course, current account deficits were still atypical and past export surpluses had made a fundamental contribution to West German affluence. It is equally instructive, moreover, to note that the post-unification boom, and therefore the accompanying import boom, were in turn dissipated by the Bundesbank's credit squeeze.

Unification changed Germany's external position almost overnight. Given the existing high rate of capital utilization in the west, it was only possible to meet the East's high demand for Western products from foreign sources. As the current account sank into deficit, the capital account oscillated in the opposite direction: capital outflows of DM 135 bn in 1989 had become an inflow of the same magnitude by 1992. West German firms increasingly sold their goods in east Germany, temporarily accepting cuts in their shares of foreign markets. Moreover, in 1990 and 1991 German imports rose by 10 and 16 per cent, respectively. Hence, as well as west Germany, other economies benefited from unification, although to differing degrees. Issing (1992, p. 4) estimates the benefit to European economies as equivalent to an average one-half percentage point increase in GNP in both 1990 and 1991. Germany thus performed a locomotive role in 1990 and 1991, a situation which changed abruptly in 1992 when German high real interest rates caused general deflation and currency speculation. The Bundesbank's high short-term interest rates thus contributed to the strength of the DM and, as a result, other economies, notably within the ERM, were also obliged to retain high rates – just as they were facing a major slowdown in growth (Chauffour *et al.*, 1992, p. 251). Two possible foreign-trade scenarios for the rest of the decade were put forward. From the German point of view, one scenario was optimistic, the other pessimistic. The optimists believed that the decline in German exports was only temporary. Others thought conflicts over income distribution were possible. Further problems like the slump in the world economy and the deterioration in the German age structure might lead to a further worsening of the current account – the latter due to dissaving by the elderly. It would now seem (Figure 7.6) that the decline was indeed temporary.

IV Conclusion

There is evidence supporting the contention that the undervalued DM was a basic feature of a growing West German economy. However, this growth model became inappropriate when the West German currency became a world 'key currency'. The impact of German unification in 1990 at least put a brake on this market constellation. At the turn of the century the transition from DM to Euro offers an historically unique opportunity for a change of monetary policy, but in Euroland as a whole. The scenario would be a somewhat overvalued Euro as the second world reserve currency, with some degree of stability towards the US dollar. This would make it easier for the eastern EU enlargement candidates to catch up with the West and would contribute to a world economy free from deflationary threats. Within Euroland (which is still not Europe) the pressure from the German economy could be a continuation of the undervaluation strategy, this time not by monetary policy, but by incomes policy. Wage moderation, in other words, *may* be an alternative beggar-thy-neighbour approach to economic policy (Owen Smith, 1999). On the other hand, the new constellation offers the opportunity to reinvent some form of socially acceptable market economy.

Notes

1. *W*est and *E*ast Germany refer to the separate German states prior to GEMSU (German Economic, Monetary and Social Union, 1 July 1990); *w*est and *e*ast Germany signify the two regions which emerged after GEMSU.
2. Note that the *quantitative* significance of the ERP (Marshall Aid) was insignificant (Ellwood, 1998, p. 33; Grünbacher and Hölscher, 1997, pp. 16–17; Knapp, 1997, p. 41; Owen Smith, 1994, p. 8; Schröder, 1990). Similarly, the draconian but crucial Currency Reform introduced by the Allies in 1948 could only succeed in stimulating dishoarding because by definition the *real* economy had been recovering and industrial bomb damage had been overestimated (Braun, 1990, p. 146; Nicholls, 1994, pp. 124–5; Owen Smith, 1994, pp. 6–7, 117–8).
3. Following the first two crude oil price shocks and, until 1992, the Bundesbank's record short-term interest rates, unemployment in the West. It may initially have been caused by demand factors but became 'structural' unemployment in the sense that the skills of the long-term unemployed become obsolete. Space does not permit an analytical digression on the complex causal factors. The Kiel view is critically examined in Owen Smith (1998b, pp. 154–9); but note that the Siemens plant in northeast England mentioned in this latter work has subsequently closed, thus undermining the cap-in-hand syndrome of British FDI policy (Owen Smith, 1999). Two years later, during a boom phase in market conditions, the mothballed plant was re-opened by the US microchip maker Amtel.
4. This is work in progress and draws upon previous joint work by Geoffrey Pugh and Grant Lewis. For a more formal statement of the methodology involved, see Lange and Pugh (1998, 170–74). Accordingly, while the method is consistent across the calculations, the data sets and periods considered differ. Work on the 1950s has so far been completed only for the sterling/DM relationship.
5. The indices are purely ordinal: the only meaning of the scale is to indicate lower (better) and higher (worse).
6. These are all *real* overvaluations: inflation rates are fully accounted for in the calculation of our equilibrium rates.
7. According to *The Economist* (11 Sept. 1993, p. 102), 'about a quarter of listed German companies' earnings are translated from dollars'.
8. Much of the following is an updated summary of the in-depth and fully referenced analysis in Owen Smith (1994, pp. 499–515).
9. See Owen Smith (1999) for a fuller comparative analysis of FDI.

Bibliography

Amitrano, A., De Grauwe, P. and Tullio, G. 'Why Has Inflation Remained So Low After the Large Exchange rate Depreciations of 1992?', *Journal of Common Market Studies*, 35/3 (Sept. 1997), 329–46.

Ark, Bart van. 'Comparative Levels of Manufacturing Productivity in Postwar Europe: Measurement and Comparison', *Oxford Bulletin of Economics and Statistics*, 52/4 (1990) 343–74.

Barclays Economics Department. *Barclays Country Report: Germany* (March 1996).

Beachill, Bob and Pugh, Geoff. 'Monetary Cooperation in Europe and the Problem of Differential Productivity Growth: an argument for a "two-speed" Europe,' *International Review of Applied Economics*, 12/3 (Sept. 1998) 445–57.

Belke, A. and Gros, D. 'EMU and EU Labour Markets: How Costly is Intra-European Exchange Rate Variability?', *IGS Discussion Papers*, No 99/13, Institute for German Studies (UK: The University of Birmingham 1999).

Bhagwati, J. *Protectionism* (Cambridge, MA: Harvard University Press, 1988).

Bhagwati, J. *The World Trading System at Risk* (Hemel Hempstead: Harvester Wheatsheaf, 1991).

Braun, H.-J. *The German Economy in the Twentieth Century* (London and New York: Routledge, 1990).

Chauffor, J.-P., Harasty, H. and Dem, J. Le. 'German Reunification and European Monetary Policy', in R. Barrell and J. Whitley, (eds), *Macroeconomic Policy Coordination in Europe: The ERM and Monetary Union* (London: SAGE Publications for the National Institute of Economic and Social Research, 1992).

De Grauwe, P. *International Money – Post-War Trends and Theories*. (Oxford: Oxford University Press, 1989).

Dresdner Bank, *Statistische Reihen* (Frankfurt, 1999).

Ellwood, D. (1998) '"You too can be like us": Selling the Marshall Plan', *History Today*, 48/2 (1998), 33–9.

Friedrich, H. and Wiedemeyer, M. *Arbeitslosigkeit – ein Dauerproblem im vereinten Deutschland? Dimensionen, Ursachen, Strategien* (Leske + Budrich, Opladen, 1992).

Frowen, S. F. (1970). 'The Unsolved Deutschmark Problem', *The Bankers' Magazine, 209* (1515), (March) pp. 137–43.

Frowen, S. F. 'The Economy of the German Democratic Republic', in Childs, David (ed). *Honecker's Germany*, London, Boston and Sydney: Allen and Unwin (1985) pp. 32–49.

Frowen, S. F. 'The Dimensions of German Economic Unification: Keynote Address', in S. F. Frowen and J. Hölscher (eds), *The German Currency Union of 1990 – A Critical Assessment* (London: Macmillan; New York: St Martin's Press, 1997, pp. 1–10.

Giersch, H., Paque, K.-H. and Schmiedling, H. *The Fading Miracle – Four decades of market economy in Germany* (Cambridge: Cambridge University Press, 1992).

Grünbacher, A. and Hölscher, J. 'From Aid to Development Finance: The German Example of Use', *IGS Discussion Papers*, No 97/17, Institute for German Studies, The University of Birmingham, UK, 1997.

Hölscher, J. *Entwicklungsmodell Westdeutschland – Aspekte der Akkumulation in der Geldwirtschaft* (Berlin: Duncker & Humbolt, 1994).

Hölscher, J. and Stephan, J. 'The German Model in Decline', in J. Hölscher and A. Hochberg, (eds), *East Germany's Economic Development since Unification – Domestic and Global Aspects*, Vol. 1 of series '*Studies in Economic Transition*', edited by J. Hölscher and H. Tomann, (London: Macmillan; New York: St Martin's Press, 1998).

Issing, O. 'The Impact of German Unification on the Members of the European Community', *Deutsche Bundesbank: Auszüge aus Presseartikeln*, 2, (1992) pp. 3–6.

JG – *Jahresgutachten* – full title: *Unterrichtung durch die Bundesregierung: Jahresgutachten 1991/92 des Sachverständigenrates zur Begutachtung der gesamtwirtschaftlichen Entwicklung* (Bonn: Deutscher Bundestag, 1976–77, 1992–93, 1993–94, 1994–95 and 1995–96).

Knapp, M. 'Vor 50 Jahren: Starthilfe für Europa durch den Marshall-Plan', *Deutschland*, 4 (1997) pp. 40–43.

Lange, T. and Pugh, G. *The Economics of German Unification – An Introduction* (Cheltenham: Edward Elgar, 1998).

Layard, R., Nickell, S. and Jackman, R. *Unemployment: Macro-economic Performance and the Labour Market* (Oxford: Oxford University Press, 1991).
Maddison, Angus. *Dynamic Forces in Capitalist Development* (Oxford: Oxford University Press, 1991).
Melitz, J. 'Monetary Discipline and Cooperation in the European Monetary System: A Synthesis', in: F. Giavazzi, S. Micossi and M. Miller (eds), *The European Monetary System* (Cambridge: Cambridge University Press, 1988).
MRDB (various): *Monthly Report of the Deutsche Bundesbank.*
Nicholls, A. J. *Freedom with Responsibility: The Social Market Economy in Germany 1918-1963*, (Oxford: Oxford University Press, 1994).
Owen Smith, E. *The German Economy* (London and New York: Routledge, 1994).
Owen Smith, E. (1998a) 'Economic Aspects of German Unification: Lessons for European Integration', in J. Hölscher and A. Hochberg (eds), *East Germany's Economic Development: Domestic and Global Aspects* (Macmillan, Basingstoke, 1998).
Owen Smith, E. (1998b) 'The Determinants of German Socioeconomic Policies', in J. R. Shackleton and T. Lange (eds) *The Political Economy of German Unification* (New York, Berghahn Books, 1998).
Owen Smith, E. (1998c): "Monetary policy in the UK and Germany under conditions of globalised money and capital markets; lessons for the personal sector and ethical considerations": Some comments', IGS *Discussion Papers*, No 98/15, Institute for German Studies, University of Birmingham.
Owen Smith, E. 'The British Third Way: some macro and microeconomic aspects', in Lothar Funk (Ed.), *The Economics and Politics of the Third Way, Essays in Honour of Eric Owen Smith*, VWL Schriftenreihe, Band 30, (Hamburg: Lit Verlag, 1999).
Richter, R. in Deutsche Bundesbank (ed.), *Fifty Years of the German Mark* (Oxford: Oxford University Press, 1998), pp. 525–71.
Riemer, J. M. *Crisis and Intervention in the West German Economy: A Political Analysis of Changes in the Policy Machinery During the 1960s and 1970s*, PhD thesis, Cornell University (Ann Arbor, Mi: 1983) University Microfilms International,.
Schröder, H.-J. (ed.), *Marshallplan und westdeutscher Wiederaufstieg* (Stuttgart: Franz Steiner Verlag, 1990).
Schuller, B.-J. 'Germany – the Paymaster of the EU and the OECD?', *IGS Discussion Papers*, No 98/16–17 (Institute for German Studies, University of Birmingham, 1998).

Comment

Jörg Bibow

The authors investigate West Germany's post war economic performance, the extent to which export performance may have been influenced by DM undervaluation, and what role the monetary policies of the Bundesbank played in this context. More precisely, the authors address the question whether West Germany's notorious trade surpluses over virtually the whole of the post war period may be indicative of a 'permanent mercantilist strategy of the Bundesbank to boost exports at the expense of domestic absorption', or whether these persistent external imbalances were due to real factors only. The hypothesis being put forward is that, 'the Bundesbank was fundamentally responsible for post war economic growth in West Germany', rather than simply securing low inflation, as conventional wisdom has it.

I take it to be a fact that export demand growth has been – and still is – of paramount importance to Germany's overall economic performance. Unfortunately, it is not at all an easy task to assess whether and to what extent Germany's strong export orientation and conspicuous trade surpluses were due to the external valuation of the Deutsche Mark. In particular, I think it is quite impossible to 'prove' that the Bundesbank deliberately orchestrated a beggar-thy-neighbour (mercantilist) strategy by persistently engineering a 'competitive', that is undervalued real exchange rate. For, as the authors frankly acknowledge, 'It would require sufficient cynicism and access to unobtainable information to test whether [DM undervaluation] was a contrived or coincidental comparative advantage'.[1] Nevertheless the authors stress that 'the notion that the Bundesbank in effect behaved in a "mercantilist" manner and German industry participated in the "neo-imperialist" dominance of world trade must explicitly and implicitly influence any meaningful analysis.' The possibility emerges here that, to some extent, we may be dealing with the 'unintended consequences' of certain actions rather than 'purposeful design'. An analysis of this possibility is fundamental to what follows.

The authors do a good job in distinguishing various phases in Germany's post war economic development, and I largely agree with their choice of timing. My observations will be more fundamentally Keynesian though, starting off from Keynes's (1936, p. 309) basic insight that, 'The long-run stability or instability of prices will depend on the strength of the upward trend of the wage-unit (or, more precisely, of the cost-unit) compared with the rate of increase in the efficiency of the productive system'. Of course, this is just the dynamic expression of the notion of the 'wage-unit' as the anchor of the price system in monetary production economies (rather than some monetary aggregate as quantity-theoretic beliefs would suggest (Scherf, 1996)).

The analysis begins with the early 1950s, the Bretton Woods era of fixed exchange rates being divided into three phases: the miracle (1953–61); employment import and capital export (1962–68); and transition to flexible exchange rates (1969–73). As to the miracle phase, it is somewhat astonishing to see that, contrary to conventional wisdom, the authors' index of DM under-/overvaluation shows a slight DM undervaluation as emerging in the late 1950s only. Yet, whether or not the Deutsche Mark actually started out at a significantly undervalued rate after 1952 may be of secondary importance, as the prime force of the German export miracle is, in my view, due to another factor, namely *relative* wage moderation. The authors point out that the miracle phase saw 'very modest real wage demands of a highly motivated and productive labour force', and they suggest that 'unions had probably underestimated the rate of improvement in productivity'.

The point is, however, that a strategy of wage moderation *relative* to external competitors stimulates both export demand and domestic capital accumulation as well, through raising profitability of home production and investment. In turn, a high rate of investment together with labour market slack make for strong productivity growth, which provides scope for a rising wage-unit without cost pressures emerging at the domestic front – the process becomes cumulative.

More remarkably, the virtuous circle was quite successfully sustained throughout the second phase lasting until the late 1960s, partly through feeding on itself (as economic growth proved conducive to satisfying growing aspirations and preserving social consensus; with real wages, in fact, rising rather strongly throughout the 1950s and 1960s), and partly through 'labour import', that is, migration from East Germany and foreign-labour influx. By contrast, the notion of 'capital export' seems rather misleading when current account surpluses are largely mirrored by the central bank's accumulation of foreign reserves while domestic capital accumulation is stronger than almost anywhere else in the world. Most importantly, the Bundesbank's role in this period was *not* to conduct monetary policy and control inflation.[2] Monetary policy was conducted by the US Fed, while the Bundesbank's part was to keep the Deutsche

Mark at its agreed US dollar parity. Price stability in Germany was secured by keeping the trend of the wage-unit roughly in line with the rate of increase in the efficiency of the productive system – *relative* wage moderation, moreover, with far-reaching unintended (?) consequences.

The fact that the Bundesbank was not in charge of price stability became quite apparent in the third phase, the transition to flexible exchange rates (1969–73). A 'climate change' had occurred at the end of the 1960s, and by the early 1970s wage growth accelerated dramatically; and so did inflation (Scherf, 1986). Yet, there was little the Bundesbank could do about it when, on the one hand, the US was pursuing her Vietnam crusade and, on the other hand, interest rate increases would have even accentuated upward pressures on the Deutsche Mark. The Bretton Woods game was up, and the Bundesbank pulled the final shot in 1973. Only from now on the Bundesbank was genuinely in charge of German (later: European) monetary policy, the Bundesbank era began in March 1973.

In my view, the authors' fourth phase 'Within a tripolar world currency system' (1974–90) should better be split up into two, with the first (i.e. fourth) phase lasting until 1980. In fact, it is on her unique (pace the Swiss National Bank) record in the mid-seventies that the Bundesbank's claim to fame as the world's number one inflation fighter must rest. For a severe monetary tightening immediately followed the demise of Bretton Woods, that is, even before the first OPEC oil price hike hit. The fourth phase of 'disinflation in an inflationary world' is also the period in which we saw the most drastic DM overvaluation, and relatively weaker growth stimuli from export demand (the concurrent *rise* in West German trade surpluses being largely a reflection of divergent macroeconomic policies which, inevitably, gave rise to international calls for a German 'locomotive' strategy in due course). With continued expansion abroad, industry responded to DM appreciation through cutting costs, that is jobs. West Germany's virtuous circle was broken, as investment plummeted while unemployment soared and persisted. At the end of the 1970s the second OPEC oil price hike made matters still worse. This time though disinflation was a concerted effort, with policies diverging only afterwards.

It was through these divergent *post*-disinflation policies in the early 1980s that the former pattern of DM undervaluation and export-led growth was being restored during the fifth phase of 'relative wage moderation cum domestic demand restriction'. As the authors point out, US expansion and dollar strength provided an important export stimulus during the first half of the eighties, being replaced during the second half by another export stimulus arising through a real depreciation of the Deutsche Mark within the stable nominal exchange rates of the ERM. Relative wage moderation provided the background, as German wage and productivity trends were in line with price stability in Germany while partner countries used the ERM as external anchor to disinflate from significantly higher wage trends. By contrast, from the early 1980s fiscal and monetary policies were kept on hold in West Germany, stabilising domestic demand at a level significantly below capacity production – with stagnating investment (capital shortage) and high unemployment (labour surplus) being the predictable consequences. The inappropriate macro policy stance only shifted towards the end of the decade, with both income tax reforms and the cautious monetary response to the stock market crash accentuating export demand-led growth. The strong investment and employment growth – at price stability and improving public finances! – seen at that time put paid to the popular 'structural' myth.

Yet, the benign scenario did not last, the situation changed dramatically in 1991. Importantly, the pending cataclysm was not so much due to unification itself, but largely to the deflationary policies that the authorities felt adequate to pursue in response (Bibow, 1998a). Export growth had weakened markedly in 1990, with the US and UK slipping into recession and stagnation in the rest of Europe. Unification thus provided a welcome consumption boost to West-Germany and its neighbours. But in 1992 fiscal policy embarked on a fateful – Maastricht inspired – deflationary crusade, while the Bundesbank had pre-emptively *hiked* interest rates in 1991; pushed up to levels which were going to break the ERM and plunge Europe into the land slide recession of 1993. The authors refer to the 'spectacular recovery of west Germany's exports after 1993'. Yet, given the strong recovery in world growth, this was not so spectacular if not for the sensational appreciation and over-valuation of the Deutsche Mark seen until 1995. One thing had to give – jobs. Roughly 1.5m jobs were wiped out during the 1990s deflationary binge in western Germany alone. And with convergence of wage and price 'inflation' in Euroland, the historical German strategy to export demand-led growth has finally ceased its effectiveness. Euroland as a whole has no-long term alternative but to generate its own *domestic* demand-led growth.

In their conclusion the authors hint at the possibility of wage moderation as an alternative beggar-thy-neighbour approach to economic policy. German experience shows that this is not an altogether new scenario, whether intended or not. Furthermore, Dutch experience since 1982 (Wassenaar Aecord) proves that it is possible to underbid the

German wage trend, whether intended or not. The point is that with inflation practically non-existent, competitive *deflation*, rather than competitive disinflation, may (have) become the new game in town. *Falling* unit-labour costs in Germany may be heralding troubles to come. Certainly the fact that Euroland's policymakers still prefer to free-ride on US growth and recovery in the rest of the world rather than generating *domestic* demand-led growth is most worrying (Bibow, 1986 and 2001).

The authors' challenging hypothesis and intriguing analysis represent a valuable contribution to the much needed de-mystification of the Bundesbank's role in Germany's post war economic performance, in particular; and to the de-bunking of German monetary mythology more generally too. The authors do a good job – but do not nearly go far enough.

Notes

1. However, Holtfrerich (1998) would seem to provide some evidence in support of this thesis as regards the situation in the 1950s, in response to the crisis of 1952 and, interestingly, partly motivated by external pressures. Of course, there is also the possibility of path dependency in the sense that policymakers subconsciously develop certain attitudes in the light of successful experiences.
2. Riese (1989, p. 110) refers to the 'myth' that the Bundesbank paid particular attention to price stability in the Bretton Woods era, pointing out a 'dilemma' in a monetary policy which tries to combine a hard currency strategy with persistent undervaluation.

Bibliography

Bibow, J. 'Geldpolitik als Inflationsursache?', in B. P. Priddat and A. Vilks (eds), *Wirtschaftstheorie und Wirtschaftswirklichkeit* (Marburg: Metropolis, 1998a).

Bibow, J. 'The new independent monetary policymaker and European unemployment or, how little should we expect from the ECB?' Paper presented at the workshop European Employment and the Single European Currency at the Wissenschaftszentrum Berlin; November 1998b.

Holtfrerich, C.-L. 'Geldpolitik bei festen Wechselkursen (1948–1970)', in Deutsche Bundesbank (ed.) *Fünfzig Jahre Deutsche Mark* (Munich, C. H. Beck, 1998), pp. 347–438.

Bibow, J. Making EMU work: some lessons from the 1990s, *International Review of Applied Economics* 15 (2001) July.

Keynes, J. M. *The General Theory of Employment, Interest and Money* (London: Macmillan, 1936).

Riese, H. 'Geldpolitik bei Preisniveaustabilität', in Ramser and H. Riese (eds), *Beiträge zur angewandten Wirtschaftsforschung* (Berlin: Springer Verlag, 1989).

Scherf, H. *Enttäuschte Hoffnungen – vergebene Chancen* (Göttingen: Vandenhoeck und Ruprecht, 1986).

Scherf, H. 'Eine Rükbesinnung auf Keynes ist dringend erforderlich', *Wirtschaftsdienst,* 5 (1996) 227–9.

8
The Fate of Key Currencies: a Strategic Approach

Stephen F. Frowen and Elias Karakitsos

Introduction

Perhaps, the least understood area of macroeconomics is the exchange rate determination. The fluctuations and trends of the major currencies – US dollar, Deutsche Mark, pound sterling and yen – experienced in the last 15 years, and since January 1999 by the euro, are hardly compatible with the main exchange rate theories. A particular determinant, say, short-term interest differentials, yield differentials, relative current account balances, money supply differentials or relative prices of goods, is generally failing to explain systematic movements in the key currencies. This failure is exemplified in models with time-varying coefficients, where a particular determinant is totally unstable. Its influence over time changes from being extremely important, compatible with the underlying theory (correct sign), to unimportant over another period and even with the wrong sign over previous periods. The general verdict among theoreticians and practitioners is that we do not know what drives currencies.

Despite the failure of the main theories to explain the observed patterns of exchange rates, we believe that their pillars and major predictions are essentially correct. The instability of determinants reflects volatile expectations rather than rejection of the main principles of the exchange rate theory. The main theories have not paid enough attention as to how expectations in the foreign exchange market are formed. In some cases the theory says nothing on how expectations are arrived at and it is left to the modeller to decide on the mechanism. In other cases the theory postulates rational expectations (or simply perfect foresight).

In this chapter we suggest that the way expectations be formed on the basis of an explicit modelling of the game pursued by the policy makers.

This strategic approach to expectations provides us with an account of the reversals in the sign and importance of the main exchange rate determinants without necessitating the rejection of the standard exchange rate theory. The exchange rate model is built on the familiar theory that the exchange rate is determined instantaneously in the assets markets under imperfect substitutability, whereas the current account determines its dynamics (see, for example, Dornbusch and Fischer, 1980).

The basic tenet is that the source of instability in the exchange rate determinants stems from the currency risk that influences the relative attractiveness of domestic to foreign assets. The currency risk is determined by the investor perceptions of the policy game among the three major areas – Europe, Japan and US. In this framework the observed instability stems from a number of factors. The first is the nature of the game. Are policy makers pursuing their objectives in a co-operative or non-co-operative manner? Do the players have the same power or does the US dominate, at least over some periods? In other words, is the assumed equilibrium Nash or Stackelberg? If the US is the leader, does it always choose the Stackelberg-leader equilibrium or does it, on occasions, prefer the follower equilibrium (after you, Alphonse)?

Some of these issues are decided by the state of each economic region in the business cycle. The extent of business cycle synchronization is therefore the second determinant of instability. If the business cycles are synchronized then the objectives of the three main players are more likely to be in conflict. For example, the pursuit of price stability when all economic regions are overheated – as was the case of West Germany during a great part of the postwar period – may require an exchange rate appreciation, but this is impossible for all three currencies. Thus, whether an interest rates hike, say, by the US would lead to a dollar appreciation would depend on the equilibrium being Nash or Stackelberg. Such choices by the policy makers, which are clearly influenced by the position of each economic region in the business cycle, can account for the correct or perverse sign of the short-term interest rate differential.

The third source of instability arises from the exact specification of the policy makers' objective function when all economies are growing at the rate of potential output – in other words when the business cycle is not an important factor. Some policy makers would assign a greater importance to, say, price stability than others would. For example, the ECB, following into the footsteps of the Deutsche Bundesbank, is more likely to be a worse anti-inflation hawk than the Fed. Japan may be the only country that is explicitly targeting its current account because of the trade frictions with the US.

The fourth source of instability arises from the time-varying priorities of the policy makers in the course of the business cycle. Thus, irrespective of the priorities the policy makers attach to the targets of economic policy at the rate of growth of potential output, they are bound to vary them in the course of the business cycle. In this framework some systematic patterns can be established. For example, every central bank would tighten monetary policy when the economy becomes overheated and would continue to hike rates until inflation is beaten. Similarly, every central bank would lower rates once inflation has peaked and would carry on trimming rates even in the recovery phase as inflation is falling.

To take account of these influences on the currencies we suggest an explicit formulation of the policy game within a stock-flow general equilibrium model of the exchange rate. This is taken up in the final section of the paper. The background and relative role of the Deutsche Mark and now the euro are explained first.

8.2 The German mark and the euro

The emergence of the Deutsche Mark

The Deutsche Mark has been Western Europe's youngest currency with a lifespan of just half a century. The Euro replaced it in January 1999. Created by the Western Allies in collaboration with German monetary experts, the Deutsche Mark took the place of the discredited Reichsmark on 20 June 1948. It is indeed fascinating to follow the Deutsche Mark's ascendancy from a newly created currency to one of the world's leading international currency, second only to the US dollar. One often hears references to the German economic miracle, the German *Wirtschaftswunder*, but with regard to the Deutsche Mark, it would be more appropriate to speak of a *Währungswunder*. And yet, the success of the Deutsche Mark, with all its ups and downs, can easily be explained in rational terms

The cradle of the Deutsche Mark was the Fritz-Erler-Kaserne in Rothwesten near Kassel, where eleven German financial experts met in a conclave from 21 April until 8 June 1948 under the chairmanship of the American officer Edward Tennenbaum. A leading member of the German team was the monetary economist Otto Pfleiderer, subsequently one of Norbert Kloten's predecessors as President of the Land Central Bank in Baden-Württemberg, Stuttgart. Pfleiderer later described Tennenbaum as the father of the Deutsche Mark. It was on the basis of the so-called Colm-Dodge-Goldsmith Plan that these experts in collaboration with representatives of the American, British and French Military Governments prepared the three *Laws for the Reorganisation of the German Monetary System* and a whole range of guiding principles (see Deutsche Bundesbank, 1999).

It is remarkable that as early as ten years after its introduction, the DM had become one of the first European currencies, together with the Swiss franc, to be made fully convertible, not only externally but for residents as well. By the 1980s the DM's role as a leading investment and reserve currency had become undisputed. In Europe it subsequently became the key and anchor currency within the European Monetary System (EMS).

It was as a result of a severe quantitative restriction that, after the emergence of initial economic problems in 1950–51, the DM soon became and remained a very strong currency despite the fact that it started as a paper currency without reserves and certainly without any international reputation. It was no doubt the combination of the wise and farsighted economic policy of Ludwig Erhard, the first post-Currency-Reform Minister of Economics and later Chancellor of the Federal Republic of Germany, plus the constructive policy of West Germany's independent central banking system, which achieved the amazing rapidity of German economic recovery.

However, this widely accepted judgement certainly had its critics, especially among some of Germany's post-Keynesian economists (see Riese, 1984 and 2000, Hölscher, 1994, and Luken-Klassen and Hölscher (1990). Jens Hölscher argues that thanks to a continuous undervaluation of the DM, West Germany achieved a self-sustaining economic expansion. This expansion was due not only to its export competitiveness, but also, so it is claimed, to the consequences of the then prevailing monetary policy of the Bundesbank. By ruling out devaluation, the acceptability of DM assets was enhanced and permitted a stable evaluation of investment opportunities (see Hölscher, Owen Smith and Pugh, 2001).

For the central bank one of the main problems was how to sterilize the effect of the inflow of money resulting from persistent export surpluses and capital inflows. This problem was a foremost one for the Deutsche Bundesbank throughout the 1960s, as the DM for most of the time remained undervalued despite its revaluation of 1961. Thus, Hölscher, Owen Smith and Pugh explain the so-called German economic miracle by the undervaluation of the Deutsche Mark, which precariously they present as a deliberate Bundesbank policy.

It would probably be more correct to ascribe the German economic miracle as being initially due more to the ingenious combination of the well designed currency reform of 1948 and the immediate abolishment of all rationing and price controls. This was Ludwig Erhard's decisive contribution to the economic recovery of West Germany. The undervaluation of the DM then ensured a persistently high level of exports and with it high economic growth rates.

Erhard's policy was assisted throughout the 1950s by a restrictive monetary policy aimed principally at controlling consumption. Thus, the export surpluses became the main motor of non-inflationary economic growth. However, the restrictive monetary policy aiming at price stability was bound, under the prevailing fixed exchange rate system, which lasted until the breakdown of the Bretton Woods System in 1973, to result in an undervaluation of the DM. It is indeed the latter, which contributed to the strong economic expansion of West Germany until 1973. Nevertheless, it is unlikely that there would have been an undervaluation of the DM in the first place had the 1953 London Debt Agreement negotiated by Hermann Abs not been a contributory factor, regardless of the Erhard reforms, which lead to the 1950–51 payments crisis.

The British Government at the time of the creation of the DM in 1948, being dominated more by Keynesian thinking, saw the greatest danger in a possible Europe-wide inflation and would have preferred West Germany to follow the British example of an adjustment inflation, eliminating suppressed inflation through a gradual increase in the price level. But the magnitude of the German suppressed inflation was such that it would have been virtually impossible to follow the British example. In retrospect, the decision to simply replace the Reichsmark by a new currency adjusted in quantity to the production protential was certainly right.

The German currency reform and its aftermath

By 1948 the introduction of a new currency was widely expected in West Germany, and yet when the great day came, it was a surprise. Of course, businesses had been storing goods they had been unwilling to sell for a valueless currency, the Reichsmark. It seemed like a miracle when on the day of the introduction of the Deutsche Mark hitherto virtually empty shop windows were filled with goods, the public had not seen since almost pre-war days, with shopkeepers only too anxious to sell against the precious new currency. The currency reform also wiped out most of Germany's national debt, which had reached phenomenal proportions. Thus, West Germany had the chance of making an entirely new start, unburdened by colossal war debts.

Britain, the victor, was not in so advantageous a position. True, a currency reform for the UK on the lines of those in other West European countries was not a necessity as it certainly had been for Germany. But more important, Britain had to honour her debt *vis-à-vis* Commonwealth countries. The accumulated sterling balances held by them could not simply be written off. The way Britain actually handled the immediate postwar years, burdened with a considerable national debt and huge overseas sterling balances, and being faced with the task to eliminate the wartime suppressed inflation, is truly remarkable. The ups and downs of the UK economy and the damaging stop-go policies in later years by successive UK governments are a different story.

West Germany had another advantage in the form of an independent central banking system, created in conjunction with the DM by the Allies at the time of the 1948 currency reform. This was a system of Land Central Banks with the Bank deutscher Länder, the forerunner of the Deutsche Bundesbank, as its central organization. The legally monostructured Deutsche Bundesbank itself came into being by the Act of the Deutsche Bundesbank of 1957. Thus, from day one of the introduction of the DM, German monetary policy was conducted consistently by a central bank totally independent of political influences and aiming solely at maintaining the stability of the DM. In fact, the 1957 Bundesbank Law imposed this objective as its principal mandate upon the Bundesbank.

At that time it seemed unlikely that the DM would, in a short period of time, gain the status of one of the world's leading international and reserve currencies. And yet the chief mandate of the Bundesbank remained directed towards maintaining internal price stability without much of a concession to either other internal macroeconomic objectives such as full employment and growth, or to the external responsibilities subsequently arising from the DM position as an international trading and reserve currency and widely expected of Germany. But to be fair it must be admitted that the Bundesbank did at times of crises frequently adopt a more pragmatic approach even at the price of not meeting its money supply target. The 1992 crisis of the European Exchange Rate Mechanism (ERM) clearly demonstrated some of the inherent conflicts (see Frowen, 2000).

Until the late 1960s sterling still counted, together with the US dollar, as the world's major international currency for private transactions, as a medium of exchange, as a unit of account and as a store of value, with the Deutsche Mark, the Swiss and French francs and the yen playing a minor role. Official transactions were dominated by the US dollar, gold, the IMF reserve positions and SDRs, with sterling taking second place. However, West Germany, having emerged as a major capital exporter arising from her impressive trade surpluses, soon saw the DM being placed ahead of sterling as an international currency for both private and official transactions. While not replacing the supremacy of the dollar, the DM now ranked second only to the dollar.

It is obvious that the way the Bundesbank has been able to use her independence in conducting monetary policy, achieving her aim of relative price stability and an average inflation rate well below those of competing countries, including the UK, has much to do with Germany's external surpluses and the international reputation of the DM. Even the oil price shocks of the 1970s did not for long interrupt the achievement of visible trade surpluses, which again rose persistently and quite dramatically until the German reunification of 1990. But even this greater shock to the West German economy did not wipe out the trade surpluses for long – even taking the reunited Germany as a whole. They again began to rise almost continuously from a low in 1991 to new post-reunification record levels in the late 1990s. Neither did the reunification weaken the DM's position as an international investment and reserve currency (see König and Willeke, 1998). The foremost external position of the DM was maintained thanks to the Bundesbank's credible and consistent policy towards monetary stability.

The Deutsche Mark as a reserve currency

Since the end of the Bretton Woods system in 1973, the DM had become the world's second most important reserve currency – after the US dollar, accounting for 15.3 per cent of total world reserves.[1] In fact, the international role of the DM started with its role as a reserve currency. By the beginning of the 1970s, the DM had replaced the pound sterling in that capacity. This was long before the DM became the anchor currency in the ERM and a leading investment currency.

Not surprisingly, the industrial countries were the major holders of foreign exchange reserves in DMs, holding just under three-fifth of the total, while oil exporting countries' DM reserves declined from a high of 30 per cent in 1970 to only 2.5 per cent in 1994; non-oil developing countries held their share of DM reserves fairly stable, fluctuating between 25 and 30 per cent.

The role of the euro

It is too soon to predict the future of the euro, which has now replaced the DM together with the other national currencies of Eurozone members. There are many difficulties ahead of the Eurozone with some member countries suffering from a lack of sustained convergence having been admitted initially. Yet, once the political decision had been taken, every effort should now concentrate on making the euro as much of a success as is possible under present conditions. The alternative would be utter chaos.

The European Central Bank (ECB) has been modelled on the Deutsche Bundesbank. Thus, price stability has by necessity and in accordance with the Maastricht Treaty (Article 105) been given overriding priority. Although this should help the euro to gain credibility, it would be too much to hope that the Bundesbank's credibility, worked-for hard and enjoyed for so long, will simply be transferred to the ECB. However, the approach to the ECB's monetary policy may have to be more pragmatic than the one the Bundesbank used to pursue.

According to the Governing Council of the ECB, the Eurosystem's stability-oriented monetary policy strategy for medium-term price stability consists of 'a quantitative definition of the primary objective of monetary policy [i.e. price stability] and "two pillars" that are used to assess risks to future price stability, namely a prominent role for money and a broadly based assessment that encompasses a wide range of indicator variables' (Issing, 2000, p. 4, Issing *et al.*, 2001, and Frowen, 2001, pp. 27–8). This is a novel approach that quite rightly avoids following into the footsteps of the more rigid Bundesbank strategy. This switch away from a total concentration on money supply control towards some kind of inflation targeting makes sense as it would have been precarious for simply applying Bundesbank policy to the ECB. The Eurozone obviously requires a more flexible approach. To achieve a key currency status, the Eurosystem's policy will also have to assist the Eurozone achieving an external creditor position through current account surpluses.

The alternatives for the euro have often been stated as either a strong euro or more unemployment, or a weaker euro as a way to, if not full employment, at least high employment levels. Thus, the ECB's policy makers with around 35 million unemployed in the Eurozone are indeed confronted with considerable ethical issues. There is at least a danger that the ECB may not in the end prove to be as independent as the Deutsche Bundesbank because of possible political pressures arising, and therefore the temptation to give in to the alternative of a weaker euro. However, the current phase of monetary tightening from the end of 1999 by a total of 225 basis points makes such accusations unfounded.

The Bundesbank's view and conviction that monetary stability is a vital prerequisite to achieve sustained growth and a high level of employment *in the long run* has been given strong support by the success of Bundesbank policies in this respect throughout the greater part of the postwar era. The question is whether in view of the severe structural unemployment, the German model can be applied successfully on a Europe-wide basis. The previous situation of West Germany being the main supplier of goods for the rest of Europe and the world at large, especially with capital and durable consumer goods, and helped by her competitive advantage, was quite different.

In Part II we present a model that attempts to explain the role of the euro (or the Deutsche Mark) on the lines discussed above, especially in relation to the US dollar.[2]

8.3 The policy-choice model

For the sake of simplicity only one currency is considered and therefore the policy choices of the two countries involved need to be explicitly modelled. It is assumed that each policy maker optimizes an objective function that is penalizing deviations of inflation from each target and deviations of growth from its target. That is, for each country *i* the utility function *U* is specified as follows:

$$U_i = \frac{1}{2}[q_{ip}(p_i - \bar{p}_i)^2 + q_{iy}(y_i - \bar{y}_i)^2] \tag{1}$$

where q_{ip} is the penalty weight that the policy makers in country $i = 1, 2$ are attaching to inflation, and q_{iy} is the penalty weight on growth. Country 1 is the US and country 2 is Europe or Germany before EMU. The bliss point is taken as the rate of growth of potential output and as inflation the rate that corresponds to potential output, i.e.

$$(\bar{p}_i, \bar{y}_i)$$

The US central bank is assumed to be balanced in its pursuit of monetary policy between the two conflicting targets of inflation and growth. On the other hand, the European Central Bank or its predecessor, the Deutsche Bundesbank, is assumed to be an anti-inflation hawk. This implies that while for the US it is assumed that $q_{1p} = q_{1y}$, for Europe it is assumed that $q_{2p} > q_{2y}$.

Each policy maker, in this case the central bank, optimizes its own objective function subject to the economic model that defines the feasible combinations of inflation and growth, given the choice of the monetary policy instrument. The model allows for the spillover effects of monetary policy from one country to the other. For the US the model is assumed to take the following form:

$$\Delta p_1 = p_1 - \bar{p}_1 = \alpha_1 \Delta y_i + \beta_1(\Delta r_2 - \Delta r_1) + \beta_1 \Delta pm \tag{2}$$

$$\Delta y_1 = y_1 - \bar{y}_1 = \lambda_1 \Delta r_1 + \mu_1 \Delta r_2 \tag{3}$$

For Europe the model is similarly defined as:

$$\Delta p_2 = p_2 - \bar{p}_2 = \alpha_2 \Delta y_2 + \beta_2(\Delta r_1 - \Delta r_2) + \beta_2 \Delta pm \tag{4}$$

$$\Delta y_2 = y_2 - \bar{y}_2 = \lambda_2 \Delta r_2 + \mu_2 \Delta r_1 \tag{5}$$

Where y_i is the growth rate; p_i is the inflation rate; r_i is the short-term interest rate, which is the instrument of monetary policy; *pm* is the price of imported raw materials (e.g. oil) expressed in foreign currency.

Growth in each country is affected by the monetary policy of the two countries, while inflation depends on the output gap and imported inflation. The latter is influenced by monetary policy as a rise in the domestic interest rate appreciates the domestic currency and depreciates the foreign currency.

In each model the following restrictions apply:

$$\alpha_i > 0, \beta_i > 0, \lambda_i < 0, \mu_i < 0, |\mu_1| < |\mu_2|, \ |\lambda_i| > |\mu_i| \tag{6}$$

The coefficient β measures the degree of supply-side openness and it is assumed that Europe is more open than the US, i.e. $\beta_2 > \beta_1$. The last inequality in (6) implies that domestic monetary policy has a bigger effect on domestic growth than the foreign one. Moreover, the penultimate inequality in (6) implies that the spillover effect of US monetary policy on Europe is bigger than the spillover effect of Europe on the US. Thus Europe is both more susceptible to imported inflation and it is also more vulnerable to 'a beggar-thy-neighbour policy' than the US.

Since the model is defined in deviation from full-employment, in the absence of shocks the objective function of each country is equal to zero; namely each economy is by definition at its bliss point. The game arises as a shock, such as the price of imported raw materials, rises above its equilibrium value. This raises inflation in both the US and Europe and the central banks respond to combat inflation.

The optimal policy for each country is obtained by minimizing the objective function subject to the economic model. Each central bank is choosing its monetary policy by taking as given the monetary policy of the other. Thus the optimal monetary policy for each country is given by the following equation:

$$\frac{\partial U_i}{\partial \Delta r_i} = \frac{\partial U_i}{\partial \Delta p_i}\left(\frac{\partial \Delta p_i}{\partial \Delta y_i}\frac{\partial \Delta y_i}{\partial \Delta r_i} + \frac{\partial \Delta p_i}{\partial \Delta r_i}\right) + \frac{\partial U_i}{\partial \Delta y_i}\frac{\partial \Delta y_i}{\partial \Delta r_i} = 0 \tag{7}$$

The US reaction function is:

$$A\Delta r_1 = B\Delta r_2 + C \tag{8}$$

where

$$A = q_{1p}(\alpha_1\lambda_1 - \beta_1)^2 + q_{1y}\lambda_1^2 > 0 \tag{9}$$

$$B = -\ (q_{1p}(\alpha_1\lambda_1 - \beta_1)(\alpha_1\mu_1 + \beta_1) + q_{iy}\lambda_1\mu_1) < 0 \tag{10}$$

$$C = -\ q_{1p}(\alpha_1\lambda_1 - \beta_1)\beta_1\Delta pm > 0 \tag{11}$$

A and C are unequivocally positive; for most parameter values B is negative.

The reaction function for Europe is

$$A\Delta r_1 = B\Delta r_2 + C \tag{12}$$

where

$$A = -\ (q_{2p}(\alpha_2\lambda_2 - \beta_2)(\alpha_2\mu_2 + \beta_2) + q_{2y}\lambda_2\mu_2) < 0 \tag{13}$$

$$B = -\ (q_{2p}(\alpha_2\lambda_2 - \beta_2)^2 + q_{2y}\lambda_2^2) < 0 \tag{14}$$

$$C = -\ q_{2p}(\alpha_2\lambda_2 - \beta_2)\beta_2\Delta pm > 0 \tag{15}$$

B and C are unequivocally negative and positive respectively; while A is for certain parameter values negative.

With the assumptions that Europe is more vulnerable to imported inflation and to 'beggar-thy-neighbour' policies than the US and that it also cares more about inflation than the US, the reaction functions of the US and Europe look like those in Figure 8.1. The US reaction function is almost flat and the reaction function of Europe is very steep. The US bliss point, denoted by A'', lies in the second quadrant of Figure 8.1.

$$A''\left(\frac{\mu_1}{\lambda_1 + \mu_1}\Delta pm,\ \frac{-\lambda_1}{\lambda_1 + \mu}\Delta pm\right)$$

On the other hand, the bliss-point for Europe, denoted by A^e, lies in the fourth quadrant

$$A^e\left(\frac{-\lambda_2}{\lambda_2 + \mu_2}\Delta pm,\ \frac{\mu_2}{\lambda_1 + \mu_2}\Delta pm\right)$$

The indifference curves of the US take the form of ellipses with centre the bliss point A''. Ellipses further away from the bliss point represent lower utility and are therefore less desirable. The US ellipses are very flat, like those in Figure 8.1. The indifference curves for Europe, on the other hand, are very steep. The slope of the indifference curves is equal to

$$\left.\frac{\Delta r_1}{\Delta r_2}\right|_u = -\frac{U_{\Delta r_2}}{u_{\Delta r_1}}$$

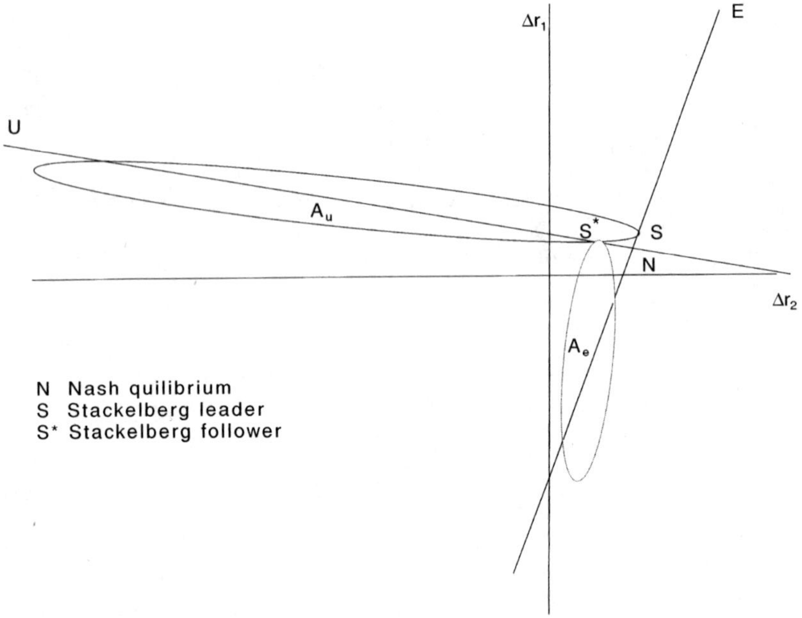

Figure 8.1 Three possible equilibriums in a game setting

Since the denominator is equal to zero for any point on the US reaction function, the US reaction function cuts the US ellipses at points where their slope is infinite. On the other hand, since the numerator is equal to zero for any point on the reaction function of Europe, the latter cuts Europe's ellipses at points where their slope is zero.

The intersection of the two reaction functions determines the Nash equilibrium, denoted by N, which is attained in quadrant 1 under the assumptions made earlier. This implies that as a result of the surge in imported raw material prices Europe is forced into tighter monetary policy than the US. This appreciates the euro (or the Deutsche Mark) against the dollar and introduces a deflationary effect in Europe with higher unemployment than the US.

The Stackelberg-leader equilibrium with the US as leader is defined as a point on the reaction function of Europe that is tangential on the US indifference curves. In Figure 8.1 the Stackelberg equilibrium is attained at point S. Clearly, this is a better solution for the US because it lies on a lower indifference curve than the one that passes through point N. This implies that the Stackelberg equilibrium with the US as a leader is Pareto efficient for the US, but not for Europe, as such equilibrium lies on a higher indifference curve for Europe.

The Stackelberg-follower equilibrium in which the US lets Europe act as a leader is defined as a point on the US reaction function that is tangential to Europe's indifference curves. In Figure 8.1 the Stackelberg equilibrium with Europe as the leader is attained at point S*. This is a better outcome for Europe, since it lies on a lower indifference curve and also for the US. Hence, the Stackelberg-follower equilibrium is Pareto-efficient for both the US and Europe.

8.4 The choice of equilibrium

Under what circumstances would the US choose each of these equilibria? That depends on the business cycle. Figure 8.2 illustrates the way in which the objective function of a central bank changes in the course of the business cycle (see for more details Karakitsos (1994). Point A represents the bliss point – defined as the rate of growth of potential output. The inflation rate that corresponds to the rate of growth of potential output is the steady state rate of inflation. Points B and D represent the peak and the trough of the business cycle in terms of the rate of growth, while points C and E the maximum and minimum rate of inflation, respectively, in the business cycle. These points divide the business cycle into five phases.

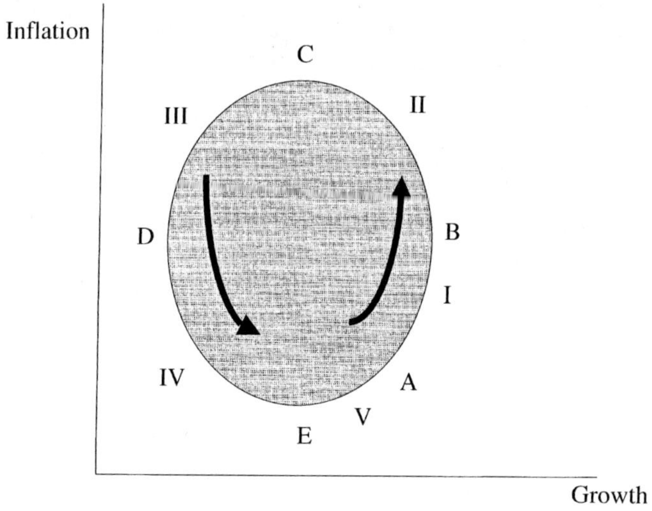

Figure 8.2 Inflation and growth in the business cycle

In phase I growth is rising above potential, the economy becomes overheated and inflation rises, usually with a lag. The correlation between inflation and growth is positive.

In phase II the economy decelerates, but inflation rises, thereby giving rise to a negative correlation between the two variables. Inflation increases in phase II, as unit labour cost continues to rise. There are two reasons why unit labour cost rises in this phase, albeit at a decreasing rate as the economy moves from B to C. First, wage-inflation is rising and, second, labour productivity growth falls. Both factors contribute to the rise in unit labour cost.

In the initial part of phase II wages are increasing as fast as inflation as employees are trying to protect the purchasing power of their wages. Immediately after point B, near the peak of the business cycle, employees are in a position to protect their real wages since their bargaining power is strong, as unemployment is low and few jobs are lost per month. However, as the economy moves towards point C the bargaining power of employees weakens, as unemployment is rising and the number of jobs lost per month is increased. Consequently, employees find it more and more difficult to protect the purchasing power of their wages. The real wage rate declines as the economy approaches point C and the wage-price spiral is finally broken.

Near the peak of the business cycle (around point B) labour productivity declines as firms lag behind in adjusting their labour force to declining demand for their products. Two reasons force firms to adjust sluggishly their labour force. First, uncertainty as to whether the drop in the demand for goods would be temporary or permanent. Second, costs of hiring and firing and training are forcing firms to see whether they can cope with reduced working hours and smaller temp-staff before they start sacking their permanent staff. However, as the fall in demand gathers pace (i.e. as the economy approaches point C) falling profitability is forcing firms to absorb into their profit margins the higher cost and decrease their labour force. Consequently, the fall in labour productivity diminishes as the economy approaches point C.

In phase III the economy goes into recession and inflation falls fast, as unit labour cost declines rapidly. Wage inflation abates as unemployment keeps rising and the number of jobs lost per month is increasing. Productivity rises as firms shed their labour force faster than the drop in demand. Profit margins are squeezed further as demand is extremely weak in the recession.

In phase IV the economy recovers, but inflation continues to fall, as unit labour cost rises, albeit at a decreasing rate. This is the inverse of phase II.

With this information as a background it is easy to see how a central bank would change its priorities in the course of the business cycle. In phases I and II the priority on inflation increases and the central bank follows tight monetary policy. In phases III and IV the central bank follows easy monetary policy as the priority on beating inflation is reduced or the priority on growth is increased. Hence, in general, interest rates rise from E to C and fall from C to E.

A central bank can be characterized as balanced, wet (or dove) and tough (or anti-inflation hawk) depending on the values it attaches to the penalty weights on inflation and growth at point A, i.e. when the economy is in the steady-state. The comparison has to be made at point A so that one is comparing like with like. This follows from the fact that the penalty weights vary in the course of the business cycle irrespective of the characterization of the central bank as balanced, wet or tough.

The central bank is balanced when the penalty weight on inflation is equal to the penalty weight on growth. The central bank is wet (or dove) when the penalty weight on growth exceeds that on inflation. The central bank is tough (or anti-inflation hawk) when the penalty weight on inflation exceeds that on growth.

If the central bank is balanced then interest rates would start falling at point C and would start rising at point E. If the central bank is wet or dove, then interest rates would start falling just before point C and would start rising after point E. If the central bank is tough or anti-inflation hawk, then interest rates would start falling after point C and would start rising before point E.

In terms of Figure 8.3 the US reaction function rotates anti-clockwise when the priority on inflation increases, i.e. when the economy is in phase I or II. When the priority on growth increases, i.e. when the economy is in phase III or IV, the US reaction function rotates clockwise. Nonetheless, the rotation of the US reaction function in the course of the business cycle is small. The US reaction function remains effectively flat.

The reaction function of Europe, on the other hand, rotates clockwise when the priority on inflation increases, i.e. when the economy is in phase I or II, see Figure 8.4. The reaction function rotates anti-clockwise when the priority on growth increases, i.e. when the economy is in phase III or IV. The European reaction function is much more sensitive than the US in the course of the business cycle.

For the sake of simplicity it is assumed that the US reaction function is fixed in the course of the business cycle, while Europe's reaction function takes three positions. It is neutral when the economy is growing at the rate of potential output (i.e. in the steady state), steeper when the economy is

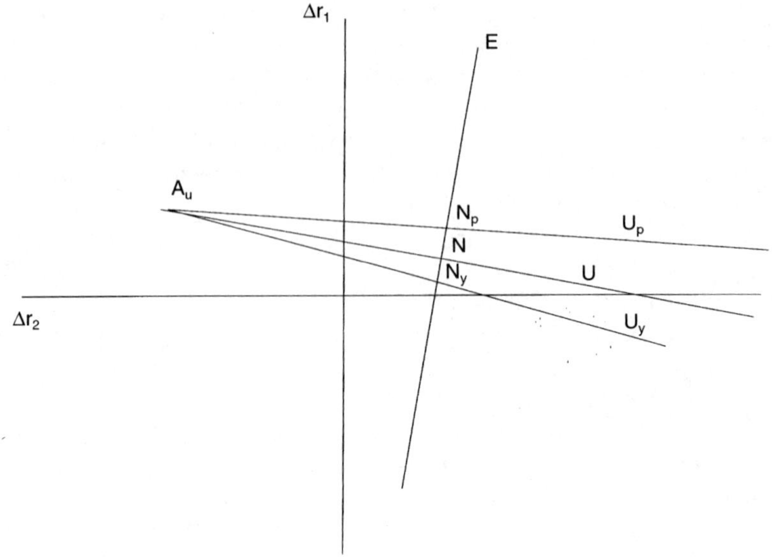

Figure 8.3 Sensitivity of equilibrium with respect of the US priorities of inflation and growth

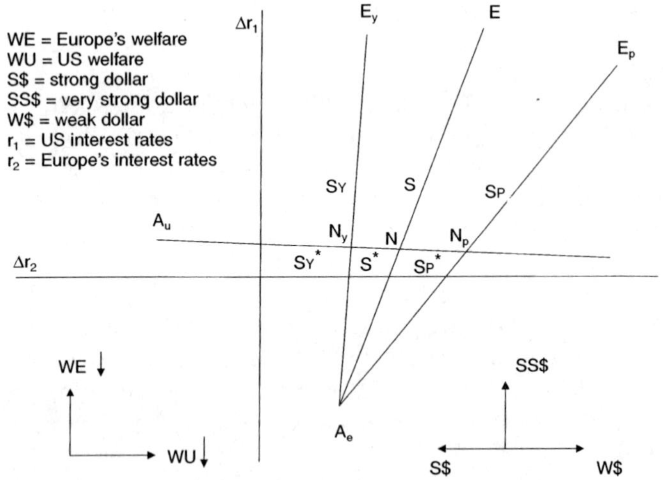

N = Nash equilibrium, S* = Stackelberg-follower, S = Stackelberg-leader, E = Europe's reaction function; A = bliss point, Y-subscript = priority on growth, P-subscript = Priority on inflation, No-subscript = neutral position

Figure 8.4 Welfare and interest rates

in recession or in recovery (i.e. in phase III or IV) and flatter when inflation is rising (i.e. in phase I or II). In Figure 8.4 E denotes Europe's reaction function in the neutral position; E_y denotes Europe's reaction function when the ECB attaches high priority in promoting growth. E_p denotes Europe's reaction function when the ECB attaches high priority in beating inflation. In each reaction function there are three equilibria if the policy game is played non-co-operatively, Nash, Stackelberg-leader and Stackelberg-follower. The assumption that the US reaction function is fixed restricts the choice of equilibrium in the policy game to just nine instead of 27 and makes the conclusions crispier by eliminating unnecessary detail.

With this information as a background it is easy to see which equilibrium the US would choose in the course of the business cycle, see Figure 8.4 and Table 8.1 for a summary. When the US is in phase I or II of its business cycle, it will choose the Stackelberg-leader equilibrium in which it acts as a leader, namely point S. The Stackelberg-leader equilibrium is Pareto efficient (i.e. welfare improving) for the US, but not for Europe. This equilibrium implies higher interest rates both for the US and Europe. The US would choose higher interest rates in order to reduce inflation, which is its primary objective in phase I or II. This would appreciate the dollar against the euro or the Deutsche Mark and would raise imported inflation in Europe. However, given the anti-inflation bias of the ECB or the Deutsche Bundesbank, interest rates would rise in Europe in order to safeguard the value of the currency against imported inflation. But this would engulf Europe into a deflationary gap, in which

Table 8.1 European reaction-function

US	Potential output F	Phase I, II E_p	Phase III, IV E_y
Phase I, II			
Choice of equilibrium	S	S_p	S_y E-Optimal
Dollar strength Compared to N	Strong	Not so weak	Even stronger
Phase III, IV			
Choice of equilibrium	S*	S^*_p E-Optimal	S^*_y
Dollar strength Compared to N	Not so strong	Weaker	Even stronger

E = Europe's reaction-function, S = Stackelberg-leader, S* = Stackelberg-follower

either unemployment would rise if the economy were in recession or unemployment would not fall if the economy were in recovery. Therefore, the Stackelberg-leader equilibrium is welfare improving for the US, but not for Europe.

This is reminiscent of the first half of the 1980s, when unemployment in Europe remained extremely high, while the dollar was very strong against the DM and all European currencies, given the role of the Bundesbank as a leader in the snake and the EMS. Many people attributed this combination to Euro-sclerosis, namely to the inflexibility of labour markets in Europe and the resulting real wage rigidity. An equally plausible, but not mutually exclusive, explanation could have been the choice of Stackelberg-leader equilibrium by the US in the face of the adverse oil shock of 1979–80. In fact, such an explanation is also consistent with the timing of the Plaza Accord, which coincided with the collapse of OPEC in 1985. The Plaza Accord represents the choice of Pareto equilibrium by the US.

If both the US and Europe are in phase I or II, then the reaction function of Europe would be flatter and point N would be further to the right to N_p in Figure 8.4. The US can still improve its welfare by choosing the Stackelberg-leader equilibrium, but its overall welfare is lower because the improvement is from a lower base (i.e. compared to N). Overall European welfare is smaller in the new Nash equilibrium N_p relative to N. It becomes even worse as the US chooses the Stackelberg-leader equilibrium S_p. The US choice of the Stackelberg-leader equilibrium is self-enforceable. Europe would be forced to choose this equilibrium as it enters into an interest rate war with the US because of the anti-inflation bias of the ECB. This is what happened in the first half of the 1980s and it is probably what has been happening since the end of 1999.

If, on the other hand, Europe is in phase III or IV when the US is in phase I or II, i.e. when the business cycles are desynchronized, then its reaction function is steeper at E_y, and point-N would lie further to the left to N_y. The US can still improve its welfare by choosing the Stackelberg-leader equilibrium, but now its overall welfare is higher because the improvement is from a higher base (i.e. compared to N). Overall European welfare is higher, but it is somewhat reduced as the US chooses the Stackelberg-leader equilibrium. An improvement in European welfare is possible only if the ECB is prepared to accept both a weaker euro and higher inflation. If the ECB is unwilling to submit to higher inflation and a weaker currency, then its reaction function would rotate clockwise (i.e. it would become flatter) as the US attempts to choose the Stackelberg-leader equilibrium. Inflation would still rise and the currency would become weaker, but by less than the original equilibrium. Both from the US and Europe's point of view desynchronization of the business cycles is preferable than synchronization.

In phase III or IV the US would always choose the Stackelberg-follower equilibrium in which Europe acts as a leader, namely point S*, irrespective of the position of Europe in the business cycle. In this case the US is exploiting the flatness of its reaction function and the steepness of the European reaction function. Given the flatness of the US reaction function, US interest rates would rise by almost the same amount as in the Nash equilibrium. However, Europe would adopt a less tight policy than at N and therefore the dollar would appreciate compared to Nash. This would allow the US to soothe the recessionary effects of the surge in raw material prices, which is its primary objective in phase III or IV, while minimizing the inflationary consequences. Since the US is adopting almost the same degree of tightening, the recessionary effects of the raw material price increase are the same in N and S*. However, by letting Europe lead the US is benefiting both in terms of inflation and growth. Inflation at S* is lower than N, because the dollar is stronger and hence imported inflation is lower. Growth is higher because domestic demand in Europe is more buoyant thereby stimulating US exports. The rise in the dollar results in a loss in US competitiveness. However, US exports still increase as the effect of the stronger domestic demand in Europe more than offsets the loss in competitiveness. Thus the US choice of Stackelberg-follower equilibrium is Pareto efficient (i.e. welfare improving) for the US. Such equilibrium is also Pareto efficient for Europe, as it lies on a lower indifference curve than the one that passes through point N, the Nash equilibrium.

If Europe lags behind the US in the business cycle as it happened in the 1980s and the 1990s, and it is in phase I or II, while the US is in phase III or IV, then Europe's reaction function would be even flatter. The choice of equilibrium now lies on E_p and therefore point N would lie, almost horizontally, further to the right to N_p in Figure 8.4. In this case there is still room for welfare improvement for both the US and Europe. The US would still choose the Stackelberg-follower equilibrium at S_p^*. However, overall welfare for the US diminishes because the improvement is from a lower base. European welfare is lower compared to N, but this is desirable since Europe attaches a high priority to reducing inflation. The dollar would still appreciate compared to the new Nash-equilibrium N_p, but it would be weaker compared to the original Nash-equilibrium, N, i.e. the equilibrium when Europe is growing at potential output. European welfare improves at S_p^* compared to N_p because the Fed is not competing with the ECB over the currency. The Fed does not lift interest rates to defend the dollar and hence the ECB tightens less than otherwise. Thus, although the dollar depreciates compared to N, it is still stronger compared to N_p. The European welfare improvement therefore reflects the smaller degree of tightening by the ECB. Such an outcome is optimal for Europe because the Fed tolerance over the dollar arises as a result of the US being in recession or in recovery and therefore the smaller the dollar appreciation the better. Hence, desynchronization of business cycles is preferable from Europe's point of view, but not from the US, as S_p^* is further away from the bliss point than S*.

If, on the other hand, the business cycle of Europe is synchronized with the US and both regions are in phase III or IV, then the European reaction function will be even steeper and the Nash equilibrium would lie, almost horizontally, further to the left of N_y in Figure 8.4. Again there is room for welfare improvement for both the US and Europe compared with the new Nash equilibrium N_y. The US will still choose the Stackelberg-follower equilibrium. But now, overall welfare for the US is enhanced since the improvement is from a higher base. Hence, synchronization of business cycles is preferable to desynchronization from the US point of view. The dollar would appreciate compared to the new Nash-equilibrium at N_y, as European interest rates do not rise a lot. The dollar would be even stronger compared to the original Nash-equilibrium N. Synchronization is preferable from the US point of view because European growth is higher at S_y^* than at N_y and hence US exports are more buoyant, in spite of the stronger dollar. The choice of Stackelberg-follower equilibrium is Pareto efficient also for Europe as the stronger dollar results in a smaller degree of tightening by the ECB.

8.5 Conclusions and lessons for Europe

We believe that Europe differs from the US in four main respects. First, Europe is more susceptible to imported inflation than the US. Second, Europe is more vulnerable than the US to 'beggar-thy-neighbour' policies. Third, the ECB is tough, while the Fed is balanced. Fourth, the US is mightier than Europe and therefore in a game framework can be considered as the leader, while Europe as the follower.

With these assumptions the US reaction function is almost flat and exhibits small variability in the course of the business cycle. However, the reaction function of Europe is more sensitive to the business cycle. It is very steep when Europe is in recession or in recovery and becomes much flatter when inflation rises. For the sake of simplicity it is assumed that the US reaction function is fixed in the course of the business cycle, while Europe's reaction function takes three positions. It is neutral when the economy is growing at the rate of potential output (i.e. in the steady state), steeper when the economy is in recession or in recovery (i. e. in phase III or IV) and flatter when inflation is rising (i.e. in phase I or II). In each reaction function there are three equilibria if the policy game is played non-co-operatively, Nash, Stackelberg-leader and Stackelberg-follower. The assumption that the US reaction function is fixed restricts the choice of equilibrium in the policy game to just nine instead of 27 and makes the conclusions crispier by eliminating unnecessary detail.

In this model the US would always choose the Stackelberg-leader equilibrium when inflation is rising (i.e. in phase I or II) and the Stackelberg-follower equilibrium when it is in recession or in recovery (i.e. in phase III or IV). The choice of equilibrium by the US is always self-enforceable. When the US prefers the Stackelberg-leader equilibrium, all it has to do is to compete with Europe over the currency. By raising its interest rates the Fed is forcing the ECB to choose the Stackelberg-leader equilibrium by entering into an interest rate race. When the US prefers the Stackelberg-follower equilibrium, all it has to do is not to compete with the ECB over the currency. By keeping rates unchanged the Fed is forcing the ECB to choose the Stackelberg-follower equilibrium, since the Fed is accepting a strong dollar.

Compared to the corresponding Nash equilibrium the US is always experiencing welfare improvement by choosing the Stackelberg equilibrium. However, for Europe welfare improves, compared to the corresponding Nash, only when the US chooses the Stackelberg-follower equilibrium. European welfare decreases, compared to the corresponding Nash, when the US chooses the Stackelberg-leader equilibrium.

When inflation in Europe rises the ECB responds by increasing the priority on beating inflation. This makes the reaction function flatter and pushes the Nash equilibrium further to the right. This diminishes the welfare of both the US and Europe and therefore the base from which any welfare improvement is measured. Therefore, any improvement, if at all, is only marginal as it takes place from a much lower base.

The dollar always appreciates compared to the corresponding Nash-equilibrium. When the US chooses the Stackelberg-follower equilibrium the dollar appreciates because Europe adopts a less tight monetary policy compared to the corresponding Nash. When the US chooses the Stackelberg-leader equilibrium the dollar appreciates because the US adopts a much tighter monetary policy than in the corresponding Nash.

However, the dollar may be weaker or stronger compared to the original

Nash equilibrium N, namely to the one obtained when both economies are growing at potential output. Compared to this yardstick the dollar is stronger when Europe is in recession or in recovery (i.e. in phase III or IV) and weaker when European inflation is rising (i.e. in phase III or IV).

What are the choices for Europe in such an environment? Two of the reasons responsible for the entrapment of Europe in a deflationary equilibrium are, first, the greater degree of supply side openness of Europe compared with the US; and second, the greater vulnerability of Europe to 'beggar-thy-neighbour' policies than the US.

EMU is improving Europe on both fronts. Europe is becoming less supply side open, as a number of countries, like the UK and Norway, are oil producing. The single market makes Europe less vulnerable to 'beggar-thy-neighbour' policies.

However, the third reason that is responsible for the deflationary equilibrium of Europe is the choice of the objective function, namely the anti-inflationary bias of the ECB compared with a more balanced Fed. If the ECB were to adopt a balanced priority between inflation and growth, like the Fed, then the reaction function of Europe would become much steeper.[3] In this case the Stackelberg equilibrium – point S – would lie vertically above N. The US in its choice of tighter monetary policy to combat imported inflation would find it easier to appreciate the dollar. Europe would accept temporarily higher inflation, but would not find itself trapped in a deflationary equilibrium, as it happened in the first half of the 1980s.

A final option for Europe is to keep its business cycle desynchronized with the US. If Europe is in recession or in recovery (i.e. in phase III or IV) while US inflation is rising (i.e. the US is in phase I or II), then the lower euro will not cause higher inflation because firms will squeeze into their profit margins the higher import prices. If Europe is in phase I or II, while the US is in phase III or IV, then the US choice of the Stackelberg-follower equilibrium will result in euro appreciation which would help Europe keep its inflation under control.

In the 1980s and in the 1990s the US was ahead of Europe in the business cycle. The US entered phase I in 1994, when Europe was in phase IV. Since the end of 1999 both the US and Europe have been in phase I. The dollar strength between 1994 and 1999 was therefore desirable, because it helped to ease inflationary pressures in the US, while it allowed Europe to recover through gains in competitiveness. However, from the end of 1999, both economies are overheated. As the dollar appreciates the ECB is raising interest rates to combat imported inflation from the weakness of the euro and the surge in the price of oil of the last twelve months. Thus the ECB is responding by choosing a flatter reaction function, as the Bundesbank did in the first half of the 1980s.

Irrespective of what Europe does the US would choose the Stackelberg-leader equilibrium, which would imply dollar strength from the corresponding Nash. If the ECB responds by increasing its priority on inflation, then the reaction function of Europe would become flatter. Europe would adopt a much tighter monetary policy at the risk of thwarting the recovery and not allowing unemployment to fall. However, that may endanger EMU, as many people would put the blame on the single currency. However, the single currency is Pareto efficient because it makes Europe less vulnerable to imported inflation and 'beggar-thy-neighbour' policies. Hence, it is becoming more important now that the ECB adopts a more balanced view between inflation and growth, like the Fed.

Note

1. For a more detailed discussion of the international role of the Deutsche Mark, see Frenkel and Goldstein, 1999, pp. 685–729.
2. For a full version of this model and its implications, see S. F. Frowen and Elias Karakitsos 'A Strategic Approach to the Euro Prospects', *Public Finance*, vol. 53, no. 1, 1998
3. In a *Central Banking* Interview, Otmar Issing stresses the ECB's dependence on the goal of price stability over the medium term set by the Maastricht Treaty. ECB restriction to '*instrument* independence' would then by implication not allow for the adoption of a balanced priority between price stability and growth. The latter will be, in the ECB view, the result of the former in the long run (see Frowen, 2001, pp. 31–33).

Bibliography

Deutsche Bundesbank *Fifty Years of the Deutsche Mark. Central Bank and the Currency in Germany since 1948* (London and New York: Oxford University Press, 1999). (Original German edition *Fünfzig Jahre Deutsche Mark. Notenbank und Währung in Deutschland seit 1948* (Munich: Verlag C. H. Beck, 1998).)

Dornbusch, R. and Fisher, S. 'Exchange rates and the Current Account', *American Economic Review*, vol. 70, no 5, (1980) pp. 960–71.

Frenkel, J. A. and Goldstein, M. 'The International Role of the Deutsche Mark', in Deutsche Bundesbank (ed.) *Fifty Years of the Deutsche Mark*, (1999) pp. 685–729.

Frowen, S. F. 'Unjustified British Critique of the Bundesbank', *Central Banking*, vol. X, no. 3 (1999–2000) pp. 40–5. (Reprinted in Deutsche Bundesbank *Auszüge aus Presseartikeln*, no. 12, 8 March 2000, pp. 15–17.)

Frowen, S. F. 'Interview: Otmar Issing', *Central Banking*, vol. XI, no. 3, February 2001, pp. 24–33. (Reprinted in Deutsche Bundesbank, *Auszüge aus Presseartikeln*, no.8, 20 February 2001, pp. 8–12.)

Frowen, S. F. and Pringle, R. *Inside the Bundesbank* (London: Macmillan; New York: St. Martin's Press, 1998).

Hölscher, J. *Entwicklungsmodell Westdeutschland: Aspekte der Akkumulation in der*

Geldwirtschaft (Berlin: Duncker & Humblot, 1994).

Hölscher, J., Owen Smith, E. and Pugh, G. (2001) 'The DM-Undervaluation and West Germany's Economic Performance' (Chapter 7 in this volume).

Issing, O. 'The Monetary Policy of the European Central Bank: Strategy and Implementation', *CES ifo Forum* (Summer 2000) pp. 3–9.

Issing, O. *et al. Monetary Policy in the Euro Area* (Cambridge: Cambridge University Press, 2001)

Karakitsos, E. 'Asset Prices in the Business Cycle', Lecture Notes, Imperial College (1994).

König, R. and Willeke, C. 'German Monetary Unification: Domestic and External Issues', in S. F. Frowen and R. Pringle (eds.) *Inside the Bundesbank* (London: Macmillan; New York: St. Martin's Press, 1998), pp. 20–31.

Luken-Klassen, M. and Hölscher, J. 'Mythos Wirtschaftswunder: Eine geldtheoretische Entzauberung', in Werner Süss (ed.) *Übergänge: Zeitgeschichte zwischen Utopie und Machbarkeit. Beiträge zu Philosophie, Gesellschaft und Politik. Festschrift for Hellmuth G. Bülow for his 65th Birthday* (Berlin: Duncker & Humblot, 1990).

Riese, H. 'Das Dilemma der Ökonomie der Bundesrepublik', in Bolte, K.-M. *et al.* (eds.) *Mitteilungen aus der Arbeitsmarkt- und Berufsforschung*. Special issue, vol. 17 (Stuttgart, Berlin, Cologne and Mainz, 1984).

Riese, H. 'The Bipolar International Monetary System and the British Pound' (Chapter 9 in this volume).

9

The Bipolar International Monetary System and the British Pound

Hajo Riese

The dollar as a model for the euro

When the euro was introduced early in 1999, the overwhelming majority of politicians and theoreticians were convinced of its success. This view reflected not only their view that the introduction of the euro was inevitable, but of greater importance was the previous year's strong position of the Deutschmark (DM) – the key currency of the European Monetary System (EMS) prior to the introduction of the euro – relative to the dollar. It was also seen that the low interest rate of the DM indicated a smooth transition from 11 European currencies to one joint currency.

It is true that there is no guarantee that the monetary process (with the European Central Bank (ECB) as a participant in this process) will create a strong euro similar to its predecessor the DM. But the Eurosceptics' traditional (and only serious) argument – that an increasing autonomy over income policy, especially fiscal and wage policies, will counter a strong price-level-centered monetary policy stabilization – must not be overestimated. Because the success of a stabilization policy does, to an extent, not just affect the regulation of the monetary process as such, but also has moderate consequences for the acceptability of the market process in adjusted national structures, with serious consequences for inadequately adjusted structures.

It seems of great importance at present that theoretical discussion and the emerging monetary policy are internally directed, centered on the stabilization of the common price level within the European Monetary Union (EMU). Thus Otmar Issing, former director of the Bundesbank, now a member of the board of the ECB remarked: 'We do not practise an exchange rate policy. But the concentration on the internal mechanism of the euro, which apparently reflects the projection of the Bundesbank model, overlooks the great importance of the introduction of the euro on the evolution of the international monetary system'. Fratianni and Hauskrecht (1999) suggest that the introduction of the euro will create a bipolar monetary system comprising the dollar and the euro, where the euro area 'will most likely encompass Central and Eastern Europe, the CFA zone, and parts of the Middle East and North Africa'.[1]

There are two aspects to this projection. The first is the ignoring of the key currency character of the yen and Swiss franc. The latter is ignored because of its role solely as an asset currency, while the ignoring of the former is based on its reduced importance as an external credit currency, while being unable to establish itself as a reserve currency (see, for example, the decisive role of the dollar as the reserve currency of the East Asian economies).[2] Following the approach of Clarida *et al.* (1998) asking for two sets of leading currencies consisting first of the G3 nations – Germany, Japan and the US – with an implicit form of inflation targeting and second the E3 nations – the UK, France and Italy – as fixed exchange rate regimes dependent on the policy of the Bundesbank, it seems remarkable that the British pound falls out of the scenario concerning the euro. This point will be discussed later. The second aspect refers to the role of the euro itself. The first point concerning the 'bipolar system' is whether the euro will be able to 'challenge the supremacy of the Dollar'.[4] Considering the contemporary size of the dollar and the lack of credibility of the ECB as an 'untested institution' compared with the Federal Reserve System (and also the former Bundesbank) it is not surprising that contra-arguments predominate.[5]

However, in the context of our current reflections this aspect remains of minor importance. Of major importance are the conditions for the dollar and the euro, as equally entitled currencies, to establish a bipolar monetary system, thus producing a break with the existing system. This break will become greater the more the supremacy of the dollar diminishes. Under these conditions the dollar and the euro will act as a duopol. Both performing the double task of managing stability and proving economies with international liquidity.[6]

Exchange rates are generally, as Fratianni and Hauskrecht have pointed out, hierarchical (with a key currency at the top of the pyramid) but not hegemonic. The key currency is related to the economic size of the issuing country; the size and depth of its financial markets and the external credit position of the country having a major effect in determining the regime's inflation rate.[7] Bearing in mind these criteria, it easy to see the large difference between a bipolar monetary system consisting of a dollar area and a euro area, compared with the existing system of the dollar's supremacy, a few key currencies of minor importance and a set of dependent currencies (together with many so-called 'weak' currencies that are not relevant to this discussion). For the first system, the twofold hierarchical structure (it is only a matter of definition if Fratianni and Hauskrecht instead speak of a *suspense* of the hierarchical structure compared with the gold standard, Bretton Woods and the EMS)[8] means greater competition between the two currencies and shifts the orientation of monetary policy to the movements of financial markets (especially asset markets). Consequentially the interest rate and the exchange rate will become the main instruments of monetary policy. This transference of the orientation of the stabilization policy from the commodity markets to the financial markets will simultaneously reduce the significance of price stability as the main target of monetary policy – in favour of a policy that will replace the stabilization of the commodity market with stabilization of the financial markets.

The Federal Reserve System has the, more or less, difficult task of managing the greater acceptance of the competing euro compared with the former EMS-currencies, while the ECB has the huge task of mastering a currency system totally changed compared with the monetary policy of autonomous nations. The model for the ECB will (and must) be the Federal Reserve System, not, as is always emphasized, the Bundesbank, a view also favoured by Frowen and Karakitsos (see Chapter 8). The bipolar character of the prospective international monetary system requires the double task of a stabilization policy while providing international liquidity. This double task is a new challenge to the successors of the Bundesbank, following her 50-year old history of combining price level stability and supporting export efforts. The task relates to becoming a world currency, competitive with the dollar, stabilizing the financial market in order to become an asset currency, while establishing the elastic maintenance of liquidity needed to become a reserve currency.

The Bundesbank has only superficially and unwillingly accepted such a monetary policy, even within the context of its controlling the key currency of the EMS.[9] *Nolens volens* the Bundesbank accepted the market process towards the internationalization of the DM in contradiction to its mercantilist instinct.[10] This was lucky for it and for Europe. It is certain that the European orientation of the Bundesbank made easier the avoidance of problems similar to those suffered by Japan, where the dollar takes the international currency role and is therefore substituted for the home currency, the yen. However, for the Bundesbank, unlike the Federal Reserve System, the internal aspects of stabilization remained dominant, with the high costs – as James Tobin continually points out – of high labour unemployment and budget deficits.

But, under the bipolar monetary system it would be impossible to maintain a nationalistic monetary policy with the accent on internal stabilization matters. The ugly alternative of inflationary target and money rule, presented both by the theoreticians and politicians suggests that the ECB will continue the defects of the Bundesbank, which under the prevailing conditions will confirm the supremacy of the dollar. This will happen because a monetary policy of internal stabilization together with the provision of an international currency provides a contradiction within the market process that defines an international currency. This will leave the euro with the status of a subaltern currency.

The challenge of the 'lender of last resort': the market solution

It seems a strange transformation from the nationalistic, internal price stability focused version of the Bundesbank to the euro as the overarching currency of a united Europe promoted as an alternative to the dollar. But in reality the mainstream of the theoretical community, seeing the DM as the model for Europe, reveals its deep-seated preference for decisive regulation of the money sphere. This view has the ECB running as a super Bundesbank. But this is a misconception. Dissentient to the adjured German idyll, an international currency run analogous to the dollar falls foul of the contradiction of obtaining internal stability and providing international liquidity. The key element of this inconsistency has the Central Bank as the lender of last resort, which requires an open re-discount window. This is Bagehot's rule, developed by him in *Lombard Street* in 1873. This market solution may be a contrast to a stabilization programme based on a money rule or inflationary target.

However, for an international currency there is no escaping the market solution satisfying the demand for this currency. This fact ensures the secondary significance of a stabilization programme (or more accurately, its derivative solution). The reason is simple, but as we will see, never understood by some theoreticians. The role of a lender of last resort means that a *national* currency has to act as an *international* currency, since only a banking system is able to operate as a lender of last resort, nationally and internationally, because commercial banks lend long while borrowing short from the central bank on the basis of the re-discount window.

That is the content of Bagehot's rule concerning the market process of providing an economy with liquidity. This is the *only* content intended by

Bagehot. But the theoreticians have no such restrictions. The misunderstanding begins with the interpretation of a lender of last resort of an *international* currency and ends with a view of the lender of last resort as a *reaction* of a short-run liquidity crisis.

First the international element: to be a lender of last resort, you must be a bank, acting within a banking system that has separate functions for the production of liquidity by a central bank and for the lending of liquidity by the commercial banks, subject to the criteria of solvency. But a banking system is a national institution that produces a national currency, not an international organization producing something similar to 'special drawing rights'.

Thus, institutions such as the International Monetary Fund (IMF) are not able to act as a lender of last resort, since they produce liquidity (in the IMF's case the so-called 'special drawing rights') on the basis of limited resources, which are bound by treaties regulating the acceptance of such rights by national central banks. The IMF works, as its name suggests, as a fund, not as a bank, lending subject to criteria of solvency not liquidity. Here there is no difference between the IMF under the Bretton Woods regime and its role since that regime's collapse in 1973. As Despres *et al.* (1996) clearly point out, the United States acted as a bank for the rest of the world, lending long and issuing short to finance that lending.[11] Of significance for the functioning of the Bretton Woods system was not the famous linkage to gold but the readiness of the Federal Reserve System, before and after 1973, to accept the role as lender of last resort via the dollar – as had, prior to 1914, the Bank of England with the British pound.

One feels that no contemporary American economist is able to understand this principle of lender of last resort.[12] This affects the second area of misunderstanding of Bagehot's rule. Contrary to current majority opinion, the open re-discount window does not appear as a reaction to a liquidity crisis. The historical background to the argument supplies the contradiction between Bagehot and Lord Overstone, whereby the latter refers to liquidity crises as an exception of the market process. As a result, he introduced the function of lender of last resort as a reaction to monetary disturbances and panics – a position fully endorsed by today's economists. But, Bagehot's rule is intended to *prevent* panics, not to react to them, and requires the re-discount window to be open continually (given the rate of interest).

The theoreticians' misunderstanding, which has them 'selling' Lord Overstone's rule as Bagehot's rule,[13] has its basis in a monetary orthodoxy that permits a deviation from the money rule (determined exogenously by the authorities) only in cases of crisis. Referring to Bagehot, this means that the theoreticians, while accepting the money rule (or equally an inflation target), at the same time refuse a market solution of monetary policy. This implies the refusal of the ability of a market process to provide international liquidity on the basis of the euro.

Given its overwhelming current power, it may be that the market process of lender of last resort, providing international liquidity, overcoming the traditional targets of price stability and so pushing an internationalization of the monetary system, will be a success for the dollar rather than the euro. Again, this will merely be a reflection of the success of the dollar relative to the DM – a transposition of the reluctant Bundesbank establishing the DM as an international asset currency to the ECB and the euro. Put briefly: the euro can challenge the supremacy of the dollar only by emulating the Federal Reserve System and providing international liquidity in the market not by teleological instruments of price stabilization, as is the Bundesbank's trademark.

The British pound in a bipolar monetary system

What of the British pound? Great Britain's monetary policy will retain its autonomy under the euro regime. This policy was formed following Britain's withdrawal from the EMS in the 1990s following the pound's devaluation. Britain is now waiting for the optimal time to join EMU. This will not be easy to achieve. Should a working bipolar monetary system develop, the pound will be subjected to the conditions of the world asset market. British monetary policy, like British economic policy in general, gives the impression that it wishes to establish so-called 'economic fundamentals' concerning a successful introduction of the euro. But, such targets are an illusion – and are, as will be shown, *la grande illusion* of the British economy since Keynes's proposal of a clearing union in the Bretton Woods negotiations at the end of the Second World War.

In short, the pound's position outside a bipolar monetary system leaves Britain with no chance of an autonomous monetary policy. There are two possible scenarios. The more realistic scenario envisages an overvalued pound – either from favourable asset markets or income dynamics – stimulating imports and limiting exports, thus leading to an import surplus. This market scenario has dominated the British economy since the Second World War, with only a few years respite (which led to suppressed overvaluation). The United States provides a corresponding stable market example, based on the worldwide dominance of the dollar as a reserve currency. Switzerland, with the Swiss franc as an asset currency, could be considered as another example. But Great Britain is neither the United States nor Switzerland. For the pound represents a system of an overvalued currency with an expected depreciation regardless of whether short-term capital imports (as in the present Asian crisis) or income effects (as in the American case) are the origin unlike the dollar and Swiss franc combining an overvalued currency with an expected appreciation. The result is an instability in the British economy which is characterized by the famous 'stop–go' policy. As will be shown later, Thatcherism was unable to overcome this cycle of instability, producing instead a suppressed overvaluation based on a restrictive monetary policy – the *stop* in the stop–go policy.

The source of this overvaluation can be traced back to the postwar income levels, where a generous wage policy and large budget deficits created an import surplus accompanied by capital imports. Naturally this will bring a currency under a threat of depreciation. Also, an ongoing condition such as this can be seen in the usual inflationary price-wage mechanism as the *go* element of the stop–go policy, producing after the devaluation a form of real appreciation – thereby recreating the overvalued currency. Considering the persistence of this market process, it will be difficult (or, as we shall see, nearly impossible) for the British economy to join EMU without an overvalued pound. Adding to this, it hardly matters whether the joint currency be overvalued or not, concerning the case of the real appreciation of the British euro sphere in view of the lasting autonomy of the income policy.

But the effect will be quite different compared with the pound's preceding regime. The current lack of a temporary devaluation will lead to a peripherization of the British economy, seemingly a persistent stop in the terminology of the stop-go-policy. *Mezzogiorno ante portas* – mezzogiorno as an example of peripherization under the conditions of a common currency. The comparisons are obvious: peripherization under Thatcherism led to the deindustrialization of Wales and Scotland, while peripherization under the euro will lead to the deindustrialization of the whole British economy.

Of course, the British economy is not a sort of mezzogiorno, and will not be. But we should not forget that the core market group representing peripherization is the Third World group. This is also the style of the postwar British economy with the commodity market exhibiting an overvalued currency and the asset market showing an expected devaluation of the currency. This results in a comparatively low real wage, with Great Britain near the bottom of the wage levels of the countries of the European Union (EU). However, there is a major difference between the postwar development of Britain and the main group of the Third World countries. Britain was able, as Schröder (1999) pointed out, to establish a creditor position in the world financial market in the past decades. This position has been founded on capital imports in British pounds, which permits the British economy to attain net receipts – an astonishing result given the dominant tendency to an expected depreciation of the pound. Britain may be viewed as an unstable Switzerland – unique in the financial firmament, maybe the final fling of the financial imperialism of the City of London that ended with the First World War, giving Britain her difference from the Third World with her debts in foreign currencies.

Nevertheless, this difference from the Third World, while so important in the constitution of an autonomous monetary policy, does not solve the dilemma of the British economy. It only makes the dilemma visible. For the paradox of the pound – on the one hand a stable asset currency and on the other a currency under threat of depreciation – will be hidden under the euro where the pound will appear as an internal currency. This matters for the British economy, because the loss of monetary autonomy, which counteracts her Third-World conditions, will push her one step nearer peripherization.

There is, of course, an alternative. The pound's overvaluation is not a divine act. The alternative must be the undervaluation of the currency. It is not sufficient to reestablish the so-called fundamentals of the commodity market (with its implication of neutral money) because these fundamentals include a tendency back to overvaluation. But it is necessary to be sceptical about the realization of this policy. The model for such a stable market format may be that of Germany or Japan in the growth period after the Second World War, founded on a combination of investment dynamics and export surplus. Such a format reduces the influence of the asset market in favour of profit inflation on the line of Keynes' treatise. Thus this will reduce the pound's position as an asset currency. And at this point scepticism is appropriate – Britain, at the start of the twenty-first century, is not able to imitate the postwar conditions of the German and Japanese economies.

Overall it is difficult to set up conditions for an undervaluation. A depreciation does not constitute an undervaluation, it creates, as we have seen, at best a temporary suppressed overvaluation (until the feedback of rising factor prices neutralizes this effect). The reasons for the instability of such a process are straightforward. The mercantilistic approach of an undervaluation of a currency involves an adaptation of factor prices, above all of nominal wages, on the basis of a fixed (undervalued) exchange rate. Inversely, it forbids determining the exchange rate on the basis of fixed factor prices. The differences between the two approaches provide the divergent market results. The differences represent the varying connections between the asset and currency markets, influenced by the expected changes in the exchange rate. In the first case stability arises – from the connection of undervaluation and expected appreciation of the currency, thereby stabilizing the undervaluation – while in the second case instability arises from the connection of undervaluation and the expected depreciation of the currency thus destroying the undervaluation.

It is hard to believe that the British government would or could impose the wage and budget constraints necessary for the establishment of an undervalued currency. Theoretically it is possible either inside or outside the euro. Outside may be easier given the greater autonomy of the exchange rate policy, but with the drawback of the asset character of the pound. Inside the euro may be easier because of the pressure for adaptation within EMU, but there is then the problem of the barriers to entry for an undervalued currency. But the main consideration must be the unforeseeable market process, which may result in the reestablishment of an overvalued currency rather than the anticipated undervaluation. The results of the Thatcher era do not dispose one to be optimistic.

Let us return to the bipolar monetary system with the dollar and euro as key currencies. There is only the slightest chance that over the next few decades Britain will be able to achieve the undervaluation scenario, combining stability with a dynamic economy as a consequence of its autonomous economic policy. The more realistic vision is that of a further depreciation of an overvalued pound, with the constitution of the bipolar monetary system with strong competition between the dollar and the euro further weakening the pound. This in turn will weaken the pound as an asset currency.

9.4 The general problem with the pound

What, in general, is the problem with the pound? I have already pointed out that, during the Bretton Woods negotiations in 1944, Keynes rejected any international monetary system that limited the autonomy of British monetary policy. This was the main thrust of his proposal of a clearing union. Keynes' position was a British reaction to what had happened after the First World War when Britain returned to the prewar parity of the gold standard. This had the effect of appreciating the pound by about 10 per cent in real terms, which in turn aggravated the effects of the Great Depression.[14]

But such an overvaluation must be distinguished from dependence in a market-based hierarchical system. Keynes' rigid position goes back to his postwar book *A Tract on Monetary Reform*, a book remarkable for the reason that he considered the weak currency position of the pound to be a *fait accompli*. With this book, not only did he reject the restoration of prewar parity, but he also wanted the United States to revalue the dollar relative to gold.

How naïve. How incredibly naïve, to think that a weak currency position permits an autonomous monetary policy, based on the annulment of market forces eliminating in particular the asset market (here to be supported by a revalued dollar) in favour of the current account, which would be financed by the international monetary system. Nevertheless, his position has had great influence on economic thinking in Britain (and on British economic policy) since the Second World War, especially with regard to an easy-money policy and fiscal policies.

But market forces took revenge for their suppression and the pound became overvalued – a widely disregarded implication of the autonomous economic policy. This disregard has characterized British governments: from the postwar Keynesian version, creating the overvaluation by stimulating imports and disappointing imports; via Thatcher's suppressed overvaluation with its consequences of diminishing skilled industries and the deindustrialization of Wales and Scotland; to Blair's helpless mixture of social engagement and rigid economic behaviour which, killing two birds with one stone, confirms the fundamentals of a matched overvaluation. The achievement of a creditor position is then no more than a drop in the ocean.

The British economy of the past half-century has cultivated an imperialistic instinct under inappropriate conditions. It is *only* a currency at the top of the hierarchy being able to practise an autonomous economic policy (taking care not to work against the hierarchical position), but the economy has passed its hierarchical position to the United States. The result of such inconsistencies is a middle-brow economy, getting closer to the Third World than the First World. In any case real wages reflect a correspondingly low productivity – at the lower end of the EU.

Concerning the pound and the euro, our analysis demonstrates that it is not sufficient to interpret the politicians' hesitation to join the euro as a necessary preparation for a frictionless integration of the British economy in the world of the new currency. On the contrary, the hesitation reflects the confirmation of an autonomous economic policy that goes back to the imperialist past before the First World War, reaffirmed again and again since the breakdown of imperialism after the First World War. The result is disintegration, disintegration in a macroeconomic sense thus affecting monetary policy. Goodbye Britain. Good luck to Britain.

Notes

1. Fratianni and Hauskrecht (1999), S. 2.
2. I think also that the mercantilist approach of the Japanese economy, accumulating dollars by export surplus (and, as a consequence, exporting capital in the form of dollars), gives the real reason for the contemporary collapse of the Japanese economy together with the Asian tigers.
3. Clarida *et al.* (1998), pp. 1033, 1052.
4. Fratianni *et al.* (1999), pp. 21ff
5. Ibid.; see further (1999), p. 20.
6. Ibid., p. 19.
7. Ibid., pp 18f.
8. Ibid., p. 19.
9. Deutsche Bundesbank (1984).
10. Deutsche Bundesbank (1988).
11. Despres *et al.* (1996); see also Fratianni and Hauskrecht (1999), p. 16.
12. For the last example, see Fischer (1999).
13. So speaks McKinnon in his historical reviews about a generally accepted Bagehot's rule, nevertheless confining it to short-run liquidity crises (and an international gold drain during the period of the gold standard). Calomiris again distinguishes exactly between liquidity crises and solvency crises, correctly rejecting the thesis of an existence of liquidity crises concerning the lending policy of the IMF – and speaks nevertheless of a lack of an 'effective' lender of last resort. The third reference in this context is to Krugman, who, considering the limited resources of the IMF, denies a 'full-scale' use of the lender of last resort, see McKinnon (1996), pp. 26, 33; Calomiris (1998), p. 13; Krugman (1998), pp. 4ff. In this context, it is remarkable that the only correct interpretation of the lender of last resort, I have ever found, was an editorial postscript to the Depres *et al.* (1996) article in *The Economist.*
14. See the instructive analysis by McKinnon (1996), pp. 38ff.

References

Calomiris, C. W. 'The IMF's imprudent role as a lender of last resort', *The Cato Journal*, vol. 17, no. 3, 1998.

Clarida, R., Gali, J. and Gertler, M. 'Monetary policy rates in practice. Some international evidence', *European Economic Review*, vol. 42 (1998) pp. 1033–67.

Despres, E., Kindleberger, C. P. and Salant, W. S. 'The dollar and world liquidity – a minority view', *The Economist*, 5 February (1996), pp. 526–9.

Deutsche Bundesbank 'The Deutsche Mark as an international investment currency', *Monthly Report*, vol. 36 no. 1, 1984.

Deutsche Bundesbank 'Forty years of the Deutsche Mark', *Monthly Report*, vol. 40, no. 1, 1998.

Fischer, S. 'On the need of an international lender of last resort', [online at] http://www.imf.org/external/np/speeches/1999/010399.HTM, 1999.

Fratianni, M. and Hauskrecht, A. 'From the gold standard to a bipolar monetary system', *Open Economics Review*, special issue 1/99, 1999.

Fratianni, M., Hauskrecht, A. and Maccario, A. 'Dominant currencies and the future of the euro', *Open Economics Review*, special issue 1/99, 1999

Krugman, P. 'Will Asia bounce back?', [online at] web.mit edu/krugman/www/suisse.html, 1998.

McKinnon, R. L. 'The rules of the game: international money and exchange rates', in *The Rules of the Game: International Money – an Historical Perspective*, Cambridge, MA/London: MIT Press (1996), pp. 23–90.

Schröder, K. *Die Stellung des britischen Pfundes in der internationalen Währungshierarchie. Eine monetäre Analyse Großbritanniens 1945–1985*. Marburg: Metropoilis, 2001.

10
Epilogue: The Meaning of Sound Money*

Sir Samuel Brittan

It is an honour for me to be asked to give the address at this dinner. Today's symposium celebrates not one, but two, anniversaries. The first of course is the 50th anniversary of the German Mark. Nothing of course is for ever. But when the Mark bids us goodbye – whether in 1999 or 2002 – it will be in the process of giving birth to the Euro, a successor framed in its image. You will have heard a great deal both about the Mark and the Euro in the course of the day; and I should like to turn to the other event.

We are also celebrating the birthday of Professor Stephen Frowen. If any of you are tactless enough to ask which birthday he is celebrating, my reply is that it is quite irrelevant. Numerous poets have declared that we should fight the 'dying of the light'; and no one has taken this advice more seriously to heart. The British poet Samuel Taylor Coleridge, who was also a student of German thought, wrote the famous poem *Youth and Age*, in which he explained how the fires of youth continued to burn, despite the change in the outward appearance. In the case of Stephen Frowen, even the appearance still shows the zest of a sparkling student. Our guest of honour has continued to work, not only from a sense of duty, but also for the sheer fun of it. And we are all better off as a result. The link between our two anniversaries is strong. Stephen Frowen has been the first Bundesbank Professor in the Free University of Berlin. Although a supporter of Bundesbank monetary principles, Stephen has followed the argument wherever it has led. So far from objecting, the Bundesbank is also honouring Stephen Frowen; and I regret that I was not able to attend a recent dinner that it gave in his honour. I have a more personal reason for admiring Stephen. For early in his career he was

* Pre-dinner speech at the Symposium '50 Years of the German Mark', in honour of Stephen F. Frowen, at the University of Birmingham, 26 June 1998

an economic journalist and editor of the distinguished monthly *The Bankers' Magazine* (now *Financial World*). He thus showed that it was possible to move from journalism to the academic world with grace and ease. Perhaps more of us should have followed his example. Yet I wonder if such a move would be possible today. I once wrote in one of my own books that the techniques of economics have been overemphasized at the expense of the underlying ideas. Work in another sphere, whether in journalism or even in government, is too often regarded as time wasted which could have been spent writing academic articles to add to one's CV. Stephen has covered a wide field. I can only highlight two or three themes. At one time he was much preoccupied with the economics of uncertainty: how decisions are made in a world where the real power to predict is very limited. This is a serious subject and cannot be brushed aside by cheap sneers at forecasts.

Our guest of honour is, however, probably best known as a keen student of monetary theory and practice, especially of the comparison between the British and German approaches, writing in the two languages and equally welcome on both sides of the North Sea. But in the last few years Stephen has been especially concerned with yet another theme: the link between ethics and economics. He is Chairman of the Finance and Ethics group of the Catholic von Hügel Institute. Indeed Cardinal Hume has expressed his personal regret that he has been unable to attend tonight, but extends his very best wishes. For two millennia there has been a gulf of incomprehension between teachings of the Church and the outlook of market economics. Stephen has always believed that they have much to learn from each other and that co-operation is more fruitful than conflict. Although I come from a different religious and philosophical background, anyone should be able to see – as a matter of logic and not of sermonizing – that it is quite impossible to advocate any economic policy at all without some ethical background. Take for instance the Bundesbank belief in sound money and low inflation. This is not a totem pole, but something which should increase human welfare – not only by promoting prosperity, but by encouraging honest dealings. These become very difficult if the measuring rod in which they are denominated is unstable and unreliable.

Deflation

I know that Stephen would not want me to sit down without making some remarks on some topical issue. And I hope those of you whose main interest is in Anglo-German political and cultural aspects will bear with me if I spend a few final minutes looking more closely at the meaning of sound money. For nearly the whole postwar period this could have been summarized as low inflation, with stable prices as a final goal. There would not be much dispute, however, that sound money involves stability in both directions: avoiding deflation as well as inflation. Over the past 50 or even 60 years inflation has been overwhelmingly the greater danger. Not only that. Numerous warnings about deflation, especially from those who remembered or read about the 1930s, turned out to be wrong or misleading. The British Prime Minister Harold Macmillan would begin Cabinet meetings by warning of the dangers of a prewar-type slump. Perhaps fortunately, the British Treasury took little notice. Macmillan himself would justify the contrast between his fears and his actions by saying that Britain could not afford to remain 'an island of inflation in a world of deflation'. (As far as that goes, this remains valid.) You all know the story of the boy who cried 'wolf' as a practical joke once too often. When a wolf really appeared no-one believed him; and he and his family were eaten. There is a similar danger that economists – having had so many false warnings – will not pay sufficient attention to signs of deflation when they really are present. These are most obvious in Japan, but are also apparent in the wider international economy.

The proverbial visitor from Mars would suppose that deflation would be much easier to fight than inflation. After all, fighting inflation involves trying to get people to spend less and accept lower pay increases, while fighting deflation means trying to get them to spend more – surely not very difficult from all we know of human nature. Moreover, the techniques of demand stimulation have been endlessly studied since the 1930s. So we have no excuse for being without contingency plans. Why then does it look as if policy makers may find it difficult?

Sound Money

There is an asymmetry between inflationary and deflationary forces. The first reflect excessive spending in money terms. The second reflects inadequate spending. But their impact is rather different. Excessive spending soon feeds into the price level both of goods and of assets. Inadequate spending, or falling spending, tends to be reflected first in falling output and employment. This is because of the rigidity of prices and pay against downward pressures. If they fall at all, they do so rather less and more slowly. Would we really wish it otherwise? Surely not. Nominal interest rates cannot fall below zero. If the general price level is falling, real interest rates will rise. A modest and gradual deflation may do little harm if the resulting level of real interest rates is appropriate in the light of savings and investment trends. For example the period between 1873 and 1896, which used to be known as the Great Depression, is now seen to have been one of reasonably rapid growth. Indeed it experienced a faster growth than the period between then and the First World War, when prices were slowly rising. But in a country facing a severe recession, like Japan today, even a modest 1–2 per cent annual fall in prices would be perverse.

There is also a problem about indices. Consumer price indices are lagging indicators. They are heavily influenced by administered prices for public services, rent and so on, and also by indirect tax changes. They may therefore provide false reassurance. Despite the weakness of the Japanese economy, the Japanese CPI has fallen only once over a full year in the 1990s – that was in 1995 and only by 0.1 per cent. Even now it is about the same as it was a year ago. Yet Japanese producer prices have been falling quite frequently and by notable amounts. They were on the last count nearly 2 per cent below a year ago and nearly 8 per cent below their level in 1991. In Britain, while the inflation target of 2 per cent has not often been met, and rarely undershot, underlying producer prices have not risen in the last year. In the US, underlying producer prices have fallen by nearly 2 per cent compared with a year ago. Unfortunately producer prices are not representative of the whole economy, as they reflect mainly manufacturing which is now little more than a fifth of the total. Probably the best underlying measure is either the GDP deflator or the gross expenditure deflator. Unfortunately these are reported late, and are erratic and subject to much revision. When inflation was in double digits, the priority was clearly to get it down; and measurement discrepancies made little difference. Now they may affect the whole direction of policy.

Despite the stickiness of some prices, output in Japan has been stagnating for most of the 1990s and Japan is now very clearly in recession. It is not a country on which I claim any expertise, but shall use it to present some stylized facts and arguments. What then is perceived to be the difficulty about reflating the Japanese economy? The two standard methods are to increase the money supply and/or to budget for a higher deficit. The usual objection to easing monetary policy is that Japanese short-term nominal interest rates are, at around 0.5 per cent, already almost as low as they can go. Japan does seem to be in what Keynes described as a liquidity trap. This is not the end of the argument on the monetary side. Several distinguished American economists have argued that, instead of confining itself to short term operations, the Bank of Japan should engage in large bond purchases which will put money directly into the hands of the non-bank public without having to go by way of the usual route of lower base rates or the equivalent. Indeed, some commentators suspect that this is what the Bank of Japan is actually doing, but view the prospect with alarm rather than hope. One objection is that the recipients of extra cash balances may neither consume more nor invest in Japanese capital assets (paper or real) but simply buy more US securities. My initial reaction is 'so what?' The impact would then be to lower the yen in the foreign exchange market and stimulate the economy by a different route.

We then come up against the domino theory. If the yen depreciates even further, it would worsen the competitive position of other East Asian economies and could in the end trigger off a Chinese devaluation and thus set off a prewar-type game of competitive depreciation in which the US and Europe would not stand idly by. There is an answer even to that. If the US and Europe were really worried about catching the deflationary disease the appropriate response would be for them to engage in monetary expansion as well. In fact US policy makers are now much more worried about potential inflationary overheating and the Wall Street bubble than they are about inadequate domestic spending. So they should welcome some easing of Japanese demand for their products. We might then have an export-led Japanese expansion and a European expansion led by domestic demand.

There would obviously be sectoral problems; but we shall always have those without a world monetary authority, and perhaps even with one. (But please do not bring up the reaction of the US Congress to an American balance of payments deficit. If all the billions that have been put into economic education in the USA still leave its legislature afraid of a current payments deficit, irrespective of its causes, then we might as well throw in the towel on human rationality and close down our universities.) Let us push the analysis a bit further. Suppose that most of the major economies of the world really were suffering from a Japanese type deflationary threat? Would competitive depreciation then matter? So long as countries try to depreciate only by means of easy money policies, it probably would not. For although the effects on the exchange rate might cancel out, the net result would be an increase in the world money supply, which – in this situation – is what the doctor ordered.

There is a further twist to the argument. Paul Krugman has said that a Japanese monetary relaxation would be more effective if the Japanese could be brought to expect gradual inflation of say 2 or 3 per cent per annum over the next few years. I do not find it shocking. General price stability is quite consistent with short to medium term periods of changing price levels. The question is how to bring about this expectation. Words would have to be supplemented by a particularly large monetary boost. One would then have to hope that such a boost would do more to boost inflationary expectations than to spread general alarm and despondency. Monetary economics has never been far away from a looking-glass world where what happens depends in part on what people expect. How about fiscal policy which has been the classic response of many followers of Keynes to a slump that does not yield easily to monetary stimulation? The main objection is that of a debt trap. In other words future taxpayers will have to pay more and more to service the interest on the national debt rather than to provide public goods and services.

The actual Japanese debt and deficit position looks like an enigma buried in a mystery, because of the complications of pension funds and a large 'second' public sector which does not figure in the official budget accounts. So my remarks on the fiscal aspect are even more stylised than they are on the monetary aspects. Faced with the threat of a slump and no inflationary danger on the horizon, governments are quite justified in borrowing from the banking system at extremely low rates of interest. I dimly recall that Milton Friedman's original postwar programme for monetary stability proposed an automatic increase in the budget deficit in a slump and an automatic surplus in a boom – as a reult of the 'built-in stabilizers'. He also envisaged that the deficits would be financed by monetary creation and the surpluses by retiring money and that this would indeed be a principal transmission mechanism for monetary policy. I do not know whether today's institutional complexities would allow such an approach. But if the Maastricht Treaty or the German inspired Growth and Stability Pact would not allow for this in Europe in an emergency, so much the worse for these pacts. Let us continue the analysis.

Suppose that because of political pressures or misguided doctrines Japanese governments do nevertheless finance deficits by long term borrowing at substantial real interest rates. Would that be dangerous? The burden of higher interest rates is normally a purely internal transfer. Nearly all the arguments about debt traps assume that output is on its trend level and at the highest rate consistent with non-accelerating inflation. But if there is a large output gap which looks like persisting for some years, there then surely is a cost-benefit calculation to be made. It is a question of weighing up the disincentive effects of higher taxes some time in the future against the stimulatory effects of a higher level of demand. At this point I would have to hand over to somebody mathematically more qualified. But before I do I would stress that the result of any such estimate is crucially dependent on whether the output gap is simply a once-for-all loss of production or whether (because of hysteresis effects), the result is a lower medium to long term rate of growth. I have just been engaged in just those long chains of arguments, which Alfred Marshall advised us to avoid and, moreover, tried to do so in words rather than algebra. What does it all amounts to?

The best summary I can make is to recall two suggestions for increasing the stock of money, due respectively to Keynes and Milton Friedman. Keynes suggested burying pound notes in the ground and leaving it to the profit motive to dig them up – thus neatly combining monetary and fiscal policy. Milton Friedman posited the dropping of dollar notes by helicopter. Keynes's suggestion was made ironically. Friedman's was meant, not as a policy proposal, but as a way of discussing the effects of different monetary strategies without getting bogged down in banking technicalities. But however they were intended, they both can and should be regarded as last resort suggestions. Rather than allow either a major economy, or the industrial world as a whole, to plunge into a deflationary spiral it would indeed be better to use the helicopter or the hole in the ground. What this amounts to saying is that however pessimistic people are, if they are given enough money they will eventually spend it. Even if they work less and take more leisure, this will be voluntary leisure and a sign of prosperity rather than slump. If you do not believe me, try your own thought experiment. If you received a modest sum of money from the government in the post you might be very suspicious. But if these kept on arriving in sufficiently large quantities, you might just try the experiment of spending a little more to see what happens. To my mind the only valid argument against experimenting with every variety of monetary and fiscal expansion is that it could stoke up a fresh round of inflation when confidence recovers and people start spending their idle balances in earnest. To which I can only reply this should indeed inhibit the monetary authorities in the face of the normal postwar type of recession; but if the deflationary danger is great enough, some of the benefits of emergency action would in the end outweigh more remote and hypothetical dangers. These arguments might seen to be taking us a long way from the Bundesbank and its cautious traditions. But although the Bundesbank has made mistakes, it has been led by rational people and, if the dangers ever came to be the opposite of what they have been in the 50 years that the Mark has existed, I am sure that those who have led the Bundesbank and who will now lead to the European Central Bank will be rational enough to employ a new bag of tricks. My only worry is whether they will do so quickly enough.

Stephen F. Frowen: Bibliographical Data

Books edited

Economic Issues: A Financial and Economic Debate in the Critical Years 1954–57, with H. C. Hillmann. (London: Waterlow & Sons, 1957) pp. xi, 231.

Enzyklopädisches Lexikon für das Geld-, Bank- und Börsenwesen (jt.ed.) (Frankfurt: Fritz Knapp Verlag, 1957) 2nd edn 1958; vol. 1, A–H, pp. v, 827; vol. 2, I–Z, pp. 1067, 3rd edn 1967. (This encyclopaedia also constitutes the second edition of Melchior Palyi and Paul Quittner (eds) *Handwörterbuch des Bankwesens*.)

Monetary Policy and Economic Activity in West Germany, with A. S. Courakis and M. H. Miller. (London: Surrey University Press in association with International Textbook Co.; New York: Wiley/Halsted Press; Stuttgart: Gustav Fischer Verlag, 1977) pp. xviii, 268.

A Framework of International Banking (Guildford: Guildford Educational Press; Würzburg and Vienna: Physica-Verlag, 1979) pp. xiv, 273.

Controlling Industrial Economies. Essays in Honour of Christopher Thomas Saunders (London: Macmillan; New York: St Martin's Press, 1983) pp. xii, 378.

Business, Time and Thought: Selected Papers of G. L. S. Shackle (London: Macmillan; New York: New York University Press, 1988) pp. xiii, 255.

Unknowledge and Choice in Economics. Proceedings of a Conference in Honour of G. L. S. Shackle (London: Macmillan; New York: St Martin's Press, 1990) pp. xxvi, 219.

Monetary Policy and Financial Innovations in Five Industrial Countries: The UK, the USA, West Germany, France and Japan, with D. Kath (London: Macmillan; New York: St Martin's Press, 1992) pp. xiv, 171.

Monetary Theory and Monetary Policy: New Tracks for the 1990s (London: Macmillan; New York: St Martin's Press, 1993) pp. xviii, 367.

Financial Decision-Making and Moral Responsibility, with F. P. McHugh (London: Macmillan; NewYork: St Martin's Press, 1995) pp. xxiv, 256.

'Understanding the Bundesbank', special issue of *Central Banking*, 6, 1, Summer 1995, 19–78 (with R. Pringle).

The German Currency Union of 1990: A Critical Assessment, with J. Hölscher (London: Macmillan; New York: St Martin's Press, 1997) pp. xxi, 269.

Welfare and Values: Challenging the Culture of Unconcern, with P. Askonas (London: Macmillan; New York: St Martin's Press, 1997) pp. xvi, 225.

Hayek: Economist and Social Philosopher – A Critical Retrospect (London: Macmillan; New York: St Martin's Press, 1997) pp. xxvi, 324.

Inside the Bundesbank, with R. Pringle (London: Macmillan; New York: St Martin's Press, 1998) pp. xxii, 188.

Risk Mangement for Central Bankers, with R. Pringle and B. Weller (London: Central Banking Publications, 2000) pp. xvi, 224.

Economics as an Art of Thought. Essays in Memory of G. L. S. Shackle, with P. E. Earl (London and New York: Routledge, 2000), pp. xxvi, 425.

Financial Competition, Risk and Accountability: British and German Experiences, with F. P. McHugh (London and New York: Palgrave, 2001) pp. xxiv, 320.

Economists in Discussion: The Correspondence between G. L. S. Shackle and S. F. Frowen, 1951–1992 (London and New York: Palgrave, 2001).

Translations from German into English

Value, Capital and Rent, by Knut Wicksell. The German original, *Über Wert, Kapital und Rente*, was first published in 1893 (London: George Allen & Unwin, 1954; New York: Augustus M. Kelley, 1970) (Reprints of Economic Classics) pp. 180.

The Role of the Economist as Official Adviser, by W. A. Jöhr and H. W. Singer (London: George Allen & Unwin, 1955) pp. xii, 150.

Translations from English into German

Die Wurzeln des Antikapitalismus, by Ludwig von Mises. The English original, *The Anti-Capitalistic Mentality*, was first published in 1956 (Princeton, NJ: Van Nostrand). (Frankfurt: Fritz Knapp Verlag, 1957; 2nd edn, 1979) pp. 125.

Contributions to books

Economic Issues: A Financial and Economic Debate in the Critical Years 1954–57 (eds Stephen Frowen and H. C. Hillmann) (London: Waterlow & Sons, 1957). Chapter titles: 'Introduction', pp. vii–viii; 'Bank Chairmen and the Credit Squeeze', pp. 83–6; 'The Future of Intra-European Payments' (with H. E. Evitt), pp. 212–15.

Enzyklopädisches Lexikon für das Geld-, Bank- und Börsenwesen, Vol. 1 (eds Stephen Frowen *et al.*) (Frankfurt: Fritz Knapp Verlag, 1957; 2nd edn 1958). Chapter titles: England 'Bank of England', pp. 515–22; 'Geld- und Kapitalmarkt', pp. 523–34; 'Londoner Börse', pp. 534–6; 'Staatshaushalt', pp. 536–45.

Zur Entwicklungshilfe: Zu aktuellen Problemen der Finanzierung im Blickwinkel der Unternehmungen (Berlin: Deutsche Gesellschaft für Betriebswirtschaft, 1962). Chapter title: 'Aktuelle Finanzierungsprobleme am Beispiel der britischen Industrie'.

Planmässige Finanzierung der Unternehmungen (Berlin: Deutsche Gesellschaft für Betriebswirtschaft, 1964). Chapter title: 'Probleme der industriellen Fremdfinanzierung im Vereinigten Königreich'.

Britannica Book of the Year 1965. Events of 1964 (London: Encyclopaedia Britannica Ltd, 1965). Chapter title: 'Stocks and Shares' (unsigned), pp. 480–82.

Die Börse: Funktionen und Organisation im internationalen Vergleich. Proceedings of the 3rd International Banking Seminar of the German Committee of AIESEC held in Düsseldorf, 23–31 July 1965; Patron: Hermann J. Abs (Cologne: AIESEC, 1965). Chapter title: 'Die Funktionen der Wertpapierbörsen in volkswirtschaftlicher Sicht'.

Die Unternehmung bei wachsender Integration der Märkte: Eine Herausforderung an die Betriebswirtschaft. Papers presented at the 18th German Betriebswirtschafter-Tag (Berlin: Deutsche Gesellschaft für Betriebswirtschaft, 1965. Chapter title: 'Probleme der Unternehmensgrösse, Kapitalbeschaffung und Exportfinanzierung im Vereinigten Königreich', pp. 192–203.

Die EWG auf dem Weg zur Wirtschaftsunion (Berlin: Deutsche Gesellschaft für Betriebswirtschaft, 1968). Chapter title: 'Sterling und die Erweiterung des gemeinsamen Marktes'.

Monetary Policy and Economic Activity in West Germany (eds S. F. Frowen, A. S. Courakis and M. H. Miller) (London: Surrey University Press in association with International Textbook Co.; New York: Wiley/Halsted Press; Stuttgart: Gustav Fischer Verlag, 1977). Chapter title: 'The Demand for and Supply of Money in the Federal Republic of Germany 1965–1974' (with P. Arestis), pp. 129–42. Comment by M. H. Miller, pp. 143–6.

A Framework of International Banking (ed. S. F. Frowen) (Guildford: Guildford Educational Press, 1979). Chapter title: 'Editor's Foreword', pp. xi–xiv.

The New International Economic Order: Philosophical and Socio-cultural Implications (International Progress Organisation. Vienna: Studies in International Relations III) (ed. H. Köchler) (Guildford: Guildford Educational Press, 1980). Chapter title: 'The New International Economic Order: Some Basic Principles and the Need for Restructuring the World Economy', pp. 64–72.

Financial Markets in the 80s. Papers from The Financial Markets Conference presented by the First Austrian Bank on 6 November 1980 at the Vienna Conference Centre (ed. A. M. Burghardt) (Vienna: First Austrian Bank, 1981). Chapter title: 'The Interaction between the International Monetary System and Financial Markets in the 1980s', pp. 7–22.

Controlling Industrial Economies. Essays in Honour of Christopher Thomas Saunders (ed. S. F. Frowen) (London: Macmillan, 1983). Chapter titles: 'Introduction', pp. vii–x; 'Impacts of Fiscal Actions on Aggregate Income and the Monetarist Controversy: an Empirical Investigation' (with P. Arestis), pp. 271–89.

Honecker's Germany (ed. David Childs) (London: Allen & Unwin, 1985). Chapter title: 'The Economy of the German Democratic Republic', pp. 32–49.

Innovationen auf Finanzmärkten (eds G. Bruns and K. Häuser) (Frankfurt: Fritz Knapp Verlag. 1986). Chapter title: 'Neuere Entwicklungen auf dem Londoner Euromarkt', pp. 89–115.

Frankfurt: Germany's Financial Centre (London: Euromoney Publications, 1988). Chapter title: 'Historical Introduction', pp. 7–10.

Business, Time and Thought: Selected Papers of G. L. S. Shackle (ed. S. F. Frowen) (London: Macmillan; New York: New York University Press, 1988). Chapter titles: 'Preface', p. x; 'Introduction', pp. xi–xiii.

Geldpolitik und ökonomische Entwicklung – Ein Symposium (eds H. Riese and H.-P. Spahn) (Regensburg. Transfer Verlag, 1990. Chapter title. 'Die Rolle Grossbritanniens im Europäischen Währungssystem', pp. 156–62.

Unknowledge and Choice in Economics. Proceedings of a Conference in Honour of G. L. S. Shackle (ed. S. F. Frowen) (London: Macmillan, 1990). Chapter titles: 'Preface', pp. xiii–xiv; 'Interest Rates and Investment Decisions', pp. 156–67.

Economic Problems of the 1990s: Europe, the Developing Countries and the United States. (eds Paul Davidson and J. A. Kregel (Aldershot: Edward Elgar, 1991). Chapter title: 'A German Perspective of a European Single Market and EMU', pp. 107–21.

La 'Rerum Novarum' e i Problemi Sociali Oggi (ed. A. Luciani) (Milan: Editrice Massimo, 1991). Chapter title: 'Rerum Novarum and the World Economy Today', pp. 75–92.

Monetary Policy and Financial Innovations in Five Industrial Countries: The UK, the USA, West Germany, France and Japan (eds S. F. Frowen and D. Kath) (London:

Macmillan. 1992). Chapter titles: 'Introduction' (with D. Kath), pp. xii–xiv; 'Financial Innovations and the Stability of the Demand for Money in Germany since 1974' (with Heinrich Schlomann), pp. 59–81.

Things Old and New: Catholic Social Teaching Revisited (eds F. P. McHugh and S. M. Natale) (University Press of America, 1993). Chapter title: 'From Rerum Novarum to John Paul II: International Economics as an Empirical Testing of Adequacies in Catholic Social Teaching', pp. 312–32.

Monetary Theory and Monetary Policy: New Tracks for the 1990s (ed. S. F. Frowen) (London: Macmillan; New York: St Martin's Press, 1993). Chapter titles: 'Introduction', pp. xxii–xxviii; 'The Demand for Money in the US, UK, Japan and West Germany: An Empirical Study of the Evidence since 1973' (with Herbert Buscher). Comments by Jürgen Siebke, pp. 123–70.

Financial Decision-Making and Moral Responsibility (eds S. F Frowen and F. P. McHugh) (London: Macmillan; New York: St Martin's Press, 1995). Chapter titles 'Introduction', pp. xxii–xxiv (with F. P. McHugh); 'The Functions of Money and Financial Credit: Their Objectives, Structure and Inbuilt Deficiencies' (with comments by A. B. Cramp and J. G. Ellis), pp. 31–56.

Neuere Entwicklungen in der Geldtheorie und Geldpolitik: Implikationen für die Europäische Währungsunion. Festschrift in Honour of Norbert Kloten (eds Peter Bofinger and Karl-Heinz Ketterer (Tübingen: J. C. B. Mohr (Paul Siebeck), 1996). Chapter title: 'Inflationsbekämpfung in Grossbritannien', pp. 225–240.

Hayek: Economist and Social Philosopher – A Critical Retrospect (ed. S. F. Frowen) (London: Macmillan; New York: St Martin's Press, 1997). Chapter title: 'Introduction', pp. xxi–xxvi.

The German Currency Union of 1990: A Critical Assessment (eds S. F. Frowen and J. Hölscher) (London: Macmillan; New York: St Martin's Press, 1997). Chapter title: 'Introduction' (with J. Hölscher), pp. xviii–xxi; 'The Dimensions of German Economic Unification: Keynote Address', pp. 1–10.

Welfare and Values: Challenging the Culture of Unconcern (eds S. F. Frowen and P. Askonas) (London: Macmillan; New York: St Martin's Press, 1997). Chapter titles: 'Welfare and Values: Setting out Markers', pp. x–xvi (with P. Askonas); 'Need for Economic Expansion'. pp. 138–43.

Visionen im Bankmanagement: Zukünftige Anforderungen an die Führung von Banken. Festschrift für Leo Schuster (eds Stephan Hörter and Andreas Wagner) (Munich: Verlag C. H. Beck, 1997). Chapter title: 'The Influence of Globalised Money and Capital Markets for the Personal Sector with Regard to Ethical Problems' (with E. Karakitsos), pp. 49–69.

Inside the Bundesbank (eds S. F. Frowen and R. Pringle) (London: Macmillan; New York: St Martin's Press, 1998). Chapter titles: 'Introduction' (with R. Pringle), pp. xix–xxii; 'Profiles of Bundesbank Presidents Hans Tietmeyer, Helmut Schlesinger and Karl Otto Pöhl', pp. 174–8.

Nachdenken über Grenzen (eds Rüdiger Görner and Suzanne Kirkbright) (Munich: iudicium verlag, 1999). Chapter title: 'Economic Margins – A Welfare and Moral Issue?', pp. 73–82.

Vermittlungen: German Studies at the Turn of the Century. Festschrift für Nigel B. R. Reeves (eds Rüdiger Görner and Helen Kelly-Holmes) (Munich: iudicium verlag, 1999). Chapter title: 'Wege zur europäischen Integration: eine kritische Betrachtung aus nationalökonomischer Sicht', pp. 163–77.

Das Menschenbild der freien Gesellschaft: Globalisierung und Europäische Integration (eds. Eduard J. M. Kroker and Bruno Dechamps) (Frankfurt: Verlag Frankfurter Allgemeine Zeitung, Verlagsbereich Buch, 2000). Chapter title: 'Europäische Integration als Gestaltungsaufgabe – Die Verantwortung für die kommenden Generationen', pp. 99–121.

Economics an an Art of Thought. Essays in memory of G. L. S. Shackle (eds P. E. Earl and S. F. Frowen) (London and New York: Routledge, 2000). Chapter title: 'Introduction' (with P. E. Earl), pp. xiii–xxvi.

Financial Turbulence and Capital Markets in Transition Countries (ed. J. Hölscher) (London and New York: Palgrave, 2000). Chapter title: 'Financial Markets in Transition Countries: Problems and Aspirations' pp. 179–85.

Nassau William Senior's 'An Outline of the Science of Political Economy' – Vademecum zu einem Klassiker der Verteilungstheorie (ed. Herbert Hax) (Düsseldorf: Verlag Wirtschaft und Finanzen, 2000). Chapter title: 'Nassau William Senior: Aspekte seiner Wert-, Geld- und Handelstheorie', pp. 43–52.

50 Years of the German Mark. Essays in Honour of Stephen F. Frowen (ed. J. Hölscher (London and New York: Palgrave, 2001) Chapter title: 'The Fate of Key Currencies: A Strategic Approach' (with Karakitsos), pp. 159–182.

Financial Competition, Risk and Accountability: British and German Experiences (eds S. F. Frowen and F. P. McHugh) (London and New York: Palgrave, 2001). Chapter titles: 'Introduction' (with F. P. McHugh), pp. xvii–xxiv; 'The Savings-Ratio Behaviour in Globalized Money and Capital Markets: A Comparison of the UK and German Experiences' (with E. Karakitsos), pp. 146–68.

Money, Macroeconomics and Keynes: Essays in Honour of Victoria Chick, vol. 1 (eds. P. Arestis, M. Desai and S. Dow (London and New York: Routledge, 2002) Chapter title: 'The Fate of Key Currencies: DM, Sterling and the Euro' (with E. Karakitsos), pp. 205–215.

Ten Years of German Unification: Transfer, Transformation, Incorporation? (eds. J. Leonhard and L. Funk). Series: The New Germany in Context, vol. 1 (Birmingham: Birmingham University Press, 2002) Chapter title: 'German Monetary Unification and its Aftermath'.

Exogenität und Endogenität: Die Geldmenge in der Geschichte des ökonomischen Denkens und in der modernen Politik. Festschrift in Honour of Karl Häuser (ed. Bertram Schefold) (Marburg: Metropolis Verlag, 2002. Chapter titles: 'Comments on Paper by Heinz Rieter "Deutsche Geldtheorie im 19. Jahrhundert – mehr als nur ein Schatten englischer Debatten?"', pp. 53–62; 'Karl Häuser – Wegweiser der Wirtschaftstheorie und politik in der Bundesrepublik Deutschland', pp. 157–160.

Articles

'Monetary Policy and Investors', *The Bankers' Magazine*, 179/1333, April 1955, 341–3.

'Balance of Payments 1954–1955', *The Bankers' Magazine*, 179/1334, May 1955, 450–55.

'The new EPU Year and Subsequent Plans', *The Bankers' Magazine*, 180/1338, Sept. 1955 (with H. E. Evitt), 177–80.

'The Autumn Budget', *The Bankers' Magazine*, 180/1340, Nov. 1955, 355–8.

'Bank Chairmen and the Credit Squeeze', *The Bankers' Magazine*, 181/1343, Feb. 1956, 103–6.

'The British Balance of Payments 1959–56', *The Bankers' Magazine*, 181/1346, 413–19.

'Suez and the Credit Squeeze', *The Bankers' Magazine*, 182/1351, Oct. 1956, 269–71.

'The Rise in Personal Savings', *The Bankers' Magazine*, 182/1353, Dec. 1956, 454–6.

'The Flow of Money', *The Bankers' Magazine*, 184/1364, Nov. 1957, 339–42. For comment, see *Manchester Guardian* (30 Oct. 1957). (Extracts reprinted in *Deutsche Bundesbank: Auszüge aus Presseartikeln*, 115, 6 Nov. 1957).

'The British Balance of Payments, 1957–58, *The Bankers' Magazine*, 185/1370, May 1958, 395–403.

'A Deflationary Budget', *The Bankers' Magazine*, 185/1370, May 1958, 389–94.

'The United Kingdom and European Integration', *Economic Reports* (Creditanstalt-Bankverein, Vienna), 11/31, May 1959, 34–6 (special issue on Austria's Relationship to the Larger European Market).

'Economic Policy after the Election', *The Bankers' Magazine*, 188/1388, Nov. 1959, 335–7.

'The Radcliffe Evidence: Medium and Long-Term Finance for Small Businesses', *The Bankers' Magazine*, 190/1398, Sept. 1960, 159–66 (for comments see A. A. Shenfield, *The Bankers' Magazine*, 190/1400, Nov. 1960, 333; Lombard, 'Doubts about a Gap Filler', *Financial Times*, 29 Aug. 1960; 'Finance for Small Business', *The Times*, 29 Aug. 1960; and Lombard, 'New Doubts about a Gap Filler', *Financial Times*, 25 Jan. 1961).

'Welthandel und regionaler Zusammenschluss', *Dokumente* (Journal of International Cooperation, Cologne), 16, 1960, 128–30.

'Entwicklungen im britischen Bankwesen', *Wirtschaftsberichte* (Creditanstalt-Bankverein, Vienna), 12/32, Nov. 1960.

'Britische Banken im Commonwealth', *Zeitschrift für das gesamte Kreditwesen*, 14/6. 1961.

'Merchant Banks', *The Bankers' Magazine*, 192/1408, July 1961, 1–10 (with T. M. Rybczynski).

'Die gegenwärtige Lage des Pfundes Sterling', *Zeitschrift für das gesamte Kreditwesen*, 14/18, 1961.

'West Berlin: Economic Aspects', *Europe House Papers*, no. 3, 1961. Proceedings of a Europe House symposium at the House of Commons (under the chairmanship of Sir Gilbert Longden, MBE) entitled 'West Berlin: What Kind of a Free City' 22 Nov. 1961, consisting of three lectures: (1) Stephen Frowen, 'Economic Aspects', (2) The Hon. Alastair Buchan, 'Strategic Aspects,' and (3) The Rt Hon. Lord Healey of Riddlesden, CH, MBE, 'Political Aspects'.

'Ein unumgängliches Mass von Planung', *Dokumente*, 17, 1961, 386–8.

'Die Problematik des Pfundes Sterling', *Konjunkturpolitik*, 8/2, 1962, 74–90.

'Das Pfund Sterling im Schatten der Wahlen', *Zeitschrift für das gesamte Kreditwesen*, 15/10, 1962.

'Das britische Börsensystem', *Zeitschrift für das gesamte Kreditwesen*, 5/13, 15 and 16, 1962.

'Die Entwicklung der britischen Banken während der ersten Jahreshälfte 1962', *Zeitschrift für das gesamte Kreditwesen*, 15, 1962.

'Industry and the NEDC', *The Manager*, May 1962, 25–7.

'London und das europäische Bankwesen', *Zeitschrift für das gesamte Kreditwesen*, 16/1, 1963.

'Das Londoner Börsenbild 1962', *Zeitschrift für das gesamte Kreditwesen*, 16/4, 1963.

'Wechselkursflexibilität und das Weltwährungssystem', *Kredit und Kapital*, 2/4 1969, 369–95.

'The Unsolved Deutschmark Problem', *The Bankers' Magazine*, 209/1515, March, 1970, 137–43.

'Some Investigations of Demand and Supply Functions for Money in the Federal Republic of Germany, 1965 to 1974, *Weltwirtschaftliches Archiv*, 112/1, 1976, 136–64 (with P. Arestis).

'The Dynamic Impacts of Government Expenditure and the Monetary Base on Aggregate Income: The West German Case, 1965 to 1974', *Kredit und Kapital*, 9/3, 1976, 368–83 (with P. Arestis).

'The Existence of a World Demand for Money Function: Preliminary Results', *Kredit und Kapital*, 10/1 1977, 1–17 (with G. Kouris).

'Die reale Geldmenge in einer volkswirtschaftlichen Produktionsfunktion', *Ifo-Studien*, 23/1–2 1977, 155–76 (with P. Arestis and E. Karakitsos).

'The Dynamic Impacts of Government Expenditure and the Monetary Base on Aggregate Income: The Case of Four OECD Countries, 1965–74', *Public Finance*, 33/1–2, 1978, 1–22 (with P. Arestis and E. Karakitsos).

'The Existence of a World Demand-for-Money Function: A Reply, *Kredit und Kapital*, 12/1, 1979, 73–82 (with G. Kouris).

'Inflation and the World Demand-for-Money Function', *Kredit und Kapital*, 13/1, 1980, 21–37 (with G. Kouris).

'Why the IMF is Increasing Its Role in Recycling', *Euromoney*, Jan. 1981, 123–32.

'Control of the UK Money Supply', *Wirtschaftsanalysen* (First Austrian Bank, Vienna), no. 2, 1981, 13–23.

'Real Money Balances in a UK Aggregate Production Function', *Revista Internazionale di Scienze Economiche e Commerciali*, 29/10–11 (Oct.–Nov. 1982, 1066–79 (with P. Arestis and E. Karakitsos).

'The Demand for Money in the US, UK, Japan and West Germany: An Empirical Study of the Evidence since 1973', University College London, Discussion Papers in Economics, no. 90–05, 1990, pp. 64 (with Herbert Buscher).

'The Ethics of Monetary Stability', *Central Banking*, 3/3, Winter 1992–93, 47–9.

'The Functions of Money and Financial Credit: Their Objectives, Structure and Inbuilt Deficiencies', *Journal of the Association of Christian Economists*, no. 14, Feb. 1993, 1–17.

'Solzhenitsyn's Message: An Evaluation', *The Month*, CCLV/1519, July 1994, 283–5. (Russian translation published in Kuranty (Moscow), no. 161 (928), 26 Aug. 1994.)

'Monetary and Fiscal Policy under Conditions of Globalised Money and Capital Markets: Lessons for the UK Personal Sector', *Public Finance*, no. 3, 1996, 305–24 (with E. Karakitsos).

'The Capital-Flows Theory of Financial Crises', *Public Finance*, no. 1, 1997, 61–88 (with E. Karakitsos).

'A Framework for Comparison of Inflation Targeting in Germany and the UK', *IGS Discussion Paper Series*, no. 96/3, p. 35. Revised and updated version: IGS Discussion Paper, no. 97/19, p. 42 (Publisher: Institute for German Studies, The University of Birmingham).

'An Evaluation of Inflation Targeting in Germany and the UK', *Kredit und Kapital*, 30/4, 1997, 501–32 (with E. Karakitsos).

'A Strategic Approach to the Euro Prospects', *Public Finance*, 53/1, 1998 (with E. Karatkisos) (published in 2001; earlier version published as *IGS Discussion Paper*, no. IGS2000/8, pp. 34 (Publisher: Institute for German Studies, The University of Birmingham).

Short articles and notes

'New Schemes to Control Banks' Liquidity – Comparison with Other Countries', *The Times*, 7 July 1958 (unsigned).

'Booming Berlin Loses Men and Money', *The Observer*, 29 Oct. 1961.

'Ein Zusammenbruch ist möglich – Stephen Frowen über Chancen und Risiken der Euromärkte', *Wirtschaftswoche*, no. 30, 23 July 1979, 79.

Comment on paper by Karl Otto Pöhl, in H. Besters, (ed.) (1984), *Währungspolitik auf dem Prüfstand. Symposia of the List Society, New Series*, vol. 9 (Baden-Baden: Nomos), pp. 138–41 (reply by Karl Otto Pöhl, pp. 151–2).

Comment on paper by Sir Edward Heath, 'International Keynesianism: The Problems of the North-South Divide', in A. P. Thirlwall (ed.), *Keynes and Economic Development. The Seventh Keynes Seminar held at the University of Kent at Canterbury (1985)* (London: Macmillan, 1987) pp. 142–4.

A note included in the report of the symposium on 'Rerum Novarum and Today's Social Problems', held in Rieti, Italy, 16–18 Nov. 1990, *Review of the Social Christian Euro-Latin American Action*, 14/1, Jan.–March 1991, 14–15.

A note included in the report of the symposium on 'L'antropologia solidaristica nella Centesimus Annus', held in Rieti, Italy, 22–27 Oct. 1991, *Review of the Social Christian Euro-Latin American Action*, 14, Oct.–Dec. 1991, 17–18.

'The Right Currency for New Jobs: Moral Arguments for Monetary Stability', *Catholic Herald* (London), 18 Dec. 1992.

'Sound Money and the Pope', *Catholic Herald* (London), 26 Feb. 1993, 5.

'Germany Should Cut Interest Rates', *The Guardian*, 24 May 1993, 11.

'In Memoriam: G. L. S. Shackle, FBA, 1903–1992 – Address given at the Service of Thanksgiving for his life and work at the Parish Church of St Peter and St Paul, Aldeburgh, Suffolk, on Wednesday, 16 September 1992', *Review of Political Economy*, 5/2, 1993, 263–6.

Profiles of Bundesbank Presidents Karl Otto Pöhl, Helmut Schlesinger and Hans Tietmeyer, *Central Banking*, 6/1, Summer 1995, 72–6 (special issue 'Understanding the Bundesbank').

'Hans Tietmeyer – A Central Banker with a Social Conscience', *Central Banking*, 10/2, 1999–2000, 62–6.

'Unjustified British Critique of the Bundesbank', *Central Banking*, 10/3, 1999–2000, pp. 40–45 (reprinted in Deutsche Bundesbank *Auszüge aus Presseartikeln*, no. 12, 8 March 2000, pp. 15–17). Reply by Norman Lamont 'Black Wednesday – the controversy continues', *Central Banking*, 10/4, 1999–2000, pp. 65–69 (comment by 'Observer', *The Financial Times*, 1 May 2000).

'Black Wednesday and the Bundesbank – Stephen F. Frowen replies to Norman Lamont', *Central Banking*, vol. 11/1, 2000, pp. 96–8.

'Interview: Otmar Issing', *Central Banking*, vol. 11/3, February 2001, pp. 24–33 (reprinted in Deutsche Bundesbank, Auszüge aus Presseartikeln, no. 8, 20 February 2001, pp. 8–12)

'Interview: Hans Tietmeyer; *Central Banking*, vol. 11/4, May 2001, pp. 11–19. (Reprinted in Deutsche Bundesbank, *Auszüge aus Presseartikeln*, May 2001.)

Dictionary entries

'Saunders, Christopher Thomas (1907–2000)', in Brian Harrison (ed.) *New Dictionary of National Biography* (Oxford: Oxford University Press, 2003).

'Shackle, George Lennox Sharman (1903–1992)', in Brian Harrison (ed.) *New Dictionary of National Biography* (Oxford: Oxford University Press, 2003).

Reviews

Title: 'The Future of Sterling'. Author: A. C. L. Day, *The Bankers' Magazine*, 177/1320, 214–16.

Title: 'Uncertainty and Business Decisions'. Eds: C. F. Carter, G P. Meredith and G. L. S. Shackle. *The Bankers' Magazine*, 177/1322, May 1954, 483–4.

Title: 'Germany's Comeback in the World Market'. Author: Ludwig Erhard. *The Bankers' Magazine*, 178/1329, Dec. 1954, 521–2.

Title: 'Britain in the World Economy'. Author: Dennis H. Robertson. *The Bankers' Magazine*, 179/1330 Jan. 1955, 48–9.

Title: 'Your Future is Now'. Author: W. J. Thorne. *The Bankers' Magazine*, 182/1350, Sept. 1956, 233–4.

Title: 'Gesundes Geld'. Author: Wilhelm Vocke. *The Bankers' Magazine*, 183/1357, April 1957, 377–8.

Title: 'Staatslexikon: Recht, Wirtschaft, Gesellschaft'. 6th edn. Ed.: Görres Gesellschaft. *The Bankers' Magazine*, 185/1366, Jan. 1958, 47–8.

Title: 'Changes in Monetary Policy and their Consequences'. Author: Otto Veit. *The Bankers' Magazine*, 185/1367, Feb. 1958, 138–9.

Title: 'Macroeconomics of North Sea Oil in the United Kingdom'. Author: Homa Motamen. *Economic Modelling*, 2/1, 1985, 74–5.

Title: 'Banking Cultures of the World'. Ed.: Leo Schuster. *Central Banking*, 7/3, Winter 1996/97, 93–5 (with F. P. McHugh).

Title: 'The Social Market Economy and Monetary Stability'. Author: Hans Tietmeyer. *Central Banking*, 10/2, 1999–2000, pp. 79–80.

Official publication

'The Economic Rationale for a New International Institution in the Field of Industrial Financing'. Paper used as a background paper for the First Meeting of the Special Advisory Group of Experts on International Industrial Financing, 27–29 January 1981, and in the further preparation of UNIDO document ID/B/261/Add.7.

Published letters

'Germany and the West', *The Economist*, 161, 6 Oct. 1951, 794.

'Britain and the Common Market', *Financial Times*, 10 June 1960 (response by G. H. Morison, *Financial Times*, 12 June 1960).

'Industrial and Commercial Finance Corporation', *Financial Times*, 14 July 1961 (response by Lord Piercy, 'I.C.F.C.', *Financial Times*, 17 July 1961).

'Advantages of Euromoney', *The Times*, 28 July 1990, 13d.

'Economic Risks in a European Monetary "Anschluss" ', *The Times*, 22 June 1991, 13d.

'Taking Out Frustrations on Minorities – A German Problem?', *Welt am Sonntag*, 24 (13 June 1993), 8.

'A Common Denominator', *Evening Standard*, 10 Jan. 1996.

'EU Central Bank', *The Times*, 5 November 1998, p. 27d.

Obituary notices

Fonseca, Fr. Aloysius (1915–1991), *The Independent*, 30 Oct. 1991, 27.
Seidel, Georg (alias Christian Ferber) (1919–1992), *The Independent*, 3 July 1992, 12.
Shackle, George Lennox Sharman (1903–1992), *The Independent*, 4 March 1992.
Prince Louis Ferdinand of Prussia (1907–1994), *The Independent*, 3 Oct. 1994.
Shackle, George Lennox Sharman (1903–1992), *New College Record 2000* (Oxford: 2001), 117–19.
Saunders, Christopher Thomas (1907–2000), Royal Economic Society *Newsletter*, March 2002.

Other references

Editors of *The Bankers' Magazine*, The *Bankers' Magazine*, 189/1390, Jan. 1960, 14–16.
G. L. S. Shackle, 'Stephen Frowen – Editor of *The Bankers' Magazine*, 1955–1960', *The Bankers' Magazine*, 189/1393, April 1960, 290.
Christian, Ferber, 'Ehemalige Deutsche, die ihre Nation gewechselt haben' (Former Germans who have changed their nationality), *Die Welt*, 8 March 1975 (supplement 'Die geistige Welt').
Philip Arestis, (ed.) *Contemporary Issues in Money and Banking. Essays in Honour of Stephen Frowen*. (London: Macmillan, 1988), 2nd edn; *Money and Banking: Issues for the Twenty-First Century* (London: Macmillan; New York: St Martin's Press, 1993).
G. L. S. Shackle, 'Foreword', in P. Arestis (ed.) *Contemporary Issues in Money and Banking*, pp. ix–x.
'Stephen Frowen 70 Jahre', *Frankfurter Allgemeine Zeitung*, 24 May 1993, 18.
'Anglo-deutscher Bankbotschafter' (Anglo-German Banking Ambassador), *FU:N – Das Magazin der Freien Universität Berlin FU:N* (Magazine of the Free University of Berlin), no. 6, 16 June 1993, 9.
Peter Hebblethwaite, 'The Church Needs its Intellectuals', *Catholic Herald*, 8 April 1994.
Contemporary Authors, vol. 180, 2000, pp. 134–6.
Hans Tietmeyer, 'Laudatio: Professor Stephen F. Frowen zum 75. Geburtstag', *Österreichisches Bankarchiv*, December 1998, pp. 988-9 (abridged version).
Hans Tietmeyer, 'Laudatio on the occasion of the 75th birthday of Professor Stephen F. Frowen', in J. Hölscher (ed.) *50 Years of the German Mark* (London and New York: Palgrave, 2001), pp. xvi–xix).
C. A. E. Goodhart, 'Keynote Speech: The DM and the Future of the Euro', in J. Hölscher (ed.) *50 Years of the German Mark* (London and New York: Palgrave, 2001), pp. 1–6).
Sir Samuel Brittan, 'Epilogue: The Meaning of Sound Money', in J. Hölscher (ed.) *50 Years of the German Mark* (London and New York: Palgrave, 2001), pp. 199–202).
Norbert Kloten, 'Stephen Frowen – An Inspired Mediator in Turbulent Times', in J. Hölscher (ed.) *50 Years of the German Mark* (London and New York: Palgrave, 2001), pp. xx–xxvii).

Name Index

Subject Index